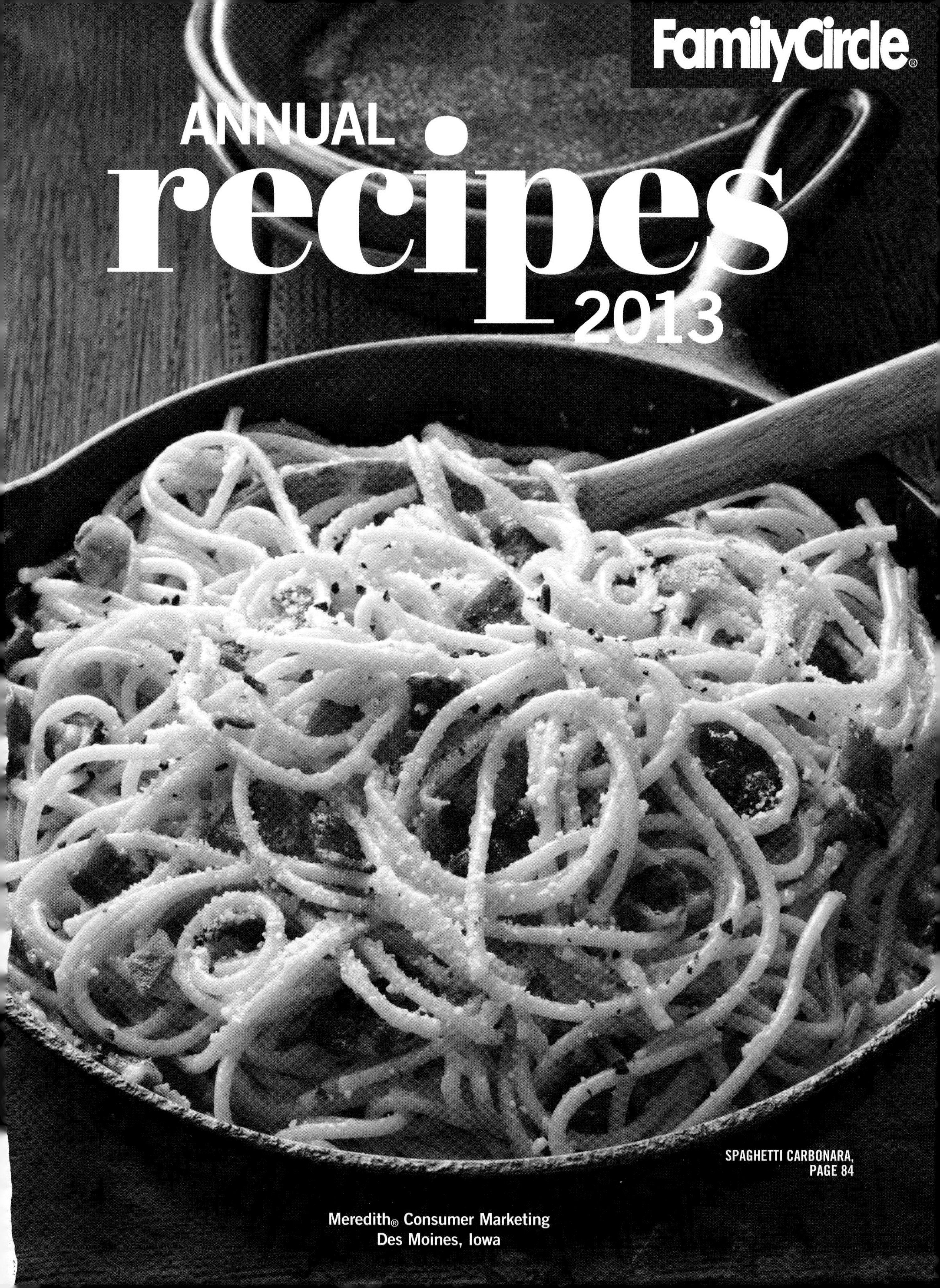

Family Circle®

ANNUAL
recipes
2013

SPAGHETTI CARBONARA,
PAGE 84

Meredith® Consumer Marketing
Des Moines, Iowa

HEIRLOOM TOMATO PIE,
PAGE 225

TOOLS FOR A GOOD LIFE

Our jobs as editors of *Family Circle*® Magazine are to provide you ideas and tools to help make your life easier, healthier and happier. One of the most important jobs you have is to feed your family. With that in mind, we've designed our food stories around principles we know you cherish because they are top-of-mind when we plan meals for our own families. Great taste is a given of every recipe in this collection, but each one also fits one or more of these additional criteria:

Healthfulness: Whether it's a classic dish that's been slimmed down (Fettuccine Alfredo, page 126) or a heart-healthy whole-foods recipe (Winter Grain and Roasted Vegetable Salad, page 45), foods that contribute to good health are of prime importance.

Convenience and/or Speed: In nearly every issue, we include recipes for the ever-popular slow cooker. For fast cooking, look to 30-minute dishes such as Chicken Stuffed with Tomato and Cheese (page 72).

Comfort: Food is more than fuel for the body. It soothes the soul too. In January, sample the Top 10 cold-weather favorites chosen by our Facebook fans, including Sharp Cheddar Shells and Cheese (page 25) and PB Chocolate Chunk Cookies (page 26).

Celebration: Throughout the year, there are special occasions to celebrate. In spring, headline a fabulous feast with Roast Chicken with Thyme-Scented Gravy (page 113). Finish it with Coconut-Strawberry Napoleons (page 114).

Budget-Consciousness: For just under $4 per serving, treat your family to Salmon Skewers over Roasted Vegetables (page 98) or creamy Enchiladas Suizas (page 97).

Everything we do is with an eye toward emerging food trends so that preparing meals for your family—one of the necessities in life—stays fresh, fun and something you look forward to. Happy cooking!

Linda

Linda Fears, Editor in Chief
Family Circle® Magazine

Family Circle Annual Recipes 2013

Meredith Consumer Marketing
Vice President, Consumer Marketing: Janet Donnelly
Consumer Marketing Product Director: Heather Sorensen
Business Director: Ron Clingman
Consumer Marketing Product Manager: Wendy Merical
Senior Production Manager: Al Rodruck

Waterbury Publications, Inc.
Editorial Director: Lisa Kingsley
Associate Editor: Tricia Bergman
Creative Director: Ken Carlson
Associate Design Director: Doug Samuelson
Graphic Designer: Mindy Samuelson
Contributing Copy Editors: Terri Fredrickson, Gretchen Kauffman
Contributing Indexer: Elizabeth T. Parson

Family Circle Magazine
Editor in Chief: Linda Fears
Creative Director: Karmen Lizzul
Food Director: Regina Ragone, M.S., R.D.
Senior Food Editor: Julie Miltenberger
Associate Food Editor: Michael Tyrrell
Assistant Food Editor: Melissa Knific
Editorial Assistant: Megan Bingham

Meredith National Media Group
President: Tom Harty

Meredith Corporation
Chairman and Chief Executive Officer: Stephen M. Lacy

In Memoriam: E.T. Meredith III (1933–2003)

LET'S EAT! Sitting down at your own table at the end of a long day to enjoy a fresh, flavorful home-cooked meal soothes away the day's stresses and satisfies on so many levels. This compilation of recipes from the 2013 issues of *Family Circle*® Magazine makes it simpler than ever to serve delicious food you cook yourself—whether it's a quick weeknight dinner or a special evening with friends. Recipes are organized by month to take advantage of what's in season and to make it easy to find just the right recipe for any occasion.

Gingered Shrimp with Soba (shown below; recipe on page 42) is part of the Heart-Smart Dinners feature in February. Japanese soba (buckwheat) noodles are tossed with shrimp and veggies in a garlicky, gingery sesame-soy sauce. Heart-Smart Dinners provide healthful whole-foods options for weeknight meals, including Chicken Sausage over Lentils, Oat-Crusted Chicken with Maple Sweet Potatoes and Salmon and Wild Rice Napoleon.

BOMBAY CHICKEN
SALAD, PAGE 182

CONTENTS

CHOCOLATE-CARAMEL
BROWNIE STACKS,
PAGE 29

JANUARY

14   22   33

TO YOUR HEALTH

Power up your defenses with these nutrient-packed meals.

POMEGRANATE
CHICKEN, PAGE 17

SALMON TACOS
WITH GUACAMOLE,
PAGE 14

MEATBALL AND BARLEY SOUP

Barley packs plenty of insoluble fiber, which lowers cholesterol and protects against cancer. All barley is nutritious, but hulled is the best.

Meatball and Barley Soup

MAKES 6 servings **PREP** 25 minutes
COOK 40 minutes

1	tablespoon olive oil
2	medium carrots, peeled and diced
2	ribs celery, diced
1	cup diced onion
3	cloves garlic, finely diced
6	cups low-sodium chicken broth
1¼	cups barley
1	pound ground pork
¾	cup shredded Parmesan cheese, plus more for garnish (optional)
2	tablespoons fresh chopped parsley
1½	teaspoons salt
½	teaspoon pepper
1	can (15.5 ounces) cannellini beans, drained and rinsed
8	cups roughly chopped escarole

• In a large pot, heat oil over medium heat. Add carrots, celery and onion; cook 8 minutes. Stir in garlic and cook 2 minutes. Add broth, 2 cups water and barley. Bring to a boil. Reduce heat to medium-low, cover and cook 25 minutes.

• Meanwhile, mix together ground pork, ¼ cup of the Parmesan, the parsley, ¼ teaspoon of the salt and ¼ teaspoon of the pepper. Roll into 30 meatballs, about 1 tablespoon each.

• Drop meatballs into soup. Stir in beans. Return to a simmer and cook 5 minutes. Stir in escarole and remaining ½ cup Parmesan, 1¼ teaspoons salt and ¼ teaspoon pepper. Ladle into bowls and garnish with grated Parmesan, if desired.

PER SERVING 450 **CAL**; 17 g **FAT** (6 g **SAT**); 23 g **PRO**; 51 g **CARB**; 13 g **FIBER**; 772 mg **SODIUM**; 46 mg **CHOL**

SWEET POTATO
SHEPHERD'S PIE

Sweet Potato Shepherd's Pie

MAKES 6 servings **PREP** 15 minutes **COOK** 19 minutes **BAKE** at 375° for 35 minutes

2½	pounds sweet potatoes, peeled and diced into ½-inch pieces
¼	cup 1% milk
3	tablespoons unsalted butter
1	teaspoon salt
½	teaspoon pepper
1½	pounds lean ground beef
2	medium carrots, finely diced
2	ribs celery, finely diced
1	small onion, finely diced
2	tablespoons all-purpose flour
2	tablespoons tomato paste
2	cups reduced-sodium beef broth
1	package (10 ounces) frozen peas
1	tablespoon chopped fresh thyme
1	tablespoon chopped fresh rosemary

• Heat oven to 375°. Add potatoes to a large lidded pot and cover with 1 inch of cold water. Bring to a boil; reduce heat to a simmer and cook, covered, 10 minutes or until fork-tender. Drain and return to pot. Add milk, 2 tablespoons of the butter, ½ teaspoon of the salt and ¼ teaspoon of the pepper. Mash until smooth. Cover and set aside.

• Meanwhile, add remaining 1 tablespoon butter to a large sauté pan over medium heat. Stir in beef, breaking apart with a spoon, as well as carrots, celery and onion. Cook 15 minutes, until vegetables are softened. Stir in flour; cook 1 minute. Stir in tomato paste, beef broth and peas. Bring to a simmer and cook 3 minutes, until liquid is slightly thickened and peas are thawed. Stir in remaining ½ teaspoon of the salt, remaining ¼ teaspoon of the pepper, the thyme and rosemary.

• Transfer meat-and-vegetable mixture to a 13 x 9 x 2-inch baking dish. Spread sweet potatoes over mixture, leaving a 1-inch border around the edge. Swirl top with back of a spoon, if desired. Bake at 375° for 30 to 35 minutes or until shepherd's pie is bubbling.

PER SERVING 429 **CAL**; 12 g **FAT** (6 g **SAT**); 32 g **PRO**; 48 g **CARB**; 8 g **FIBER**; 701 mg **SODIUM**; 86 mg **CHOL**

SALMON TACOS
WITH GUACAMOLE

Quinoa is high in magnesium, which is known to reduce headaches and help regulate blood sugar.

Quinoa-Stuffed Peppers

MAKES 4 servings **PREP** 10 minutes
COOK 16 minutes **BAKE** at 375° for 55 minutes

7	**sweet peppers (red, orange and yellow)**
1	**cup Bob's Red Mill whole grain quinoa**
1	**tablespoon olive oil**
1	**cup diced sweet onion**
1	**teaspoon ground cumin**
½	**teaspoon cinnamon**
1	**cup dried figs, roughly chopped**
½	**cup unsalted cashews, roughly chopped**
¾	**teaspoon salt**
¼	**teaspoon pepper**

• Heat oven to 375°. Seed and dice 1 of the cooked peppers. Slice remaining 6 peppers from stem to bottom; seed.

• In a medium lidded pot, bring 2 cups water to a boil. Stir in quinoa; return to a boil. Cover, reduce to medium-low and cook 10 minutes. (If using another brand of quinoa, cook ⅔ time shown on package.) Drain; set aside.

• Return pot to stove; place over medium heat. Add olive oil. Stir in the 1 diced pepper and onion. Cook 5 minutes. Mix in cumin and cinnamon; cook 1 more minute. Stir in figs, cashews, quinoa, salt and pepper. Fill pepper halves with quinoa mixture and place cut side up in a 9 x 13-inch baking dish. Cover with foil and bake at 375° for 25 minutes. Remove foil and bake another 30 minutes or until peppers are tender.

PER SERVING 482 g **CAL**; 15 g **FAT** (2 g **SAT**); 12 g **PRO**; 83 g **CARB**; 13 g **FIBER**; 466 mg **SODIUM**; 0 mg **CHOL**

Salmon Tacos with Guacamole

MAKES 4 servings **PREP** 15 minutes **COOK** 15 minutes **LET STAND** 5 minutes **BAKE** at 400° for 15 minutes

1	**cup Texmati rice blend (red, white, brown and wild rice)**
1	**tablespoon plus 2 teaspoons olive oil**
¾	**teaspoon salt**
¼	**teaspoon pepper**
1	**ripe avocado**
1	**teaspoon lime juice**
1	**clove garlic, grated**
1	**tablespoon chopped cilantro, plus more for garnish (optional)**
1	**pound salmon (four 4-ounce fillets)**
½	**teaspoon ground coriander**
½	**teaspoon sweet paprika**
8	**small corn tortillas**
½	**cup Cilantro-Lime Yogurt (recipe at right)**
	Lime wedges (optional)

• Heat oven to 400°. In a small, lidded pot, combine 1½ cups water, rice and 1 tablespoon of the oil. Bring to a boil, then reduce heat to low and cook, covered, 15 minutes. Remove from heat and let stand 5 minutes. Fluff with a fork and stir in ¼ teaspoon of the salt and ⅛ teaspoon of the pepper. Cover and set aside.

• Meanwhile, make guacamole. Mash avocado in a bowl. Stir in lime juice, garlic, cilantro and ¼ teaspoon of the salt. Set aside.

• Pat salmon dry. Place on a foil-lined baking sheet and rub with remaining 2 teaspoons olive oil. In a small bowl, combine coriander, paprika, remaining ¼ teaspoon salt and remaining ⅛ teaspoon pepper. Rub onto salmon. Bake at 400° for 15 minutes or until fish flakes easily with a fork.

• Wrap tortillas in foil; place in oven for a few minutes until warmed through. To assemble, flake salmon into large pieces, leaving skin on foil, and place on warm tortillas with guacamole, Cilantro-Lime Yogurt and, if desired, cilantro and lime wedges. Serve rice on side.

Cilantro-Lime Yogurt: Combine 1 container (6 ounces) fat-free plain Greek yogurt with 1 teaspoon lime juice, 1 teaspoon lime zest, 1 tablespoon chopped cilantro and ⅛ teaspoon salt.

PER SERVING 446 **CAL**; 18 g **FAT** (8 g **SAT**); 30 g **PRO**; 41 g **CARB**; 8 g **FIBER**; 598 mg **SODIUM**; 89 mg **CHOL**

QUINOA-STUFFED PEPPERS

APPLE, SAUSAGE AND
WALNUT PASTA

Reap the most benefits from folate-rich leafy greens by eating them raw or barely cooked.

POMEGRANATE CHICKEN

Apple, Sausage and Walnut Pasta

MAKES 6 servings **PREP** 10 minutes
COOK 15 minutes

1	pound whole wheat penne
½	cup walnuts
3	links (3 ounces each) Italian chicken sausage, removed from casings
1	tablespoon all-purpose flour
1	cup low-sodium chicken broth
2	apples, diced into ½-inch pieces
1	bag (6 ounces) baby spinach
½	cup grated Asiago cheese
½	teaspoon salt
¼	teaspoon pepper

• Bring a large pot of lightly salted water to boiling. Cook pasta according to package directions. Drain and set aside.

• Meanwhile, add walnuts to a large nonstick sauté pan over medium heat; toast 5 minutes, stirring occasionally. Remove to a cutting board to cool, then roughly chop.

• In same pan, add chicken sausage. Cook over medium heat 5 to 7 minutes, breaking apart with a wooden spoon, until browned. Stir in flour; cook 1 minute. Add broth and bring to a simmer over medium-high heat. Mix in apples and cook 2 minutes. Stir in spinach until wilted. Mix in walnuts, Asiago, salt and pepper. Transfer to a bowl with pasta; stir to combine. Serve immediately.

PER SERVING 464 **CAL**; 15 g **FAT** (3 g **SAT**); 16 g **PRO**; 67 g **CARB**; 5 g **FIBER**; 644 mg **SODIUM**; 41 mg **CHOL**

Pomegranate Chicken

MAKES 4 servings **PREP** 15 minutes **COOK** 15 minutes

1	cup wheat berries (quick cooking)
3	cups low-sodium chicken broth
¾	cup pomegranate seeds (about 1 pomegranate)
¼	cup chopped parsley
1	teaspoon salt
½	teaspoon pepper
1¼	pounds boneless, skinless chicken breasts (4 breasts)
1	tablespoon olive oil
1½	cups plus 2 teaspoons pomegranate juice
2	teaspoons cornstarch
1	tablespoon unsalted butter

• In a medium pot, combine wheat berries and 2½ cups of the chicken broth. Cover and bring to a boil. Reduce heat to a simmer and cook 15 minutes. Drain and return to pot. Stir in pomegranate seeds, 3 tablespoons of the parsley, ¼ teaspoon plus ⅛ teaspoon of the salt and ¼ teaspoon of the pepper. Cover and set aside.

• Meanwhile, season chicken with ½ teaspoon of the salt and ¼ teaspoon of the pepper. Heat oil in a large sauté pan over medium-high heat. Add chicken and cook 4 to 5 minutes per side or until cooked through. Remove to a plate and set aside.

• In same pan, add the 1½ cups pomegranate juice and remaining ½ cup chicken broth. Bring to a boil. In a small bowl, stir together remaining 2 teaspoons pomegranate juice and the cornstarch. Whisk into boiling pomegranate mixture; cook 4 minutes until thickened. Remove from heat; stir in butter and remaining ⅛ teaspoon salt. Return chicken to pan; toss to coat. Serve chicken over wheat berries. Drizzle with extra pomegranate sauce and garnish with remaining 1 tablespoon parsley.

PER SERVING 479 **CAL**; 9 g **FAT** (3 g **SAT**); 42 g **PRO**; 55 g **CARB**; 5 g **FIBER**; 742 mg **SODIUM**; 89 mg **CHOL**

COMFORT ZONE

Tuck into these Top 10 cold-weather favorites chosen by our Facebook fans.

SHARP CHEDDAR
SHELLS AND
CHEESE, PAGE 25

MEATLOAF AND
BUTTERMILK MASHED
POTATOES, PAGE 26

CHICKEN AND DUMPLINGS

Chicken and Dumplings

MAKES 8 servings **PREP** 15 minutes
COOK 35 minutes

1	whole chicken, cut up (about 3½ pounds)
3	large carrots, peeled and cut into ½-inch pieces
1	medium onion, diced
1	rib celery, trimmed and sliced
2	small chicken bouillon cubes
2¼	cups all-purpose flour
3	tablespoons chopped chives
1	teaspoon salt
½	teaspoon baking soda
1	cup half-and-half
1	box (10 ounces) frozen peas, thawed
½	teaspoon black pepper

• Place chicken, meaty side down, in a large stockpot. Add carrots, onion, celery, bouillon cubes and 8 cups water. Bring to a simmer over medium-high heat. Reduce heat to medium and simmer 30 minutes.

• Meanwhile, make dough for dumplings. In a large bowl, whisk together flour, chives, ¾ teaspoon of the salt and the baking soda. Pour in half-and-half and stir until mixture begins to hold together. Transfer dough to a lightly floured surface. With a floured rolling pin, roll out into a 10 x 8-inch square.

• Remove the chicken from the pot to a cutting board; reduce the heat under pot to low. Let chicken stand until cool enough to handle. Remove and discard skin and bones. Cut meat into bite-size pieces and return to pot. Increase the heat to medium-high and bring the soup to a simmer.

• Cut dumpling dough into 1-inch pieces. Drop into simmering soup along with thawed peas, black pepper and remaining ¼ teaspoon salt. Return to a simmer and cook dumplings 5 minutes; serve warm.

PER SERVING 567 **CAL**; 17 g **FAT** (6 g **SAT**); 61 g **PRO**; 37 g **CARB**; 4 g **FIBER**; 790 mg **SODIUM**; 180 mg **CHOL**

GRILLED CHEESE AND TOMATO WITH CHIPOTLE MAYO

Grilled Cheese and Tomato with Chipotle Mayo

MAKES 6 servings **PREP** 15 minutes **COOK** 6 minutes per batch

12	slices farmhouse white bread
4	tablespoons unsalted butter, softened
¼	cup jarred chipotle mayonnaise
6	ounces cheddar cheese, shredded (1½ cups)
1	large tomato, sliced
6	ounces Gouda cheese, shredded (1½ cups)

• Spread bread slices on a large cutting board. Spread 1 teaspoon butter on one side of each slice. Place slices, buttered sides down, back on board. Divide chipotle mayonnaise among slices, 1 teaspoon on each.

• Divide shredded cheddar among 6 of the slices, ¼ cup on each, compacting slightly so that cheese sticks together. Top each with sliced tomato and ¼ cup of the shredded Gouda, compacting slightly. Sandwich with remaining bread slices, mayo side down.

• Heat a large, lidded nonstick skillet over medium-low heat. Once heated, add 2 sandwiches to skillet. Cover and cook 2 to 3 minutes, compressing gently with spatula. Flip sandwiches and cook 2 to 3 more minutes.

PER SERVING 534 **CAL**; 29 g **FAT** (16 g **SAT**); 20 g **PRO**; 48 g **CARB**; 2 g **FIBER**; 1,050 mg **SODIUM**; 84 mg **CHOL**

SHRIMP AND GRITS

Shrimp and Grits

MAKES 4 servings PREP 20 minutes COOK 20 minutes LET STAND 5 minutes

1	pound cleaned raw shrimp
1½	teaspoons Old Bay seasoning
¼	teaspoon salt
1	cup coarse ground corn grits
2	slices bacon, cut into thin strips
3	cloves garlic, sliced
1	can (14 ounces) creamed corn
¾	cup heavy cream
2	scallions, trimmed and sliced

• In a medium bowl, toss shrimp with Old Bay seasoning. Set aside.

• Bring 3 cups water and the salt to a boil in a large, lidded saucepan. Gradually stir in grits and reduce heat to medium. Partially cover and cook, stirring occasionally, 10 minutes.

• Meanwhile, heat a large stainless-steel skillet over medium-high heat. Add bacon and cook until just crisp, about 6 minutes. Remove bacon with a slotted spoon to drain on paper towels.

• Reduce heat under skillet to medium and add garlic. Cook 30 seconds to a minute. Add shrimp and cook 3 minutes, turning, until pink. Remove shrimp and garlic to a bowl with a slotted spoon. Stir creamed corn into grits. Reduce heat to medium-low, cover and cook 5 minutes. Let stand 5 minutes.

• Pour heavy cream into skillet, scraping up any browned bits from bottom of pan. Simmer 4 minutes until slightly thickened. Stir in shrimp and garlic and bacon pieces. Cook 1 minute.

• Pour grits onto platter. Top with shrimp mixture and scatter scallions over top.

PER SERVING 535 CAL; 24 g FAT (12 g SAT); 30 g PRO; 47 g CARB; 4 g FIBER; 974 mg SODIUM; 241 mg CHOL

Slow Cooker Pot Roast

MAKES 4 servings PREP 25 minutes
SLOW COOK on HIGH for 6½ hours or LOW for 8 hours COOK 3 minutes

1	medium onion, sliced
2	pounds boneless beef chuck roast
2	teaspoons chopped fresh rosemary
½	teaspoon salt
½	teaspoon garlic powder
½	teaspoon black pepper
3	carrots, peeled and cut into 1-inch pieces
1	package (12 ounces) small potatoes, larger ones halved
1	cup beef broth
2	tablespoons Worcestershire sauce
2	tablespoons all-purpose flour

• Scatter half the onion slices in bottom of a 4- or 5-quart slow cooker. Season roast with 1 teaspoon of the rosemary, the salt, garlic powder and pepper. Add to slow cooker on top of onion.

• Place carrots, potatoes and remaining onion slices around and on top of roast in slow cooker. Sprinkle with remaining 1 teaspoon rosemary. Whisk together broth and Worcestershire and pour over vegetables. Cover and cook on HIGH for 6½ hours or on LOW for 8 hours.

• With a slotted spoon, transfer vegetables to a serving platter. With a large spatula, lift out roast, trying to keep in one piece. Place on top of vegetables and strain liquid into a fat separator or measuring cup. Transfer remaining vegetables to platter.

• Skim fat from liquid and transfer to a small saucepan. Combine flour and 3 tablespoons water in a small bowl. Whisk mixture into saucepan. Bring to a simmer over medium heat. Cook 3 minutes and serve alongside pot roast and vegetables.

PER SERVING 434 CAL; 12 g FAT (4 g SAT); 51 g PRO; 29 g CARB; 4 g FIBER; 768 mg SODIUM; 110 mg CHOL

SLOW COOKER
POT ROAST

Chicken Pot Pie

MAKES 6 servings **PREP** 15 minutes
COOK 15 minutes **BAKE** at 400° for 35 minutes
COOL 10 minutes

CRUST

- 2 cups all-purpose flour
- ½ teaspoon salt
- ¾ cup solid vegetable shortening

FILLING

- 1 tablespoon olive oil
- 1 potato (6 ounces), peeled and diced
- 1 small onion, chopped
- 2 ribs celery, chopped
- 2 large carrots, peeled and sliced
- 1½ cups chicken broth
- 2 tablespoons all-purpose flour
- 2 teaspoons fresh thyme leaves, chopped
- ¼ teaspoon each salt and black pepper
- 2 cups cubed cooked chicken breast

• Heat oven to 400°. **Crust:** Combine flour and salt in a food processor. Drop in pieces of shortening and process in on-and-off bursts until combined. Drizzle with 3 to 4 tablespoons ice water; process until crust comes together in a ball. Divide in two, with one portion just slightly larger.

• With a floured rolling pin, roll larger dough into a 12-inch circle on a floured sheet of waxed paper. Invert into a 10½-inch cast-iron skillet, patching any cracks. Roll remaining dough into an 11-inch circle. Refrigerate while making filling.

• **Filling:** Heat oil in a large nonstick skillet over medium heat. Add potato, onion, celery and carrots. Cook, stirring, 5 minutes.

• Blend broth and flour; add to skillet along with thyme, salt and pepper. Simmer 10 minutes. Stir in chicken; remove from heat.

• Pour filling into bottom crust. Top with remaining crust. Pinch edge together and tuck down slightly into pan. Cut slits into top crust.

• Bake at 400° for 35 minutes until lightly browned and bubbly. Cool 10 minutes.

PER SERVING 512 **CAL**; 28 g **FAT** (7 g **SAT**); 19 g **PRO**; 42 g **CARB**; 3 g **FIBER**; 585 mg **SODIUM**; 36 mg **CHOL**

SHARP CHEDDAR SHELLS AND CHEESE

Sharp Cheddar Shells and Cheese

MAKES 6 servings **PREP** 15 minutes **COOK** 8 minutes

- 1 box (16 ounces) medium shells
- 3 tablespoons unsalted butter
- ½ medium onion, chopped
- 3 tablespoons all-purpose flour
- 2 cups 2% milk
- ½ teaspoon mustard powder
- ½ teaspoon salt
- ¼ teaspoon ground white or black pepper
- ¾ pound sharp white cheddar cheese, grated (3 cups)
- 1 cup crushed pretzels or barbecue kettle potato chips

• Bring a large pot of salted water to a boil. Add shells; cook about 8 minutes, following package directions. Drain.

• Meanwhile, melt butter in a medium saucepan over medium heat. Add onion and cook 5 minutes. Whisk in flour. While whisking, add milk in a thin stream. Whisk in mustard powder, salt and pepper.

• Bring to a simmer, whisking occasionally. Simmer 3 minutes. Remove from heat and whisk in cheese. Top with crushed pretzels.

PER SERVING 682 **CAL**; 28 g **FAT** (17 g **SAT**); 30 g **PRO**; 76 g **CARB**; 5 g **FIBER**; 752 mg **SODIUM**; 82 mg **CHOL**

MEATLOAF AND BUTTERMILK MASHED POTATOES

PB Chocolate Chunk Cookies

MAKES 28 servings PREP 15 minutes
BAKE at 350° for 18 minutes per batch

2	cups all-purpose flour
½	teaspoon salt
½	teaspoon baking soda
¼	teaspoon baking powder
½	cup (1 stick) unsalted butter, softened
½	cup creamy peanut butter
¾	cup packed dark brown sugar
½	cup granulated sugar
2	large eggs
1	tablespoon vanilla extract
1	bag (11 ounces) semisweet chocolate chunks
1	cup dry-roasted peanuts, chopped

• Heat oven to 350°. In a medium bowl, blend flour, salt, baking soda and baking powder. Set aside.

• Cream together butter and peanut butter until smooth. Add both kinds of sugar and beat until fluffy, about 2 minutes. Beat in eggs, one at a time. On low speed, beat in vanilla.

• Add flour mixture and beat on low speed until combined. Stir in chocolate chunks and peanuts. Drop by scant ¼ cupfuls onto baking sheets. Bake at 350° for 18 minutes per batch. Cool on wire racks.

Note: These are great served warm. If desired, microwave on a paper towel for 15 seconds.

PER COOKIE 229 CAL; 12 g FAT (5 g SAT); 5 g PRO; 26 g CARB; 2 g FIBER; 97 mg SODIUM; 24 mg CHOL

Meatloaf and Buttermilk Mashed Potatoes

MAKES 6 servings PREP 15 minutes COOK 12 minutes BAKE at 375° for 1 hour LET REST 10 minutes

2	slices whole wheat bread, crumbled
1⅓	cups low-fat buttermilk
1	large egg
1½	pounds meatloaf mix (ground beef, pork and veal)
½	pound mild bulk Italian sausage
1	small onion, finely chopped
2	tablespoons Worcestershire sauce
½	teaspoon dried oregano
1½	teaspoons garlic salt
1	teaspoon black pepper
2½	pounds russet potatoes, peeled and cut up
¼	cup unsalted butter
1	package (.87 ounce) brown gravy mix

• Heat oven to 375°. In a bowl, combine bread crumbs, ⅓ cup of the buttermilk and the egg. Let soak 5 minutes.

• In large bowl, combine meatloaf mix, crumbled sausage, onion, Worcestershire, oregano, ½ teaspoon of the garlic salt and ½ teaspoon of the pepper. Gently stir in bread crumb mixture. Fit meat mixture into a 9 x 5 x 3-inch loaf pan and smooth top.

• Bake at 375° for 1 hour or until meatloaf is 150°. Let rest, covered, 10 minutes.

• Meanwhile, place potatoes in a large pot and add enough cold water to cover by an inch. Salt water and bring to a boil over high heat. Cook 12 minutes or until tender. Drain and return to pot. Add remaining 1 cup buttermilk, the butter, remaining 1 teaspoon garlic salt and remaining ½ teaspoon pepper. Mash to desired consistency.

• Prepare gravy mix following package directions. Remove meatloaf from pan, discarding drippings. Slice and serve with mashed potatoes and gravy.

PER SERVING 581 CAL; 29 g FAT (13 g SAT); 34 g PRO; 46 g CARB; 4 g FIBER; 924 mg SODIUM; 153 mg CHOL

PB CHOCOLATE
CHUNK COOKIES

CHOCOLATE-CARAMEL
BROWNIE STACKS

Chocolate-Caramel Brownie Stacks

MAKES 16 servings **PREP** 15 minutes
MICROWAVE 1 minute, 50 seconds
BAKE at 325° for 35 minutes
LET STAND 5 minutes **REFRIGERATE** 2 hours

- 1½ cups all-purpose flour
- ½ cup unsweetened cocoa powder
- ¾ teaspoon baking soda
- ½ teaspoon salt
- ¾ cup (1½ sticks) unsalted butter
- 3 ounces semisweet chocolate, broken up
- 1¼ cups sugar
- 3 large eggs
- 2 teaspoons vanilla extract
- 4 ounces (½ package) cream cheese, softened
- ⅓ cup caramel sauce, plus more for drizzling
- ½ teaspoon unflavored gelatin
- 1½ cups heavy cream
-   Chocolate sauce
-   Caramel popcorn

• Heat oven to 325°. Line a 9 x 9 x 2-inch baking pan with foil.

• Whisk flour, cocoa, baking soda and salt. Combine butter and chocolate in a large glass bowl. Microwave in three 30-second increments, stirring until smooth.

• Whisk in sugar and flour mixture, then eggs and vanilla. Spread into prepared pan.

• Bake at 325° for 35 minutes or until pick inserted in center comes out clean. Cool in pan for 10 minutes; use foil to lift from pan to a wire rack. Cool completely.

• With a serrated knife, slice in half horizontally. Line pan with plastic wrap and insert top layer, cut side up, in pan.

• In a medium bowl, beat cream cheese and caramel sauce. Sprinkle gelatin over 2 tablespoons water in a small glass bowl and let stand 5 minutes. Microwave 15 to 20 seconds until dissolved. Beat into cream cheese mixture. Whip 1 cup of the heavy cream to stiff peaks. Fold into cream cheese mixture. Spread onto brownie layer in pan and top with remaining layer, cut side down. Refrigerate 2 hours.

• Whisk remaining ½ cup cream to stiff peaks. Use plastic to lift stacked brownie from pan. With serrated knife, cut into squares. Top each square with a dollop of whipped cream, some of the caramel sauce, chocolate sauce and caramel popcorn. Serve immediately.

PER SERVING 400 **CAL**; 23 g **FAT** (13 g **SAT**); 5 g **PRO**; 46 g **CARB**; 1 g **FIBER**; 211 mg **SODIUM**; 101 mg **CHOL**

Cinnamon Streusel Coffee Cake

MAKES 16 servings **PREP** 20 minutes
BAKE at 350° for 65 minutes

TOPPING
- 1 cup packed light brown sugar
- 1 cup all-purpose flour
- 2 teaspoons cinnamon
- ¼ teaspoon salt
- 1 stick (½ cup) cold unsalted butter, cut up

CAKE
- 2¼ cups all-purpose flour
- 1 teaspoon baking powder
- ½ teaspoon baking soda
- ¼ teaspoon salt
- ½ cup (1 stick) unsalted butter, softened
- 1 cup sugar
- 2 eggs
- 1 teaspoon vanilla extract
- 1 cup buttermilk (or 2 tablespoons white vinegar and ¾ cup plus 2 tablespoons milk)

• Heat oven to 350°. Line a 9-inch square pan with foil; coat foil with nonstick cooking spray. Prepare **Topping:** In a bowl, blend brown sugar, flour, cinnamon and salt. Work butter into flour mixture with your fingertips until crumbly. Refrigerate while preparing cake batter.

• **Cake:** Combine flour, baking powder, baking soda and salt. Set aside. Beat butter and sugar until smooth, 2 to 3 minutes. Beat in eggs, one at a time. Mix in vanilla.

• On low speed, beat in half the flour mixture, the buttermilk and then remaining flour mixture. Spread half the batter into prepared pan. Top with 1 cup of the topping, finely crumbling to cover batter. Top with remaining batter, spreading to cover topping. Crumble remaining 2 cups topping over batter.

• Bake at 350° for 55 to 65 minutes or until toothpick inserted in center comes out clean. Cool in pan on a wire rack.

PER SERVING 312 **CAL**; 12 g **FAT** (8 g **SAT**); 4 g **PRO**; 47 g **CARB**; 1 g **FIBER**; 169 mg **SODIUM**; 57 mg **CHOL**

CINNAMON STREUSEL COFFEE CAKE

STEWPENDOUS

Five easy slow cooker suppers warm up winter.

CHICKEN BRUNSWICK STEW

Chicken Brunswick Stew

MAKES 6 servings **PREP** 10 minutes
SLOW COOK on HIGH for 6 hours or LOW for
8 hours

2	**pounds skinless, bone-in chicken thighs**
1	**pound potatoes, cut into 1-inch pieces**
1	**large onion, chopped**
2	**cups reduced-sodium chicken broth**
1	**can (15 ounces) diced tomatoes**
¼	**cup tomato paste**
1	**teaspoon dried oregano**
1	**teaspoon salt**
½	**teaspoon black pepper**
1	**can (15.5 ounces) butter beans, rinsed and drained**
1	**cup frozen sliced okra, thawed**

• Coat slow cooker bowl with nonstick cooking spray. Place chicken, potatoes and onion in bottom of slow cooker. In a medium bowl, stir together broth, tomatoes, tomato paste, oregano, ½ teaspoon of the salt and ¼ teaspoon of the black pepper. Pour over chicken and potatoes.

• Cover and cook on HIGH for 6 hours or LOW for 8 hours. One hour before end of cooking time, stir in beans, okra and remaining ½ teaspoon salt and ¼ teaspoon pepper.

• Shred chicken off bones and serve with vegetables.

PER SERVING 314 **CAL**; 9 g **FAT** (3 g **SAT**); 28 g **PRO**; 34 g **CARB**; 6 g **FIBER**; 970 mg **SODIUM**; 76 mg **CHOL**

IRISH LAMB STEW

Irish Lamb Stew

MAKES 6 servings **PREP** 15 minutes **SLOW COOK** on HIGH for 6 hours or LOW for 8 hours

2	**pounds boneless lamb shoulder or lamb steak, cut into 1-inch pieces**
3	**tablespoons all-purpose flour**
1	**pound potatoes, peeled and cut into 1-inch pieces**
½	**pound turnips, peeled and cut into ½-inch pieces**
1	**onion, chopped**
3	**carrots, peeled and cut into ½-inch pieces**
2	**ribs celery, cut into 1-inch pieces**
2	**cups beef broth**
1	**cup dry red wine**
¼	**cup tomato paste**
1	**teaspoon salt**
½	**teaspoon black pepper**
½	**teaspoon dried thyme**
1	**package (10 ounces) frozen peas, thawed**
	Biscuits (optional)

• Coat slow cooker bowl with nonstick cooking spray. Toss lamb with flour and place in bottom of slow cooker. Add potatoes, turnips, onion, carrots and celery, in that order.

• Combine broth, wine, tomato paste, ½ teaspoon of the salt, ¼ teaspoon of the pepper and the thyme. Pour over contents of slow cooker.

• Cover and cook on HIGH for 6 hours or LOW for 8 hours. Stir in peas and remaining ½ teaspoon salt and ¼ teaspoon pepper during last 15 minutes of cooking time. Serve with warm biscuits, if desired.

PER SERVING 494 **CAL**; 21 g **FAT** (9 g **SAT**); 35 g **PRO**; 34 g **CARB**; 6 g **FIBER**; 883 mg **SODIUM**; 109 mg **CHOL**

Chipotle Pork and Sweet Potato Stew with Cornbread

MAKES 6 servings   **PREP** 15 minutes   **SLOW COOK** on HIGH for 6 hours or LOW for 8 hours, 15 minutes

2	pounds boneless country pork ribs, cut into 2-inch pieces
1	teaspoon chipotle chili powder
1	teaspoon dried oregano
1	teaspoon ground cumin
1	teaspoon salt
1	onion, chopped
4	cloves garlic, sliced
1¼	pounds sweet potatoes, peeled and cut into 1-inch pieces
1	green pepper, cored, seeded and thinly sliced
2	cups reduced-sodium chicken broth

CORNBREAD

½	cup cornmeal
½	cup all-purpose flour
2	teaspoons sugar
1	teaspoon baking powder
⅛	teaspoon salt
2	tablespoons cold butter, cut into small pieces
½	cup milk
2	tablespoons chopped cilantro

• Coat slow cooker bowl with nonstick cooking spray. Season pork with chili powder, oregano, cumin and ½ teaspoon of the salt. Place in slow cooker; add onion, garlic, sweet potatoes and green pepper, in that order. Pour broth over top.

• Cover and cook on HIGH for 6 hours or LOW for 8 hours.

• Add remaining ½ teaspoon salt 45 minutes before end of cooking time; drop cornbread batter (see below) in heaping tablespoons on top. If cooking on LOW, add 15 minutes.

• **Cornbread:** In a large bowl, whisk together cornmeal, flour, sugar, baking powder and salt. Cut in butter until mixture resembles coarse meal. Stir in milk until just moistened; fold in cilantro.

PER SERVING 472 **CAL**; 17 g **FAT** (7 g **SAT**); 34 g **PRO**; 43 g **CARB**; 4 g **FIBER**; 796 mg **SODIUM**; 109 mg **CHOL**

CHIPOTLE PORK AND SWEET POTATO STEW WITH CORNBREAD

SAN FRANCISCO–STYLE
CIOPPINO

Tex-Mex Beef Taco Stew

MAKES 6 servings **PREP** 10 minutes
SLOW COOK on HIGH for 6 hours or LOW for
8 hours

2	pounds beef chuck, cut into 1-inch pieces
1	onion, sliced
2	cans (14.5 ounces) diced tomatoes with jalapeño
1	packet (1 ounce) reduced-sodium taco seasoning
1	can (15.5 ounces) pinto beans, drained and rinsed
1	can (15.5 ounces) kidney beans, drained and rinsed
1	package (10 ounces) frozen corn, thawed
	Sour cream, sliced scallions and tortilla chips for garnish (optional)

• Coat slow cooker bowl with nonstick cooking spray. Place beef and onion in bottom of slow cooker. Combine tomatoes and taco seasoning; pour over beef.

• Cover and cook on HIGH for 6 hours or LOW for 8 hours. One hour before end of cooking time, stir in beans and corn.

• Serve with sour cream, sliced scallions and tortilla chips, if desired.

PER SERVING 412 **CAL**; 8 g **FAT** (3 g **SAT**); 41 g **PRO**; 42 g **CARB**; 11 g **FIBER**; 1,010 mg **SODIUM**; 64 mg **CHOL**

TEX-MEX BEEF
TACO STEW

San Francisco–Style Cioppino

MAKES 6 servings **PREP** 15 minutes **SLOW COOK** on HIGH for 6 hours or LOW for 8 hours

1	can (28 ounces) crushed tomatoes
1	can (28 ounces) whole tomatoes, broken up
½	cup dry red wine
2	cans (6.5 ounces each) minced clams
1	large onion, chopped
1	sweet red pepper, cored, seeded and chopped
4	cloves garlic, chopped
2	teaspoons sugar
1	teaspoon dried oregano
½	teaspoon salt
⅛	teaspoon cayenne pepper
1	pound medium shrimp, shells removed and deveined
1	pound medium sea scallops
½	cup parsley, chopped
	Sourdough bread (optional)

• Coat slow cooker bowl with nonstick cooking spray. Add crushed tomatoes, whole tomatoes, red wine, juice from 1 can of clams, onion, red pepper, garlic, sugar, oregano, salt and cayenne. Break up tomatoes with a wooden spoon.

• Cover and cook on HIGH for 6 hours or LOW for 8 hours.

• Thirty minutes before end of cooking time, stir in shrimp, scallops and drained clams. Just before serving, stir in parsley. Serve with sourdough bread, if desired.

PER SERVING 347 **CAL**; 4 g **FAT** (1 g **SAT**); 48 g **PRO**; 26 g **CARB**; 5 g **FIBER**; 1,008 mg **SODIUM**; 181 mg **CHOL**

CHICKEN SAUSAGE OVER
LENTILS, PAGE 41

FEBRUARY

45   53   63

THIS SPUD'S FOR YOU

Taste pure comfort with this budget-friendly recipe based on potatoes.

Gnocchi with Butter, Sage and Walnuts

MAKES 6 servings **PREP** 30 minutes **BAKE** at 400° for 55 minutes **REFRIGERATE** 30 minutes **COOK** 4½ minutes

2	**pounds baking potatoes**
2	**egg yolks, beaten**
½	**teaspoon salt**
¼	**teaspoon ground nutmeg**
1½	**cups all-purpose flour**
6	**tablespoons unsalted butter**
¼	**cup fresh sage leaves, coarsely chopped**
½	**cup toasted walnuts, chopped**
½	**cup shredded Parmesan**
	Freshly ground pepper

• Heat oven to 400°. Scrub potatoes and pierce with a fork. Bake at 400° for 55 minutes. Remove from oven and cool slightly. Spoon flesh into a large bowl and mash until smooth. Cool to room temperature.

• Make a well in potatoes. Add egg yolks, ¼ teaspoon of the salt and the nutmeg. With a fork, gently mix egg into potatoes. Slowly stir in flour. Knead in bowl a few times until dough comes together. Turn out onto a floured surface and continue to knead for 2 to 3 minutes until soft and smooth. Cover with plastic wrap and refrigerate for 30 minutes.

• Divide dough into 8 equal pieces. On a floured surface, roll 1 piece into a rope about 18 inches in length. Cut into 1-inch pieces and roll over tines of a fork. Transfer to a floured baking sheet. Repeat with remaining dough.

• Bring a large pot of lightly salted water to a boil. Add half the gnocchi and return to a simmer; when gnocchi float to the top, about 1 to 2 minutes, remove to a large bowl with a slotted spoon. Repeat with remaining gnocchi.

• Melt butter in a skillet; add sage and remaining ¼ teaspoon salt. Cook 30 seconds.

• Toss butter mixture with gnocchi. Add nuts, Parmesan and pepper and serve.

PER SERVING 444 **CAL**; 22 g **FAT** (10 g **SAT**); 12 g **PRO**; 53 g **CARB**; 4 g **FIBER**; 301 mg **SODIUM**; 104 mg **CHOL**

HEART-SMART DINNERS

Pump up your menu with these healthful, whole-foods meals.

GINGERED SHRIMP
WITH SOBA, PAGE 42

WINTER GRAIN
AND ROASTED
VEGETABLE SALAD,
PAGE 45

TOMATO AND
EGGPLANT FUSILLI

Tomato and Eggplant Fusilli

MAKES 6 servings PREP 15 minutes
COOK 30 minutes

¼	cup olive oil
4	cups cherry tomatoes
1	large eggplant (about 1¼ pounds), cut into ½-inch cubes
3	large cloves garlic, sliced
¾	teaspoon salt
1	pound whole wheat fusilli
1	cup fresh basil, torn
1	heaping cup (4 ounces) shredded ricotta salata

• In a large lidded skillet, heat 2 tablespoons of the oil over medium heat. Stir in tomatoes and eggplant. Cook, covered, 15 minutes. (If skillet does not have a lid, try covering tightly with aluminum foil or a baking sheet.) Stir in garlic and ¼ teaspoon of the salt; cover and cook another 10 to 15 minutes until tomatoes are slightly wilted.

• Meanwhile, bring a pot of lightly salted water to a boil. Cook fusilli according to package directions, reserving ¾ cup of the pasta water. Using a slotted spoon, transfer fusilli to skillet with tomato-eggplant mixture. Stir in ½ cup of the pasta water, ¾ cup of the basil, ¾ cup of the ricotta salata, the remaining 2 tablespoons oil and remaining ½ teaspoon salt. (If pasta seems dry, stir in ¼ cup pasta water.) Garnish with remaining ¼ cup basil and ¼ cup ricotta salata.

PER SERVING 434 CAL; 13 g FAT (3 g SAT); 13 g PRO; 67 g CARB; 11 g FIBER; 474 mg SODIUM; 8 mg CHOL

CHICKEN SAUSAGE OVER LENTILS

Chicken Sausage over Lentils

MAKES 4 servings PREP 15 minutes COOK 25 minutes

1¼	cups dried French green lentils
1	bay leaf
1	sprig fresh thyme
3	tablespoons olive oil
1	cup finely diced fennel
1	medium onion, finely diced
1	large carrot, peeled and finely diced
1	rib celery, finely diced
2	cloves garlic, chopped
2	tablespoons red wine vinegar
1	tablespoon Dijon mustard
½	teaspoon salt
¼	teaspoon pepper
1	package (12 ounces) fully cooked roasted garlic chicken sausage
	Fresh parsley, chopped (optional)

• In a medium lidded pot, combine lentils, bay leaf, thyme sprig and 6 cups lightly salted water; bring to a boil. Reduce heat to medium-low and simmer 20 to 25 minutes until lentils are tender (they should be slightly firm, not mushy). Drain and remove herbs.

• Meanwhile, heat 2 tablespoons of the oil in a large sauté pan over medium heat. Add fennel, onion, carrot and celery. Cook 10 minutes or until softened. Add garlic; cook 2 minutes. Stir in drained lentils, remaining 1 tablespoon oil, the vinegar, mustard, salt and pepper.

• Prepare chicken sausage per package directions. Slice on the bias in ¼-inch pieces. Serve over lentils. Garnish with parsley, if desired.

PER SERVING 453 CAL; 18 g FAT (3 g SAT); 29 g PRO; 45 g CARB; 11 g FIBER; 795 mg SODIUM; 65 mg CHOL

Gingered Shrimp with Soba

MAKES 6 servings **PREP** 20 minutes
COOK 11 minutes

- 2 packages (8 ounces each) Eden Organic Soba Pasta
- 2 tablespoons olive oil
- 1 pound shrimp, peeled and deveined
- 1 piece (5 inches) ginger, grated (¼ cup)
- 4 cloves garlic, chopped
- 1 bag (8 ounces) shredded carrots (2½ cups)
- 1 head napa cabbage, sliced into 2-inch strips (10 cups)
- 1¼ cups sliced scallions
- 1 cup vegetable broth, chilled
- 3 tablespoons low-sodium soy sauce
- 2 tablespoons rice vinegar
- 1 teaspoon cornstarch
- 1 teaspoon sesame oil

• Bring a pot of lightly salted water to a boil. Add soba pasta; cook 6 minutes. Drain and rinse well with cold water. Set aside.

• Meanwhile, add 1 tablespoon of the oil to a large sauté pan over medium heat. Add shrimp, ginger and garlic. Cook 2 to 3 minutes until shrimp are cooked through. Remove to a very large bowl.

In the same sauté pan, add remaining 1 tablespoon oil over medium heat. Stir in carrots; cook 2 minutes. Stir in cabbage; cook 4 minutes, until wilted. Stir in 1 cup of the scallions; cook 1 minute. Remove vegetables to bowl with shrimp.

• Whisk together cold vegetable broth, soy sauce, vinegar, cornstarch and sesame oil until smooth. Pour into same sauté pan over medium heat, scraping the bottom of the pan to break up the bits. Bring to a boil and cook 1 minute. Pour into bowl with shrimp and vegetables; stir in cooked soba pasta. Serve sprinkled with remaining ¼ cup scallions.

PER SERVING 438 **CAL**; 8 g **FAT** (1 g **SAT**); 26 g **PRO**; 63 g **CARB**; 6 g **FIBER**; 800 mg **SODIUM**; 112 mg **CHOL**

Oat-Crusted Chicken with Maple Sweet Potatoes

MAKES 4 servings **PREP** 20 minutes
COOK 26 minutes

- 1½ pounds sweet potatoes, peeled and cut into 1-inch pieces
- 1 tablespoon unsalted butter
- ¼ cup skim milk
- ¼ cup maple syrup, plus more for drizzling (optional)
- 1¼ teaspoons salt
- 1 cup old-fashioned oats
- 2 cloves chopped garlic
- 1 tablespoon fresh rosemary
- 1 tablespoon fresh thyme
- ½ teaspoon pepper
- ¼ cup shredded Parmesan, plus more for garnish
- 1 egg
- ¼ cup all-purpose flour
- 4 small boneless, skinless chicken breasts (1 pound)
- 2 tablespoons olive oil
  Arugula (optional)

• Place sweet potatoes in a medium lidded pot; cover with cold water by 1 inch. Bring to a boil; reduce heat to medium and simmer, covered, for 10 to 12 minutes, until fork-tender. Drain, return to pot and mash. Stir in butter, milk, maple syrup and ½ teaspoon of the salt.

• Meanwhile, in a food processor, combine oats, garlic, rosemary, thyme, ½ teaspoon of the salt and the pepper. Pulse several times until ingredients are roughly chopped. Pour into a bowl and add Parmesan. In a second bowl, beat egg with 2 tablespoons water. In a third bowl, blend flour and ¼ teaspoon of the salt.

• Pound chicken breasts to ½-inch thickness. Coat each breast on both sides with flour. Dip into beaten egg, allowing excess to drip off chicken. Finally, coat with oat mixture and place on a baking sheet.

• In a large nonstick skillet, heat 1 tablespoon of the oil over medium-high heat. Add 2 of the chicken breasts; cook 4 minutes. Flip over and reduce heat to medium; cook 3 minutes. Repeat with remaining 1 tablespoon olive oil and 2 chicken breasts.

• Top chicken with Parmesan and, if desired, drizzle with warm maple syrup. Serve with sweet potatoes and, if desired, arugula.

PER SERVING 487 **CAL**; 14 g **FAT** (4 g **SAT**); 34 g **PRO**; 57 g **CARB**; 6 g **FIBER**; 783 mg **SODIUM**; 103 mg **CHOL**

GINGERED SHRIMP WITH SOBA

OAT-CRUSTED
CHICKEN WITH MAPLE
SWEET POTATOES

SALMON AND WILD RICE
NAPOLEON

Salmon and Wild Rice Napoleon

MAKES 4 servings
PREP 15 minutes   COOK 50 minutes
BAKE at 400° for 8 minutes

- 1 **bag (5 ounces) wild rice (about 1 cup)**
- 2½ **cups low-sodium chicken broth**
- ½ **cup dried cranberries**
- ⅓ **cup plus 2 tablespoons pistachios, roughly chopped**
- ¼ **teaspoon salt**
- ¼ **teaspoon pepper**
- 4 **4-ounce center-cut salmon fillets (1 pound total)**
- ½ **teaspoon celery salt**
- ½ **teaspoon ground mustard**
- ¼ **teaspoon ground allspice**
  Celery leaves, chopped (optional)

• Heat oven to 400°. In a small lidded pot, combine wild rice and chicken broth. Cover and bring to a boil. Reduce to a simmer and cook 50 minutes until kernels puff. Drain and return to pot. Stir in cranberries, ⅓ cup of the pistachios, the salt and ⅛ teaspoon of the pepper. Cover; set aside.

• Meanwhile, prepare salmon. Slice each fillet in half lengthwise, and place all 8 pieces on a foil-lined baking sheet coated with nonstick cooking spray. In a small bowl, combine celery salt, ground mustard, allspice and remaining ⅛ teaspoon pepper. Spritz salmon with nonstick cooking spray and rub spice mixture evenly on each piece. Bake at 400° for 8 minutes or until salmon flakes easily with a fork.

• To serve, spoon ⅓ cup of the rice on each plate; place bottom half of a salmon fillet over rice. Spoon another ⅓ cup rice on top and finish layering with top half of a salmon fillet. Garnish each dish with remaining 2 tablespoons pistachios and, if desired, celery leaves.

PER SERVING 449 CAL; 16 g FAT (2 g SAT); 35 g PRO; 44 g CARB; 4 g FIBER; 355 mg SODIUM; 72 mg CHOL

WINTER GRAIN AND ROASTED VEGETABLE SALAD

Winter Grain and Roasted Vegetable Salad

MAKES 6 servings   PREP 20 minutes   ROAST at 425° for 40 minutes   COOK 15 minutes

- 1 **bunch fresh beets (with stems and leaves), about 1¾ pounds**
- 3 **tablespoons plus 2 teaspoons olive oil**
- 1 **tablespoon chopped fresh thyme plus 1 sprig**
- 2 **teaspoons chopped fresh rosemary plus 1 sprig**
- 1½ **teaspoons salt**
- 1 **pound parsnips, peeled and diced into 1-inch pieces**
- ¾ **cup pearled farro**
- ¾ **cup quick-cooking bulgur wheat**
- 1 **medium onion, diced**
- ½ **cup pecans, chopped**
- ½ **teaspoon black pepper**
- 2 **ounces soft goat cheese**

• Heat oven to 425°. Trim beet stems and leaves; set aside. Scrub beets and dry; quarter and toss with 1 tablespoon of the oil, 1 sprig each of the thyme and the rosemary, and ¼ teaspoon of the salt. Wrap tightly in foil and place packet on a baking sheet. Toss parsnips in 1 tablespoon of the oil and ¼ teaspoon of the salt; place unwrapped next to beets. Roast at 425° for 35 to 40 minutes or until fork-tender.

• Allow beets to cool slightly; carefully peel and discard skins using a paper towel. Dice beets into 1-inch pieces and place in a large bowl with accumulated juices and roasted parsnips.

• In a medium lidded pot, combine farro, bulgur and 5 cups water. Cover and bring to a boil; reduce heat to medium-low. Simmer 15 minutes or until grains are cooked. Drain and rinse under cold water. Stir into bowl with beets and parsnips.

• Meanwhile, remove beet greens from stems; roughly chop greens and cut stems into 1-inch pieces. Wash well. Add 1 tablespoon of the olive oil to a large skillet. Stir in beet stems; cook 6 minutes. Add onion and remaining 1 tablespoon thyme and 2 teaspoons rosemary; cook 5 minutes. Stir in beet greens; cook 3 minutes or until greens are wilted. Season with ¼ teaspoon of the salt. Stir into bowl with grains and roasted vegetables. Mix in pecans, remaining 2 teaspoons olive oil and ¾ teaspoon salt and the pepper. Crumble goat cheese over each serving.

PER SERVING 426 CAL; 18 g FAT (3 g SAT); 12 g PRO; 59 g CARB; 15 g FIBER; 815 mg SODIUM; 4 mg CHOL

SOUPER SUPPERS

A bowl of steaming soup or stew does wonders to take the edge off winter.

LOADED BAKED
POTATO SOUP,
PAGE 53

BLACK BEAN AND
SAUSAGE STEW,
PAGE 54

SHRIMP AND CORN
CHOWDER

Whether it's creamy or brothy, a bowl of soup soothes and satisfies like no other food can.

Shrimp and Corn Chowder

MAKES 6 servings   **PREP** 15 minutes
COOK 28 minutes

2	tablespoons unsalted butter
2	small leeks, cleaned and sliced
1	large baking potato (about 12 ounces), peeled and cubed
3	cups reduced-sodium chicken broth
4	cups corn kernels
1½	cups half-and-half
2	tablespoons cornstarch
2	teaspoons Old Bay seasoning
1	sweet yellow pepper, cored, seeded and thinly sliced
1	sweet orange pepper, cored, seeded and thinly sliced
1	pound medium shrimp, shelled, deveined and cut into thirds
1	tablespoon lemon juice
½	teaspoon hot sauce

• In a large pot, melt butter over medium heat and add leeks; cook 8 minutes, stirring occasionally. Add potato, broth and corn kernels. Simmer 15 minutes, stirring occasionally.

• Combine half-and-half and cornstarch; stir into pot. Add Old Bay seasoning and bring to a simmer. Add peppers and shrimp; simmer 5 minutes, stirring occasionally. Stir in lemon juice and hot sauce. Serve immediately.

PER SERVING 377 **CAL**; 13 g **FAT** (7 g **SAT**); 23 g **PRO**; 47 g **CARB**; 5 g **FIBER**; 603 mg **SODIUM**; 147 mg **CHOL**

TORTELLINI EN BRODO

Tortellini en Brodo

MAKES 6 servings   **PREP** 5 minutes   **COOK** 10 minutes

5	cups reduced-sodium chicken broth
1	package (20 ounces) refrigerated herb chicken tortellini (such as Buitoni)
1	pound plum tomatoes, seeds removed, chopped
1	cup frozen peas, thawed
1	bag (6 ounces) baby spinach
	Shredded basil and shaved Parmesan cheese (optional)

• Place broth and 1 cup water in a large pot and bring to a boil. Add tortellini and tomatoes; simmer 7 to 9 minutes or until tortellini are tender.

• Stir in peas. Add spinach gradually. Sprinkle basil and Parmesan over top, if desired. Serve immediately.

PER SERVING 346 **CAL**; 9 g **FAT** (2 g **SAT**); 14 g **PRO**; 54 g **CARB**; 5 g **FIBER**; 766 mg **SODIUM**; 34 mg **CHOL**

BEEF STEW WITH
ROOT VEGETABLES

Hearty Chicken Noodle Soup

MAKES 6 servings PREP 30 minutes
COOK 1 hour, 28 minutes

BROTH

8	large bone-in, skinless chicken thighs (about 3 pounds)
2	large onions, peeled and cut into wedges
2	carrots, cut into 1-inch pieces
2	ribs celery, cut into 1-inch pieces
4	cloves garlic, smashed
2	bay leaves
15	whole peppercorns
2	sprigs fresh thyme

SOUP

2	carrots, peeled and sliced
2	ribs celery, sliced
2	small chicken bouillon cubes
½	teaspoon salt
4	ounces broad egg noodles
¼	cup parsley, chopped

• **Broth:** In a large pot, combine chicken, onions, carrots, celery, garlic, bay leaves, peppercorns, thyme and 12 cups water.

• Bring to a boil; reduce heat and simmer, covered, 20 minutes. Remove chicken thighs to a cutting board and shred meat from bones. Reserve meat and add bones back to pot. Continue to simmer, covered, 60 minutes. Strain broth into a second large pot. Discard bones and other solids.

• **Soup:** Skim broth; bring to a boil. Add carrots, celery, bouillon cubes and salt. Stir in noodles and cook about 7 minutes or until noodles and vegetables are tender. Stir in parsley and reserved chicken. Cook 1 minute to heat chicken.

PER SERVING 384 CAL; 15 g FAT (4 g SAT); 36 g PRO; 25 g CARB; 3 g FIBER; 864 mg SODIUM; 137 mg CHOL

Beef Stew with Root Vegetables

MAKES 6 servings PREP 25 minutes SLOW COOK on HIGH for 5 hours or LOW for 7 hours

2	pounds beef chuck, cut into 2-inch pieces
1	teaspoon salt
¼	teaspoon plus ⅛ teaspoon black pepper
1	large onion, chopped
2	cloves garlic, chopped
½	pound baby carrots
2	parsnips (about ¾ pound), peeled and cut into 2-inch pieces
2	turnips (about ½ pound), peeled and cut into 1-inch pieces
1	pound small (about 1 inch in diameter) multicolor potatoes
½	teaspoon dried thyme
2½	cups unsalted beef broth
3	tablespoons cornstarch

• Coat slow cooker bowl with nonstick cooking spray. Season beef with ½ teaspoon of the salt and ¼ teaspoon of the pepper. Place in bottom of slow cooker.

• Scatter onion, garlic, carrots, parsnips, turnips, potatoes and thyme over beef, in that order. Pour broth over top.

• Cover and cook on HIGH for 5 hours or LOW for 7 hours. Drain liquid from slow cooker into a small saucepan and bring to a simmer. In a small bowl, combine cornstarch with 2 tablespoons water and stir until combined. Slowly stir into saucepan and simmer 1 minute or until thickened. Season with remaining ½ teaspoon salt and ⅛ teaspoon pepper. Stir liquid back into slow cooker and serve.

PER SERVING 364 CAL; 7 g FAT (3 g SAT); 35 g PRO; 36 g CARB; 6 g FIBER; 574 mg SODIUM; 64 mg CHOL

HEARTY CHICKEN
NOODLE SOUP

MINESTRONE WITH TUBETTINI
AND CAPICOLA

Minestrone with Tubettini and Capicola

MAKES 6 servings PREP 25 minutes
COOK 21 minutes

2	tablespoons olive oil
1	onion, chopped
3	cloves garlic, sliced
3	carrots, cut into small dice
3	ribs celery, sliced
1	medium zucchini, diced
1	medium summer squash, diced
1	can (14.5 ounces) no-salt-added diced tomatoes
½	teaspoon dried Italian seasoning
2	large vegetable bouillon cubes, from a 2.1-ounce package
¾	cup tubettini (such as Ronzoni)
1	can (15 ounces) chickpeas, drained and rinsed
1	can (15 ounces) kidney beans, drained and rinsed
¼	pound capicola, cut into ribbons Grated Parmesan cheese (optional)

• Heat oil in a large pot over medium-high heat. Add onion and garlic; cook 5 minutes, stirring occasionally.

• Add carrots, celery, zucchini, squash, tomatoes, Italian seasoning, bouillon cubes and 8 cups hot water. Simmer, partially covered, 5 minutes, stirring occasionally. Stir in pasta and simmer an additional 9 minutes or until vegetables and pasta are tender. Stir in chickpeas, kidney beans, and capicola; heat through, about 2 minutes.

• Top each portion with grated Parmesan cheese, if desired. Serve immediately.

PER SERVING 331 CAL; 9 g FAT (2 g SAT); 16 g PRO; 48 g CARB; 11 g FIBER; 1,111 mg SODIUM; 11 mg CHOL

LOADED BAKED POTATO SOUP

Loaded Baked Potato Soup

MAKES 6 servings PREP 20 minutes BAKE at 400° for 50 minutes COOK 22 minutes BROIL 3 minutes

2½	pounds baking potatoes
½	pound sliced bacon
2	tablespoons unsalted butter
1	small onion, finely chopped
2	tablespoons all-purpose flour
4	cups 2% milk
½	teaspoon salt
¼	teaspoon black pepper
¼	teaspoon nutmeg
¼	teaspoon cayenne pepper
3	cups shredded white cheddar cheese
4	scallions, thinly sliced
6	teaspoons sour cream

• Heat oven to 400°. Pierce potatoes with a fork and bake at 400° for 50 minutes until tender. Allow to cool slightly. Scoop potato flesh into a bowl and mash.

• Meanwhile, cook bacon in a large nonstick skillet until crisp, about 8 minutes. Remove bacon and crumble; set aside. Reserve 2 tablespoons of bacon fat.

• In a large pot, add butter and reserved bacon fat. Heat over medium heat. Add onion and cook 3 minutes; sprinkle flour over onion and cook 1 minute. Gradually whisk in milk; stir in salt, pepper, nutmeg and cayenne. Add reserved mashed potatoes and bring to a simmer. Reduce heat to medium-low and simmer 10 minutes, stirring occasionally. Stir in 2 cups of the cheese, half the reserved bacon and half the scallions.

• Heat broiler. Divide soup equally among 6 flameproof onion soup crocks. Sprinkle remaining cup of cheese over tops of crocks. Broil 4 inches from heat source for 3 minutes until cheese melts.

• Garnish each with 1 teaspoon sour cream and remaining bacon and scallions.

PER SERVING 577 CAL; 31 g FAT (17 g SAT); 29 g PRO; 48 g CARB; 3 g FIBER; 933 mg SODIUM; 100 mg CHOL

BLACK BEAN AND
SAUSAGE STEW

Butternut Squash and Carrot Soup

MAKES 6 servings **PREP** 15 minutes
BAKE at 425° for 30 minutes

1	**large onion, cut in eighths**
3	**cloves garlic, whole**
1	**butternut squash (2½ pounds), peeled, seeded and cut into 1-inch pieces**
½	**pound carrots, peeled and cut into 1-inch pieces**
2	**tablespoons olive oil**
¾	**teaspoon salt**
¼	**teaspoon black pepper**
4	**cups reduced-sodium chicken broth**
1	**tablespoon brown sugar**
¼	**teaspoon ground nutmeg**

• Heat oven to 425°. Toss vegetables with oil, ¼ teaspoon of the salt and ⅛ teaspoon of the pepper. Spread vegetables on a baking sheet and bake at 425° for 30 minutes, turning after 15 minutes.

• Puree vegetables and broth in 2 batches until smooth; transfer to large pot. Bring to a simmer. Stir in brown sugar, nutmeg and remaining ¼ teaspoon salt and ⅛ teaspoon pepper. Serve with Sourdough Croutons (recipe below), if desired.

PER SERVING 144 **CAL**; 5 g **FAT** (1 g **SAT**); 3 g **PRO**; 26 g **CARB**; 6 g **FIBER**; 629 mg **SODIUM**; 0 mg **CHOL**

Sourdough Croutons: Toss 4 cups sourdough bread cubes with 1 tablespoon olive oil and ¼ teaspoon garlic salt. Bake at 400° for 8 minutes, turning once. Toss with an additional tablespoon olive oil before serving.

Black Bean and Sausage Stew

MAKES 6 servings **SOAK** overnight **PREP** 15 minutes **COOK** 1 hour, 10 minutes

1	**pound black beans**
1	**tablespoon vegetable oil**
½	**pound sweet Italian sausage, casings removed, crumbled**
1	**large onion, chopped**
4	**cloves garlic, chopped**
4	**cups reduced-sodium vegetable broth**
1	**teaspoon chili powder**
1	**teaspoon dried oregano**
1	**teaspoon cumin**
1	**sweet red pepper, cored, seeded and chopped**
	Chopped cilantro, avocado, tomato and sweet red pepper for garnish (optional)

• Cover beans with water and soak overnight, or follow quick-soak method on packaging.

• Heat oil in a large pot over medium-high heat. Add sausage and cook 5 minutes, stirring occasionally. Add onion and garlic; cook 5 minutes, stirring occasionally.

• Stir in broth, 2 cups water, soaked beans, chili powder, oregano and cumin. Simmer, covered, 60 minutes or until beans are tender; add red pepper during last few minutes of cooking.

• Remove about 1 cup of the mixture to a blender and puree; return to pot.

• Garnish each serving with chopped cilantro, avocado, tomato and sweet red pepper, if desired.

PER SERVING 358 **CAL**; 7 g **FAT** (2 g **SAT**); 24 g **PRO**; 52 g **CARB**; 18 g **FIBER**; 531 mg **SODIUM**; 11 mg **CHOL**

BUTTERNUT SQUASH
AND CARROT SOUP

TOMATILLO
PORK STEW

A jar of tomatillo salsa makes a shortcut sauce in this delicious Mexican-style stew.

Tomatillo Pork Stew

MAKES 6 servings **PREP** 15 minutes
SLOW COOK on HIGH for 6 hours or LOW for 8 hours

2	pounds boneless pork shoulder or pork butt, cut into 2-inch pieces
1	teaspoon dried oregano
1	teaspoon cumin
½	teaspoon salt
¼	teaspoon black pepper
2	onions, halved and sliced
4	cloves garlic, chopped
2	green peppers, cored, seeded and sliced
1	jar (16 ounces) tomatillo salsa
2	tablespoons cornmeal
3	cups cooked white rice
	Sour cream and cilantro (optional)

• Coat slow cooker bowl with nonstick cooking spray. Place pork in bottom of slow cooker and toss with oregano, cumin, salt and pepper. Scatter onions, garlic and green peppers over pork, in that order. Pour salsa evenly over top.

• Cover and cook on HIGH for 6 hours or LOW for 8 hours. Stir in cornmeal during last 15 minutes. Serve with rice and, if desired, top with sour cream and cilantro.

PER SERVING 373 **CAL**; 9 g **FAT** (3 g **SAT**); 32 g **PRO**; 37 g **CARB**; 3 g **FIBER**; 912 mg **SODIUM**; 91 mg **CHOL**

BEEF BARLEY SOUP

Beef Barley Soup

MAKES 6 servings **PREP** 20 minutes **COOK** 1 hour, 40 minutes

1	tablespoon vegetable oil
1¼	pounds beef chuck for stew, cut into 1-inch pieces
1	teaspoon salt
⅛	teaspoon black pepper
1	large onion, sliced
3	cloves garlic, chopped
1	container (26 ounces) unsalted beef stock (such as Swanson), about 3¼ cups
2	large carrots, peeled and sliced
2	ribs celery, sliced
1	can (14.5 ounces) no-salt-added diced tomatoes
8	ounces sliced white mushrooms
¾	cup barley
½	teaspoon dried thyme
1	cup frozen peas, thawed
	Chopped parsley (optional)

• Heat oil in a large pot over medium-high heat. Season beef with ¼ teaspoon of the salt and the black pepper and add to pot; sauté 5 minutes, turning once. Add onion and garlic; cook 3 minutes, stirring occasionally.

• Add stock, 3 cups water, carrots and celery. Cover and simmer 60 minutes, stirring occasionally. Add tomatoes, mushrooms, barley, remaining ¾ teaspoon of the salt and the thyme. Simmer 30 minutes, covered, stirring occasionally.

• Stir in peas and simmer 2 minutes. Garnish with parsley, if desired.

PER SERVING 304 **CAL**; 7 g **FAT** (2 g **SAT**); 27 g **PRO**; 33 g **CARB**; 8 g **FIBER**; 724 mg **SODIUM**; 40 mg **CHOL**

SCORE!

No matter the outcome of the game, this Super Bowl spread is a winner!

WARM LAYERED DIP

Warm Layered Dip

MAKES 16 servings PREP 15 minutes
BAKE at 375° for 30 minutes
MICROWAVE 45 seconds

2	cans (16 ounces each) refried beans
1	cup jarred salsa verde
1	package (8 ounces) shredded Mexican cheese blend
2	teaspoons ancho or regular chili powder
1	cup sour cream
½	red onion, finely chopped
3	tablespoons white vinegar
½	teaspoon sugar
2	plum tomatoes, seeded and diced
1	cup shredded lettuce (about 6 ounces)
1	avocado, peeled, pitted and diced
	Traditional tortilla chips or tortilla scoops, for dipping

• Heat oven to 375°. Coat a 1½-quart baking dish with nonstick cooking spray. Spread 1 can of the refried beans into prepared dish. Top with ½ cup of the salsa and 1 cup of the cheese. Stir remaining can of beans to loosen, then carefully spread over cheese layer. Top with remaining ½ cup salsa and 1 cup cheese.

• Cover dish with foil and bake at 375° for 30 minutes. Meanwhile, microwave chili powder in a small glass dish for 45 seconds until toasted. Stir into sour cream.

• In a small bowl, combine red onion, vinegar and sugar. Set aside.

• Remove warm dish from oven. Uncover and top with sour cream, tomatoes, lettuce, avocado and pickled red onions. Serve with chips.

PER SERVING 257 CAL; 14 g FAT (6 g SAT); 8 g PRO; 24 g CARB; 5 g FIBER; 404 mg SODIUM; 27 mg CHOL

MAC AND CHEESE CUPS

Mac and Cheese Cups

MAKES 16 servings PREP 15 minutes COOK 8 minutes BAKE at 375° for 18 minutes

1	box (16 ounces) elbow macaroni
2	tablespoons unsalted butter
2	tablespoons all-purpose flour
2½	cups milk
1	tablespoon Dijon mustard
2	teaspoon onion powder
¼	teaspoon salt
¼	teaspoon pepper
	Pinch nutmeg
	Pinch cayenne
¼	pound sliced American cheese
1	bag (8 ounces) shredded cheddar cheese
1	egg, lightly beaten

• Heat oven to 375°. Bring a large pot of lightly salted water to a boil. Add macaroni and cook 8 minutes or per package directions. Drain and return to pot.

• Meanwhile, melt butter in a saucepan over medium heat. Add flour and cook 1 minute. Whisk in milk in a thin stream. Whisk in mustard, onion powder, salt, pepper, nutmeg and cayenne. Bring to a simmer; cook 3 minutes, whisking occasionally.

• Remove from heat and whisk in American cheese and 1 cup of the shredded cheddar cheese. Whisk a little of the cheese sauce into the egg to temper. Whisk egg mixture back into the cheese sauce.

• Stir sauce into macaroni. Coat indents of 16 standard muffin cups with nonstick cooking spray. Divide macaroni among prepared cups. Top each with 1 tablespoon of the remaining cheddar cheese. Bake at 375° for 18 minutes until lightly browned. Cool slightly before running a thin spatula around edge and spooning out of pans.

PER SERVING 229 CAL; 10 g FAT (6 g SAT); 10 g PRO; 25 g CARB; 1 g FIBER; 258 mg SODIUM; 41 mg CHOL

Chili Bar

MAKES 16 servings **PREP** 10 minutes **COOK** 33 minutes

- **2** tablespoons olive oil
- **1** large onion, chopped
- **2** cloves garlic, sliced
- **⅓** cup mild chili powder
- **1** teaspoon dried oregano
- **½** teaspoon ground cumin
- **3** pounds ground beef
- **¼** cup packed dark brown sugar
- **1** ounce unsweetened chocolate
- **1** can (29 ounces) tomato sauce
- **¾** teaspoon salt
- **¼** teaspoon cayenne pepper
- **2** cans (15 ounces each) dark red kidney beans, drained and rinsed

Baked potatoes, hot dogs and buns, hard taco shells and fully cooked rice
Shredded cheddar cheese, sliced scallions and sour cream

• Heat oil in a large, lidded pot over medium heat. Add onion and cook 5 minutes. Stir in garlic, chili powder, oregano and cumin. Cook 1 minute.

• Increase heat to medium-high. Crumble in ground beef. Cook 5 minutes, stirring occasionally. Add brown sugar and chocolate and cook until dissolved. Stir in tomato sauce, salt and cayenne and bring to a simmer. Partially cover and simmer over medium-low heat for 20 minutes, stirring occasionally.

• Uncover and stir in beans. Cook 2 minutes to heat through. Serve spooned over baked potatoes or hot dogs, inside hard taco shells or over rice. Garnish with shredded cheese, scallions and/or sour cream.

PER ¾ CUP CHILI 292 **CAL**; 16 g **FAT** (6 g **SAT**); 20 g **PRO**; 18 g **CARB**; 6 g **FIBER**; 581 mg **SODIUM**; 58 mg **CHOL**

CHILI BAR

ONION-MUSTARD DIP

GARDEN VEGGIE DIP

CHIPOTLE BASIL DIP

TRIO OF DIPS

A sour cream mixture is the starter for three dip variations.

Sour Cream Base

MAKES 3 cups   PREP 5 minutes

1	container (16 ounces) sour cream
1	cup light mayonnaise
2	tablespoons milk
1	tablespoon fresh lemon juice
¼	teaspoon salt
¼	teaspoon black pepper
	Assorted veggies, for dipping

• In a medium bowl, blend sour cream, mayo, milk, lemon juice, salt and pepper. Combine 1 cup with each of the three dip flavors. Refrigerate until serving with assorted veggies alongside.

Chipotle Basil

MAKES 1¼ cups   PREP 5 minutes

• Combine 2 chipotle chiles in adobo, seeded; 1 cup basil leaves; and 1 cup Sour Cream Base in a mini chopper or blender. Puree until smooth.

PER TABLESPOON 30 CAL; 3 g FAT (1 g SAT); 0 g PRO; 1 g CARB; 0 g FIBER; 57 mg SODIUM; 6 mg CHOL

Onion-Mustard

MAKES 1¼ cups   PREP 5 minutes

• Melt 1 tablespoon unsalted butter in a 10-inch skillet over medium heat. Add 1 cup chopped onion and ½ teaspoon sugar and cook 15 minutes (you may need to lower heat to medium-low) until very soft. Remove from heat and add 2 tablespoons Dijon mustard and a

pinch of nutmeg. Stir in 1 cup Sour Cream Base.

PER TABLESPOON 39 CAL; 3 g FAT (1 g SAT); 0 g PRO; 2 g CARB; 0 g FIBER; 81 mg SODIUM; 8 mg CHOL

Garden Veggie

MAKES 1¼ cups   PREP 5 minutes
REFRIGERATE 20 minutes

• Combine ½ sweet red pepper, finely chopped; 3 tablespoons minced chives; 3 tablespoons chopped parsley; 1 tablespoon milk or water; and ¾ teaspoon garlic powder with 1 cup Sour Cream Base. Refrigerate 20 minutes or until serving.

PER TABLESPOON 31 CAL; 3 g FAT (1 g SAT); 0 g PRO; 1 g CARB; 0 g FIBER; 45 mg SODIUM; 7 mg CHOL

FRIED PICKLES

Fried Pickles

MAKES 16 servings   **PREP** 15 minutes
COOK 3 minutes per batch

- **3**   **cups vegetable oil**
- **¾**   **cup cornmeal**
- **⅓**   **cup plus ½ cup all-purpose flour**
- **¼**   **teaspoon black pepper**
- **¼**   **teaspoon cayenne pepper**
- **⅛**   **teaspoon salt**
- **⅔**   **cup milk**
- **1**   **large egg**
- **1**   **jar (32 ounces) dill pickles**
       Bottled ranch dressing

• Heat oil in a deep pot over medium heat until it registers 370° to 375° on a deep-fat fry thermometer.

• Mix cornmeal, ⅓ cup of the flour, the pepper, cayenne and salt in a large resealable plastic bag.

• Whisk milk and egg together in a medium bowl.

• Cut pickles into spears (about 8 per pickle). Blot spears dry on paper towels and toss in a bowl with remaining ½ cup flour.

• Dip 8 to 10 spears in egg mixture, then add to bag with cornmeal mixture. Shake to coat pickles. Spread spears onto a rack and continue with all spears (in batches of 8 to 10).

• Fry one batch of pickles for 3 minutes until golden. Transfer to a paper towel and repeat with all batches, returning oil to 375° before adding each batch. Serve with ranch dressing.

PER SERVING 142 **CAL**; 9 g **FAT** (2 g **SAT**); 2 g **PRO**; 12 g **CARB**; 1 g **FIBER**; 595 mg **SODIUM**; 16 mg **CHOL**

GRIDIRON GRILLED VEGGIE SANDWICHES

Gridiron Grilled Veggie Sandwiches

MAKES 16 servings   **PREP** 15 minutes   **GRILL** 14 minutes   **REFRIGERATE** overnight
BAKE at 350° for 35 minutes

- **1**   **eggplant (1 pound), trimmed and sliced ¼ inch thick lengthwise**
- **½**   **teaspoon salt**
- **2**   **tablespoons white balsamic vinegar**
- **1**   **teaspoon Dijon or grainy mustard**
- **5**   **tablespoons olive oil**
- **¼**   **teaspoon black pepper**
- **1**   **sweet onion, peeled, trimmed and cut into ¼-inch rings (about 5)**
- **1**   **large zucchini (12 ounces), trimmed and sliced ¼ inch thick lengthwise**
- **2**   **loaves (1 pound each) roasted garlic or traditional oval bread (unsliced)**
- **1**   **cup jarred pesto**
- **7**   **to 8 ounces smoked or traditional mozzarella cheese, sliced**
- **1**   **cup jarred roasted red peppers**

• Heat grill or grill pan to medium-high. Spread eggplant slices on a sheet of paper towels and sprinkle with ¼ teaspoon of the salt. Set aside to drain. Blot with paper towels.

• In a small bowl, blend remaining ¼ teaspoon salt, the vinegar and mustard. While whisking, add oil in a thin stream. Whisk in pepper.

• Brush eggplant and onion with some of the dressing and grill 4 minutes per side, turning once. Remove to a platter. Brush zucchini with dressing and grill 3 minutes per side, turning once (this may need to be done in batches). Transfer to platter. Refrigerate overnight.

• Heat oven to 350°. Slice bread lengthwise in half. Spread each cut side with ¼ cup of the pesto. Divide eggplant slices between loaves. Top with zucchini, onion, cheese and roasted peppers. Replace top crusts and wrap loaves in foil.

• Bake at 350° for 20 minutes, weighing down with a cast-iron skillet or foil-wrapped brick. Unwrap loaves and bake an additional 10 to 15 minutes, until cheese is melted and sandwiches are warm throughout. Cut each loaf into 8 slices.

PER SERVING 303 **CAL**; 16 g **FAT** (4 g **SAT**); 11 g **PRO**; 30 g **CARB**; 4 g **FIBER**; 523 mg **SODIUM**; 16 mg **CHOL**

Touchdown Cupcakes

MAKES 16 servings **PREP** 15 minutes **BAKE** at 325° for 20 minutes

CUPCAKES

2¼	cups all-purpose flour
1	teaspoon baking soda
½	teaspoon salt
½	teaspoon baking powder
1	stick (½ cup) unsalted butter, softened
1⅓	cups sugar
½	cup cream cheese, softened
½	cup boiling water
2	large eggs
1	teaspoon vanilla extract
⅓	cup unsweetened cocoa powder

DECORATIONS

1	stick (½ cup) unsalted butter, softened
½	cup cream cheese, softened
2	cups confectioners' sugar
2	tablespoons milk
1	teaspoon vanilla extract
	Green food coloring
	#233 or #234 piping tip (grass tip) or a medium star tip
16	chocolate-covered almonds

• **Cupcakes:** Heat oven to 325°. Line 16 cups of 2 muffin tins with paper or foil liners. Blend flour, baking soda, salt and baking powder in a bowl.

• In a large bowl, beat butter and sugar. In a separate bowl, beat cream cheese with ¼ cup of the boiling water. Beat eggs, one at a time, into butter mixture, beating well after each addition. Beat in vanilla.

• On low, beat in half the flour mixture, then the cream cheese mixture, followed by remaining flour mixture.

• Remove 1 cup of the batter to a small bowl. Whisk remaining ¼ cup boiling water into cocoa powder. Fold into smaller portion of batter.

• Fill cupcake liners half full of vanilla batter. Divide chocolate batter evenly among cups. Swirl with a knife. Bake at 325° for 18 to 20 minutes. Cool on a wire rack.

• **Decorations:** Beat butter and cream cheese until smooth. On low, beat in confectioners' sugar, milk and vanilla. Separate ½ cup of the frosting and place in a resealable plastic bag. Tint remaining frosting green. Transfer to a piping bag fitted with #233, #234 or star tip. Pipe onto cupcakes to resemble grass (alternately, spread green frosting onto cupcakes). Snip a tiny corner off bag with white frosting and pipe lines and numbers on cupcakes. Place a chocolate-covered almond on each cake and pipe on laces with white frosting.

PER SERVING 372 **CAL**; 19 g **FAT** (11 g **SAT**); 5 g **PRO**; 48 g **CARB**; 1 g **FIBER**; 223 mg **SODIUM**; 73 mg **CHOL**

SPAGHETTI CARBONARA,
PAGE 84

MARCH

69   83   91

QUICK FIXES

Eat well on busy weeknights with these delicious 30-minute meals.

TURKEY SAUSAGE AND
SPINACH ORECCHIETTE,
PAGE 75

Shrimp and Sweet Pepper Fajitas

MAKES 4 servings **PREP** 10 minutes **COOK** 15 minutes

1	tablespoon vegetable oil
1	pound medium shrimp, shelled and deveined
1	tablespoon Southwest seasoning blend
6	cups sliced fresh peppers and onions
⅛	teaspoon salt
1	cup quinoa, uncooked
8	warm corn tortillas
½	cup reduced-fat sour cream
¼	cup jarred salsa verde
2	limes, cut into wedges
4	scallions, sliced

• Heat oil in a large nonstick skillet over medium-high heat. Season shrimp with 1 teaspoon of the Southwest seasoning. Add to skillet and cook 2 minutes on each side. Remove to a plate.

• Add peppers and onions to skillet. Season with salt and 1 teaspoon of the Southwest seasoning. Cook 10 minutes or until tender, stirring often. Add up to ¼ cup water if mixture becomes too dry. Stir in shrimp.

• Meanwhile, cook quinoa following package directions, about 15 minutes, adding remaining 1 teaspoon Southwest seasoning. Remove from heat.

• Wrap shrimp-and-pepper mixture in tortillas and serve with quinoa, sour cream, salsa, limes and scallions.

PER SERVING (2 fajitas) 484 **CAL**; 12 g **FAT** (3 g **SAT**); 29 g **PRO**; 65 g **CARB**; 8 g **FIBER**; 738 mg **SODIUM**; 184 mg **CHOL**

HONEY-SOY GLAZED SALMON

Brown rice can be made ahead: Cook, then spread on a baking sheet to cool. Store in recipe-size portions in the refrigerator up to 3 days. Reheat as needed.

PORK MEDALLIONS WITH APPLES

Honey-Soy Glazed Salmon

MAKES 4 servings **PREP** 10 minutes
BAKE at 450° for 15 minutes

½	**cup honey, slightly heated**
2	**tablespoons reduced-sodium soy sauce**
2	**tablespoons jarred chopped garlic**
1	**tablespoon lime juice**
4	**salmon fillets (about 5 ounces each)**
2	**cups cooked brown rice**
2	**scallions, sliced**
½	**cup cilantro, chopped**
	Steamed snow peas (optional)

• Heat oven to 450°. Line a baking dish with aluminum foil and spray with nonstick cooking spray.

• In a small bowl, whisk together honey, soy sauce, garlic and lime juice. Place salmon, skin side down, in prepared dish and spoon half the sauce over top. Bake at 450° for 10 minutes. Spoon some of the remaining sauce over salmon; bake for an additional 5 minutes. Broil salmon 1 minute, if desired, until lightly browned.

• To serve, garnish salmon and rice with scallions and cilantro. Drizzle remaining sauce over salmon and rice. Serve with steamed snow peas, if desired.

PER SERVING 427 CAL; 6 g FAT (1 g SAT); 34 g PRO; 59 g CARB; 2 g FIBER; 415 mg SODIUM; 81 mg CHOL

Pork Medallions with Apples

MAKES 4 servings **PREP** 10 minutes **COOK** 20 minutes

POTATOES

1	**pound small red-skinned potatoes, halved**
1	**tablespoon vegetable oil**
¼	**teaspoon salt**
⅛	**teaspoon black pepper**

PORK

8	**thin boneless pork cutlets (about 1¼ pounds total)**
¾	**teaspoon salt**
¼	**teaspoon black pepper**
1	**teaspoon dried rosemary**
2	**tablespoons vegetable oil**
2	**Gala apples, peeled, cored and thinly sliced**
1	**cup frozen chopped onion, thawed**
1	**tablespoon jarred chopped garlic**
1	**tablespoon plus 1 teaspoon cornstarch**
2½	**cups apple cider**
2	**teaspoons Dijon mustard**
	Steamed green beans (optional)

• **Potatoes.** Heat oven to 450°. Toss potatoes with oil, salt and pepper. Place on a rimmed baking pan and roast for 20 minutes or until tender. Turn after 10 minutes.

• **Pork.** Meanwhile, season pork with ½ teaspoon of the salt, ⅛ teaspoon of the pepper and ¾ teaspoon of the rosemary. Heat oil in a large nonstick skillet over medium-high heat. Add pork; cook 2 minutes per side. Remove to a plate; keep warm.

• Add apples, onion and garlic to skillet; cook 5 minutes, stirring occasionally. Combine cornstarch and cider; add to skillet. Stir in remaining ¼ teaspoon each salt and rosemary and remaining ⅛ teaspoon pepper. Simmer 1 minute until thickened; stir in mustard.

• Serve pork chops and potatoes with apples and sauce spooned over and, if desired, green beans on the side.

PER SERVING 491 CAL; 17 g FAT (4 g SAT); 33 g PRO; 52 g CARB; 4 g FIBER; 750 mg SODIUM; 88 mg CHOL

BROCCOLI-ONION PIE

Broccoli-Onion Pie

MAKES 6 servings PREP 5 minutes BAKE at 400° for 25 minutes

¾ cup 2% milk

4 eggs

3 tablespoons vegetable oil

½ cup shredded Parmesan cheese

1 teaspoon dried oregano

¾ teaspoon garlic salt

⅛ teaspoon ground nutmeg

⅛ teaspoon black pepper

¾ cup reduced-fat baking mix

4 cups small fresh broccoli florets

1 cup chopped frozen onions, thawed

Tossed salad and sliced tomato (optional)

• Heat oven to 400°. Coat six 6-ounce ceramic ramekins with nonstick cooking spray.

• In a large bowl, whisk together milk, eggs, oil, 6 tablespoons of the cheese, the oregano, garlic salt, nutmeg and pepper. Whisk in baking mix until smooth; fold in broccoli and onions.

• Divide mixture equally among ramekins. Bake at 400° for 15 minutes. Sprinkle remaining 2 tablespoons cheese over tops of ramekins and bake for an additional 10 minutes or until internal temperature reaches 160°. Let cool slightly. Run a small knife or an offset spatula around edge of each ramekin and gently unmold.

• Serve with tossed salad and sliced tomato, if desired.

PER SERVING 236 CAL; 14 g FAT (3 g SAT); 11 g PRO; 18 g CARB; 2 g FIBER; 430 mg SODIUM; 149 mg CHOL

Chicken Stuffed with Tomato and Cheese

MAKES 4 servings PREP 15 minutes BROIL 10 minutes COOK 4 minutes

4 boneless, skinless chicken breasts (about 4 ounces each)

½ teaspoon salt

¼ teaspoon black pepper

¾ cup shredded part-skim mozzarella cheese

1 plum tomato (8 slices)

8 large basil leaves

⅓ cup bread crumbs

2 tablespoons grated Parmesan cheese

2 egg whites, lightly beaten

2 teaspoons olive oil

1 tablespoon chopped garlic

1 can (14 ounces) reduced-sodium diced tomatoes

¼ cup torn basil

½ pound angel hair pasta, cooked following package directions

• Heat broiler to high. Set oven rack about 8 inches from heat source. Coat a broiler pan with nonstick cooking spray.

• Slice each chicken breast in half horizontally, leaving one side attached. Open like a book and season with ¼ teaspoon of the salt and ⅛ teaspoon of the pepper. On one side of each breast, layer mozzarella, tomato and basil. Fold over.

• Combine bread crumbs and Parmesan on a plate. Dip both sides of chicken in egg whites and coat with bread crumb mixture; place on prepared broiler pan. Lightly spritz with nonstick cooking spray and broil for 4 to 5 minutes per side or until temperature reaches 160°.

• Meanwhile, in a medium saucepan heat oil over medium-high heat; add garlic and cook 30 seconds. Stir in tomatoes and remaining ¼ teaspoon salt and ⅛ teaspoon pepper. Simmer 3 minutes; add basil.

• Serve chicken with cooked angel hair and sauce.

PER SERVING 487 CAL; 11 g FAT (4 g SAT); 42 g PRO; 53 g CARB; 3 g FIBER; 683 mg SODIUM; 76 mg CHOL

CHICKEN STUFFED WITH
TOMATO AND CHEESE

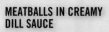
MEATBALLS IN CREAMY DILL SAUCE

Meatballs in Creamy Dill Sauce

MAKES 4 servings **PREP** 15 minutes
COOK 14 minutes

1	**pound lean ground beef**
1	**egg**
⅓	**cup bread crumbs**
¼	**cup fat-free milk**
½	**teaspoon salt**
½	**teaspoon black pepper**
1	**medium onion, thinly sliced**
2	**cups reduced-sodium beef broth**
2	**tablespoons all-purpose flour**
1	**can (4 ounces) sliced mushrooms, drained**
¼	**cup reduced-fat sour cream**
2	**tablespoons snipped fresh dill**
6	**ounces egg noodles, cooked following package directions**
	Steamed broccoli (optional)

• In a large bowl, combine ground beef, egg, bread crumbs, milk and ¼ teaspoon each of the salt and pepper. Form into 16 meatballs.

• Heat a large nonstick skillet over medium-high heat; coat with nonstick cooking spray. Add onion and cook 2 minutes. Combine broth and flour; add to skillet. Bring to a simmer. Add mushrooms, meatballs and remaining ¼ teaspoon each salt and pepper. Cook 12 minutes, turning meatballs once, until temperature reaches 160°. Remove from heat; stir in sour cream and dill.

• Serve with noodles and, if desired, steamed broccoli.

PER SERVING 448 **CAL**; 12 g **FAT** (5 g **SAT**); 37 g **PRO**; 45 g **CARB**; 3 g **FIBER**; 789 mg **SODIUM**; 181 mg **CHOL**

TURKEY SAUSAGE AND SPINACH ORECCHIETTE

Turkey Sausage and Spinach Orecchiette

MAKES 6 servings **PREP** 10 minutes **COOK** 12 minutes

4	**sweet Italian turkey sausages (about ¾ pound), casings removed, crumbled**
1	**cup frozen chopped onions, thawed**
2	**tablespoons jarred chopped garlic**
2	**cups sliced sweet red and yellow peppers**
½	**teaspoon dried Italian seasoning**
1	**can (8 ounces) no-salt-added tomato sauce**
1	**pound orecchiette**
1	**bag (6 ounces) baby spinach**
⅓	**cup shredded Asiago cheese**

• Heat a large nonstick skillet over medium-high heat. Add sausage, onions and garlic; cook 5 minutes, stirring occasionally. Stir in peppers and Italian seasoning; cook an additional 5 minutes, stirring occasionally. Add tomato sauce and simmer 2 minutes.

• Meanwhile, cook orecchiette following package directions, about 10 minutes. Drain, reserving 1 cup cooking water.

• Gradually stir spinach into skillet. In pasta pot, combine pasta and sausage sauce, adding some of the reserved cooking water if needed to loosen sauce.

• To serve, spoon pasta into a large serving bowl. Top with shredded Asiago.

PER SERVING 457 **CAL**; 9 g **FAT** (3 g **SAT**); 24 g **PRO**; 68 g **CARB**; 6 g **FIBER**; 459 mg **SODIUM**; 39 mg **CHOL**

USE YOUR NOODLE

These Mediterranean-style pasta dishes are destined to become family favorites.

30-MINUTE BOLOGNESE,
PAGE 87

MEDITERRANEAN RIGATONI,
PAGE 84

PIPETTE WITH SAUSAGE
AND FENNEL

Pipette with Sausage and Fennel

MAKES 6 servings
PREP 15 minutes **COOK** 20 minutes

- **1** pound pipette or mezzi rigatoni
- **12** ounces hot Italian sausage, casings removed
- **2** tablespoons olive oil
- **1** large fennel bulb, halved, cored and thinly sliced, fronds chopped and reserved
- **1** medium sweet onion, halved and thinly sliced
-   Juice and zest from 1 orange (about ¼ cup juice and 1 tablespoon zest)
- **¾** cup grated Parmesan
- **¼** teaspoon salt

• Bring a large pot of lightly salted water to a boil. Add pipette and cook 8 minutes or according to package directions. Drain, reserving 1 cup of the pasta water.

• Meanwhile, brown sausage in a large sauté pan over medium-high heat, stirring occasionally, 5 to 7 minutes. Remove sausage to a plate with a slotted spoon.

• Reduce heat to medium. Add oil to the same pan; stir in fennel and onion. Cook 10 to 12 minutes, until vegetables are softened. Pour in orange juice and zest, scraping bottom of pan to release any brown bits. Stir in sausage, pasta, ½ cup of the reserved pasta water (add remaining water ¼ cup at a time if it seems dry), ½ cup of the Parmesan and the salt. Garnish with remaining ¼ cup Parmesan and the reserved fennel fronds.

PER SERVING 509 **CAL**; 17 g **FAT** (5 g **SAT**); 21 g **PRO**; 67 g **CARB**; 5 g **FIBER**; 626 mg **SODIUM**; 25 mg **CHOL**

CAMPANELLE WITH MUSHROOMS AND KALE

Campanelle with Mushrooms and Kale

MAKES 6 servings **PREP** 20 minutes **COOK** 25 minutes

- **1** pound campanelle
- **6** tablespoons unsalted butter
- **1½** pounds mixed mushrooms (such as shiitake, cremini and button), sliced
- **1** large shallot, finely diced
- **12** ounces fresh kale (1 large bunch), stems removed and thinly sliced (about 12 cups)
- **3** tablespoons all-purpose flour
- **3** cups 1% milk
- **1** teaspoon salt
- **¼** teaspoon pepper
- **⅛** teaspoon ground nutmeg

• Bring a large pot of lightly salted water to a boil. Cook campanelle 10 minutes or according to package directions. Drain; set aside.

• Melt 3 tablespoons of the butter in a large sauté pan over medium-high heat. Add mushrooms and shallot, stirring occasionally; cook 10 to 12 minutes until most of the liquid is absorbed. Add kale, stirring until wilted and slightly tender, about 3 minutes.

• Meanwhile, in drained pot, melt remaining 3 tablespoons butter over medium heat. Add flour; cook 2 minutes. Pour in milk in a thin stream, whisking constantly. Bring to a simmer and cook 7 minutes, until thickened, whisking occasionally. Stir in salt, pepper and nutmeg. Stir mushroom-kale mixture and pasta into sauce and serve.

PER SERVING 535 **CAL**; 15 g **FAT** (8 g **SAT**); 20 g **PRO**; 81 g **CARB**; 6 g **FIBER**; 504 mg **SODIUM**; 36 mg **CHOL**

PASTA ALLA VODKA

Pasta shapes are designed to complement the sauce with which they're served. Cup shapes are perfect for chunky sauces.

Tortellini Arrabbiata

MAKES 6 servings PREP 15 minutes COOK 21 minutes

2	tablespoons olive oil
2	green bell peppers, seeded and diced
1	medium onion, chopped
3	cloves garlic, chopped
1	teaspoon Italian seasoning
¼	teaspoon black pepper
1	can (28 ounces) fire-roasted crushed tomatoes
5	jarred pepperoncini, trimmed and sliced
½	cup dry red wine
1	package (20 ounces) plus 1 package (9 ounces) refrigerated cheese tortellini
2	tablespoons grated Parmesan

• Heat oil in a large pot over medium heat. Add green peppers and onion and cook 5 minutes. Add garlic, Italian seasoning and black pepper. Cook 1 minute.

• Stir in crushed tomatoes, pepperoncini and red wine. Simmer 15 minutes.

• Meanwhile, bring a large pot of lightly salted water to a boil. Add tortellini and cook 7 minutes or per package directions. Drain and transfer to a platter. Top with sauce and grated Parmesan.

PER SERVING 552 CAL; 16 g FAT (6 g SAT); 25 g PRO; 76 g CARB; 6 g FIBER; 1,040 mg SODIUM; 77 mg CHOL

Pasta alla Vodka

MAKES 6 servings PREP 10 minutes COOK 17 minutes

1	box (1 pound) small shaped pasta
2	tablespoons olive oil
1	package (6 ounces) Canadian bacon, diced
1	medium onion, finely chopped
1	can (15 ounces) diced tomatoes
1	can (28 ounces) crushed tomatoes in puree
½	cup vodka
¼	cup fresh basil, chopped
2	teaspoons sugar
¼	teaspoon salt
¼	teaspoon black pepper
½	cup heavy cream
2	tablespoons grated Parmesan

• Bring a large pot of lightly salted water to a boil. Add pasta and cook 10 minutes or per package directions. Drain and return to pot.

• Meanwhile, heat oil in a large skillet over medium-high heat. Add Canadian bacon and brown on both sides, about 4 minutes total. Remove to a plate with a slotted spoon.

• Reduce heat to medium and add onion to skillet. Cook 5 minutes. Stir in diced tomatoes, crushed tomatoes, vodka, basil, sugar, salt and pepper and bring to a simmer. Cook 8 minutes.

• Add Canadian bacon back to skillet along with heavy cream. Heat through and spoon over pasta. Top with grated Parmesan.

PER SERVING 499 CAL; 15 g FAT (6 g SAT); 16 g PRO; 62 g CARB; 3 g FIBER; 771 mg SODIUM; 41 mg CHOL

TORTELLINI ARRABBIATA

GEMELLI WITH
MINT-PEA PESTO

Spring vegetables such as peas and asparagus add an eye-catching touch of green—as well as good nutrition—to these yummy pasta dishes.

Gemelli with Mint-Pea Pesto

MAKES 6 servings **PREP** 10 minutes **COOK** 12 minutes

1	bag (14.4 ounces) frozen peas
2	cups fresh mint
¼	cup plus 2 tablespoons olive oil
½	cup sliced almonds
1	tablespoon lemon juice
2	teaspoons lemon zest
2	tablespoons Pecorino-Romano cheese
½	teaspoon salt
⅛	teaspoon pepper
1	pound gemelli

• Bring a large pot of lightly salted water to a boil. Add peas; blanch 30 seconds. Remove from pot with a slotted spoon and run under cold water until cool; set aside. Reserve water (cover with a lid to keep hot).

• In a food processor or blender, combine 1½ cups of the peas, the mint, oil, ¼ cup of the almonds, the lemon juice and lemon zest. Process until well combined. Transfer to a bowl and stir in cheese, salt and pepper.

• Bring reserved pot of water to a boil; add gemelli. Cook 12 minutes or according to package directions. Meanwhile, add pesto to a large sauté pan over medium-low heat. Drain pasta, reserving 1 cup of the water; transfer pasta immediately to pan. Stir in reserved water and the remaining peas and ¼ cup almonds. Serve immediately.

PER SERVING 533 **CAL**; 20 g **FAT** (4 g **SAT**); 19 g **PRO**; 70 g **CARB**; 9 g **FIBER**; 287 mg **SODIUM**; 5 mg **CHOL**

LINGUINE WITH ASPARAGUS, ARTICHOKES AND PANCETTA

Linguine with Asparagus, Artichokes and Pancetta

MAKES 6 servings **PREP** 10 minutes **COOK** 13 minutes

1	pound linguine
4	ounces diced pancetta
1	box (8 ounces) frozen artichokes
1	pound fresh asparagus, trimmed and cut into ½-inch bias slices
1	tablespoon lemon juice
1	cup heavy cream
½	cup fresh parsley, chopped
¾	teaspoon salt
	Freshly cracked pepper

• Bring a large pot of lightly salted water to a boil. Cook linguine 9 minutes or according to package directions. Drain and set aside.

• Meanwhile, add pancetta to a large sauté pan over medium heat; cook 5 to 7 minutes. Remove with slotted spoon to a plate. Increase heat to medium-high. Add artichokes; cook 2 minutes. Stir in asparagus; cook 2 minutes. Add lemon juice, scraping bottom of pan to release any brown bits. Add cream; bring to a simmer and cook 1 to 2 minutes, until slightly thickened. Stir in pancetta, parsley and salt. Garnish with freshly cracked pepper. Serve immediately.

PER SERVING 506 **CAL**; 22 g **FAT** (12 g **SAT**); 16 g **PRO**; 62 g **CARB**; 5 g **FIBER**; 647 mg **SODIUM**; 68 mg **CHOL**

MEDITERRANEAN RIGATONI

With a variety of dried pastas in the pantry, dinner is just a few fresh ingredients—and a few minutes—away.

Spaghetti Carbonara

MAKES 6 servings **PREP** 15 minutes
COOK 10 minutes

1	**pound spaghetti**
6	**slices bacon, diced**
1	**cup milk**
2	**large eggs plus 2 egg yolks**
½	**teaspoon salt**
1	**tablespoon all-purpose flour**
¾	**cup grated Parmesan cheese**
1½	**teaspoons freshly cracked black pepper**

• Bring a pot of lightly salted water to a boil. Add spaghetti and cook 10 minutes or per package directions. Drain, reserving 1 cup of the pasta water.

• Meanwhile, add bacon to a large sauté pan. Cook over medium heat 6 minutes or until slightly crispy. Drain on paper towels, reserving 2 tablespoons of the drippings.

• Blend milk, eggs, egg yolks and salt.

• Heat bacon drippings over medium heat. Whisk in flour; cook 1 minute. Quickly pour in milk mixture, whisking constantly to keep eggs from scrambling. Cook 2 to 3 minutes until thickened. Remove from heat and whisk in ½ cup of the cheese.

• Toss drained pasta with sauce, bacon, remaining ¼ cup cheese and some of the reserved pasta water. Sprinkle with black pepper just before serving.

PER SERVING 468 **CAL**; 15 g **FAT** (6 g **SAT**); 20 g **PRO**; 61 g **CARB**; 3 g **FIBER**; 629 mg **SODIUM**; 127 mg **CHOL**

Mediterranean Rigatoni

MAKES 6 servings **PREP** 15 minutes **COOK** 11 minutes

1	**box (16 ounces) rigatoni**
1	**pound boneless, skinless chicken breasts, cut into ½-inch pieces**
⅔	**cup feta cheese cubes packed in oil, drained, oil reserved**
1	**cup grape tomatoes, halved**
½	**cup pitted Kalamata olives, halved**
1	**teaspoon fresh oregano, chopped**
1	**tablespoon lemon juice plus 1 teaspoon grated lemon zest**
¼	**teaspoon black pepper**
⅛	**teaspoon salt**

• Bring a large pot of lightly salted water to a boil. Add rigatoni and cook 11 minutes or per package directions. Drain, reserving ½ cup of the pasta water.

• Meanwhile, toss chicken with 2 tablespoons of the oil from the feta. Heat a large stainless steel skillet over medium-high heat. Add chicken and cook 4 to 5 minutes, until no longer pink.

• Stir in tomatoes, olives and oregano and heat through. Remove from heat and toss with rigatoni, feta cheese, ¼ cup (or more) of the pasta water, the lemon juice and zest, pepper and salt.

PER SERVING 577 **CAL**; 23 g **FAT** (5 g **SAT**); 29 g **PRO**; 59 g **CARB**; 2 g **FIBER**; 938 mg **SODIUM**; 54 mg **CHOL**

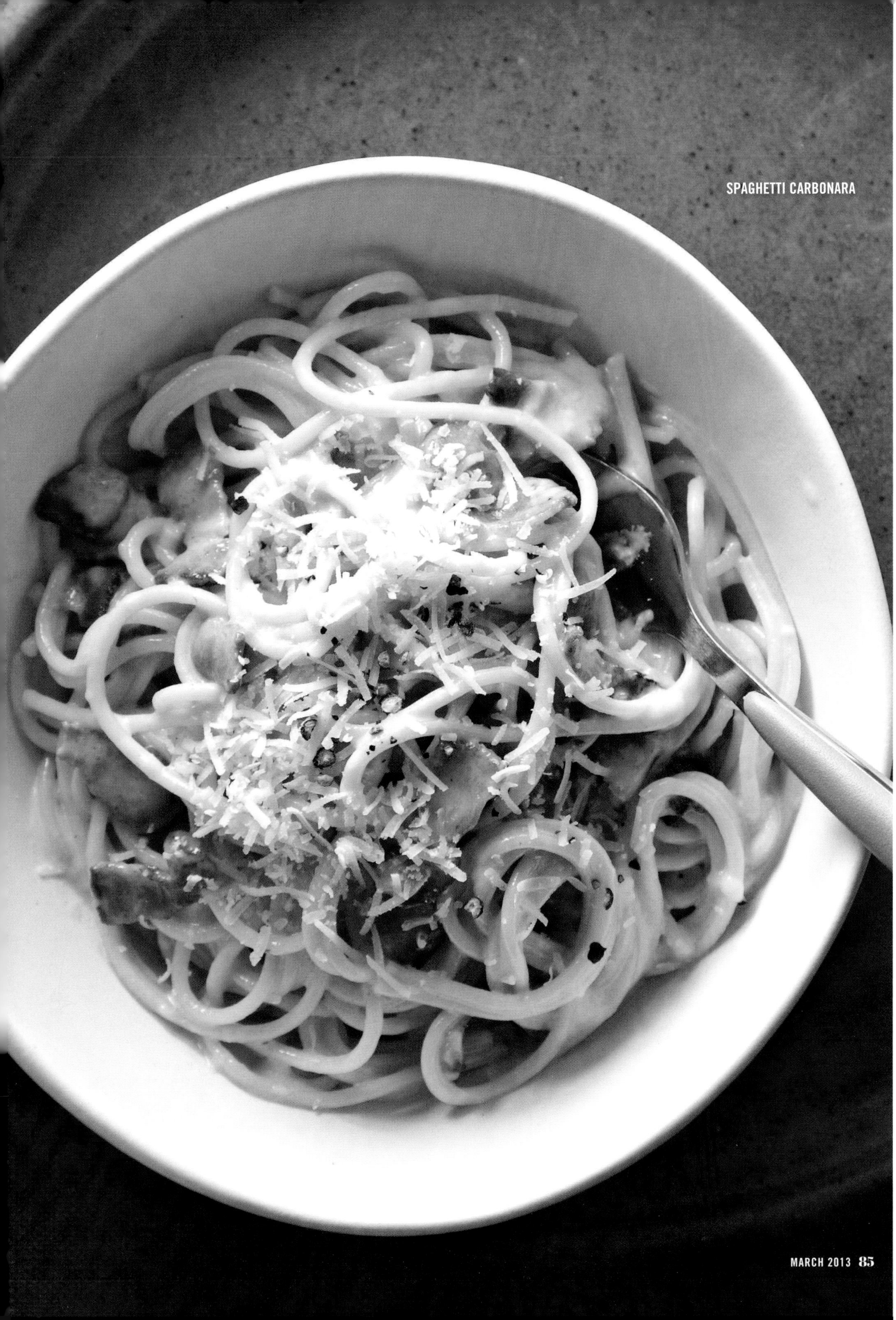

SPAGHETTI CARBONARA

SHRIMP FETTUCCINE WITH
CREAMY CAPER SAUCE

Shrimp Fettuccine with Creamy Caper Sauce

MAKES 4 servings **PREP** 15 minutes
COOK 12 minutes

- **1** **box (12 ounces) spinach fettuccine**
- **1** **tablespoon olive oil**
- **1** **small red onion, halved and sliced**
- **2** **cloves garlic, sliced**
- **1** **pound cleaned raw shrimp, thawed if frozen**
- **⅔** **cup garden vegetable cream cheese**
- **⅓** **cup heavy cream**
- **2** **tablespoons fresh dill, chopped**
- **2** **tablespoons capers**
- **2** **tablespoons lemon juice**
- **½** **teaspoon black pepper**
- **¼** **teaspoon salt**

• Bring a large pot of lightly salted water to a boil. Add fettuccine and stir so strands do not stick together. Cook 12 minutes or per package directions. Drain, reserving ½ cup of the pasta water.

• Meanwhile, heat oil in a large nonstick skillet over medium heat. Add onion and garlic and cook 5 minutes. Stir in shrimp, cream cheese, cream, dill, capers, lemon juice, pepper and salt. Cook 3 to 5 minutes, until shrimp are cooked through.

• Stir cooked pasta into sauce, along with some of the reserved pasta water. Serve immediately.

PER SERVING 597 **CAL**; 23 g **FAT** (12 g **SAT**); 33 g **PRO**; 66 g **CARB**; 4 g **FIBER**; 745 mg **SODIUM**; 221 mg **CHOL**

30-MINUTE BOLOGNESE

30-Minute Bolognese

MAKES 6 servings **PREP** 10 minutes **COOK** 30 minutes

- **1** **medium onion, roughly chopped**
- **2** **ribs celery, roughly chopped**
- **1** **medium carrot, roughly chopped**
- **3** **cloves garlic**
- **1** **tablespoon olive oil**
- **8** **ounces sweet Italian sausage, casings removed**
- **8** **ounces ground beef**
- **8** **ounces ground veal**
- **1** **cup dry red wine**
- **1** **can (14.5 ounces) crushed tomatoes**
- **1** **bay leaf**
- **¼** **teaspoon salt**
- **¼** **teaspoon pepper**
- **1** **pound long fusilli or papardelle**
  Ricotta (optional)
  Fresh parsley, chopped (optional)

• Add onion, celery, carrot and garlic to a food processor. Pulse several times until vegetables are in very small pieces.

Heat oil in a large sauté pan over medium-high heat. Add sausage, beef and veal. Cook 8 minutes, stirring occasionally and breaking up meat. Add vegetables; cook 5 minutes. Pour in wine. Bring to a simmer and cook 2 minutes, scraping bottom of pan to release any brown bits. Stir in tomatoes and bay leaf. Reduce heat to medium-low and simmer 15 minutes. Remove bay leaf. Stir in salt and pepper.

• Meanwhile, bring a pot of lightly salted water to a boil. Add pasta and cook according to package directions. Drain and stir into Bolognese sauce.

• If desired, garnish each serving with a large dollop of ricotta and chopped fresh parsley.

PER SERVING 575 **CAL**; 17 g **FAT** (6 g **SAT**); 30 g **PRO**; 67 g **CARB**; 5 g **FIBER**; 504 mg **SODIUM**; 68 mg **CHOL**

STRESS-FREE SLOW COOKER SUPPERS

Set the timer for 10 hours and dinner will be ready when you walk through the door.

BBQ Short Ribs

MAKES 6 servings **PREP** 15 minutes **SLOW COOK** on LOW for 10 hours

5	**pounds short ribs**
1	**large onion, chopped**
2	**cloves garlic, chopped**
1	**cup ketchup**
1	**cup unsalted beef broth**
2	**tablespoons sugar**
2	**tablespoons white vinegar**
2	**tablespoons Worcestershire sauce**
1	**teaspoon dry mustard**
¼	**teaspoon black pepper**

Mashed potatoes and sautéed Swiss chard (optional)

• Spray slow cooker bowl with nonstick cooking spray. Place ribs in bottom of slow cooker.

• Scatter onion and garlic over ribs. Combine ketchup, broth, sugar, vinegar, Worcestershire sauce, mustard and black pepper. Pour over ribs. Cover and cook on LOW for 10 hours.

• Remove ribs from slow cooker. Skim fat from sauce (there will be more than 1 cup).

• Serve ribs with sauce and, if desired, mashed potatoes and sautéed Swiss chard.

PER SERVING 727 **CAL**; 39 g **FAT** (16 g **SAT**); 73 g **PRO**; 17 g **CARB**; 1 g **FIBER**; 772 mg **SODIUM**; 223 mg **CHOL**

SMOKY NAVY BEAN SOUP

CHICKEN AND HOMINY CHILI BOWL

Smoky Navy Bean Soup

MAKES 8 servings **PREP** 15 minutes
SOAK overnight **SLOW COOK** on LOW for
10 hours

1	pound navy beans, soaked overnight
2	cups chopped smoked ham, about 8 ounces
1	large onion, chopped
3	ribs celery, thinly sliced
3	carrots, peeled and thinly sliced
1	can (14.5 ounces) petite diced tomatoes with chipotle or jalapeño pepper
½	teaspoon dried thyme
1	teaspoon salt
¼	teaspoon black pepper
1	bag (5 ounces) baby spinach

• Coat slow cooker bowl with nonstick cooking spray.

• Drain beans and add to slow cooker bowl. Stir in 6 cups water, ham, onion, celery, carrots, tomatoes and thyme. Cover and cook on LOW for 10 hours.

• Remove 2 cups of the soup, puree and return to slow cooker. Add salt and pepper; gradually add spinach and stir until wilted.

PER SERVING 264 **CAL**; 2 g **FAT** (1 g **SAT**); 18 g
PRO; 43 g **CARB**; 16 g **FIBER**; 744 mg **SODIUM**;
15 mg **CHOL**

Chicken and Hominy Chili Bowl

MAKES 6 servings **PREP** 15 minutes **SLOW COOK** on LOW for 10 hours and on HIGH for 15 minutes

6	large bone-in, skinless chicken thighs (about 6 ounces each)
1	teaspoon salt
1	teaspoon ground cumin
½	teaspoon black pepper
½	teaspoon dried oregano
1	onion, chopped
3	cloves garlic, chopped
1	jalapeño pepper, seeded and chopped
1	green bell pepper, cored, seeded and chopped
2	cups reduced-sodium chicken broth
1	can (15 ounces) hominy, drained and rinsed
2	tablespoons cornmeal
½	cup cilantro, chopped, plus more for serving (optional)
	Tortilla chips and sour cream (optional)

• Spray slow cooker bowl with nonstick cooking spray. Place chicken in bottom of slow cooker and season with ½ teaspoon each of the salt and cumin and ¼ teaspoon each of the black pepper and oregano.

• Scatter onion, garlic, jalapeño and green pepper over chicken. Pour broth over top. Cover and cook on LOW for 10 hours.

• Stir in hominy, cornmeal and remaining ½ teaspoon each salt and cumin and ¼ teaspoon each black pepper and oregano. Cook on HIGH for 15 minutes.

• To serve, stir in cilantro. If desired, accompany with tortilla chips, sour cream and additional chopped cilantro.

PER SERVING 263 **CAL**; 10 g **FAT** (3 g **SAT**); 26 g
PRO; 18 g **CARB**; 3 g **FIBER**; 929 mg **SODIUM**;
86 mg **CHOL**

BALSAMIC POT ROAST

Balsamic Pot Roast

MAKES 6 servings **PREP** 15 minutes **SLOW COOK** on LOW for 10 hours

1	**beef chuck or bottom round roast, about 3¼ pounds**
½	**teaspoon salt**
½	**teaspoon dried thyme**
⅛	**teaspoon black pepper**
1	**onion, chopped**
3	**carrots, chopped**
3	**ribs celery, chopped**
3	**cloves garlic, chopped**
2	**cups unsalted beef stock**
⅔	**cup balsamic vinegar**

Prepared polenta and sautéed sweet peppers (optional)

• Spray slow cooker bowl with nonstick cooking spray. Season roast with salt, thyme and black pepper. Place in bottom of slow cooker.

• Scatter onion, carrots, celery and garlic over roast. Pour stock and balsamic vinegar over top. Cover and cook on LOW for 10 hours.

• Remove roast and allow to rest 15 minutes before slicing. Skim fat from cooking liquid. Mash vegetables in cooking liquid to slightly thicken sauce.

• Serve sliced roast with sauce and, if desired, polenta and sautéed peppers.

PER SERVING 371 CAL; 11 g FAT (4 g SAT); 53 g PRO; 11 g CARB; 2 g FIBER; 256 mg SODIUM; 103 mg CHOL

GREEN DAY

Charm with these cake-like cookies, an Irish take on the classic black-and-white treat.

St. Patrick's Day Green-and-White Cookies

In a medium bowl, whisk together 2 cups all-purpose flour, 1 teaspoon baking powder, 1/2 teaspoon baking soda and 1/4 teaspoon salt. In a large bowl, beat 10 tablespoons unsalted butter and 1/2 cup each light brown sugar and granulated sugar for 2 minutes. Add 1/3 cup buttermilk, 1 egg and 1 1/2 teaspoons vanilla and beat until smooth; gradually beat in dry ingredients until combined. Chill batter for 15 minutes. Drop batter in 2-tablespoon mounds onto ungreased baking sheets, about 3 inches apart. Bake at 375° for 12 to 13 minutes, until just set. Remove from sheet onto a wire rack and cool. Beat together 2 1/2 cups confectioners' sugar and 3 tablespoons milk until smooth and a good spreading consistency, adding an extra 1 or 2 teaspoons milk if needed. Into half the icing, beat 1/8 teaspoon mint extract and a few drops green food coloring. Spread half of the flat side of each cookie with white icing; let dry. Spread other half with green icing and allow to dry. Makes 24 cookies.

VANILLA AND CHOCOLATE
CUPCAKES, PAGES 116–117

APRIL

97   107   118

ON THE MONEY

Make a nutritious, delicious meal for just under $4 a serving.

SALMON SKEWERS OVER
ROASTED VEGETABLES,
PAGE 98

Beans and Greens

MAKES 6 servings **PREP** 15 minutes **COOK** 16 minutes

1	box (12 ounces) penne pasta
8	ounces bacon (10 slices), cut crosswise in pieces
2	cloves garlic, sliced
2	heads (1 pound each) escarole, trimmed, washed, dried and chopped
1	can (15.5 ounces) Great Northern beans, drained and rinsed
½	teaspoon salt
¼	teaspoon pepper
1	tablespoon grated Parmesan

• Bring a large pot of lightly salted water to a boil. Add pasta and cook according to package directions, about 10 minutes. Drain, reserving ½ cup of the pasta water.

• Meanwhile, cook bacon in a large lidded skillet over medium-high heat for 8 to 9 minutes until crispy. Remove with a slotted spoon and reserve 3 tablespoons of the drippings in the pan.

• Set drippings over medium heat and add garlic. Cook 1 minute. Add escarole and cook, stirring occasionally, partially covered, for 5 minutes. Uncover and stir in beans, bacon, salt and pepper. Heat through, adding reserved pasta water if dry.

• Place pasta on a platter and add escarole mixture. Top with Parmesan.

PER SERVING 410 **CAL**; 13 g **FAT** (4 g **SAT**); 18 g **PRO**; 64 g **CARB**; 15 g **FIBER**; 506 mg **SODIUM**; 18 mg **CHOL**

ENCHILADAS SUIZAS

Enchiladas Suizas

MAKES 6 servings **PREP** 25 minutes
COOK 14 minutes **BAKE** at 375° for 25 minutes

1	**package (20.8 ounces) lean ground turkey**
1	**zucchini (about 8 ounces), grated**
1	**small onion, chopped**
¾	**teaspoon salt**
½	**teaspoon dried oregano**
½	**teaspoon black pepper**
¼	**teaspoon ground cumin**
1	**jar (16 ounces) medium salsa verde (tomatillo salsa)**
¾	**cup half-and-half**
4	**ounces Monterey Jack cheese, grated (1 cup)**
12	**corn tortillas**
	Chopped cilantro (optional)

• Heat oven to 375°. Coat a 13 x 9 x 2-inch baking dish with nonstick cooking spray.

• Coat a 12-inch nonstick skillet with nonstick spray and place over medium heat. Crumble in ground turkey and add zucchini and onion. Cook until turkey is no longer pink and most of the liquid has evaporated, 10 minutes. Season with ½ teaspoon of the salt, the oregano, ¼ teaspoon of the pepper and the cumin.

• Meanwhile, combine salsa, half-and-half and remaining ¼ teaspoon each of the salt and pepper in a blender and pulse until smooth. Stir ¾ cup of the sauce into skillet and heat through. Remove from heat and stir in ¼ cup of the cheese.

• Pour ⅔ cup of the sauce over prepared dish, tilting to coat bottom. Heat a small nonstick skillet over medium-high heat and add 1 tortilla. Heat, flipping, 20 seconds. Transfer to a work surface and spoon ¼ cup of the turkey mixture down center. Roll up to enclose filling and transfer, seam side down, to prepared dish. Repeat with remaining tortillas and filling.

• Pour remaining sauce over enchiladas and top with remaining ¾ cup cheese. Bake at 375° for 25 minutes. Serve warm. Garnish with cilantro, if desired.

PER SERVING 408 **CAL**; 18 g **FAT** (8 g **SAT**); 26 g **PRO**; 33 g **CARB**; 4 g **FIBER**; 773 mg **SODIUM**; 108 mg **CHOL**

TURKEY AND TABBOULEH

Turkey and Tabbouleh

MAKES 4 servings **PREP** 20 minutes **LET STAND** 1 hour **GRILL** 4 minutes

1	**cup garden vegetable broth**
1	**cup quick-cooking bulgur**
2	**plum tomatoes, seeded and diced**
1	**cucumber, peeled, seeded and diced**
½	**cup (2 ounces) crumbled feta cheese**
¼	**cup fresh mint, chopped**
¼	**cup fresh parsley, chopped**
3	**tablespoons lemon juice plus 1 teaspoon lemon zest**
2	**cloves garlic, minced**
1	**teaspoon honey**
½	**teaspoon salt**
¼	**teaspoon black pepper**
¼	**cup olive oil**
1	**pound turkey cutlets**

• Bring vegetable broth to a boil. Pour over bulgur in a large bowl. Cover with plastic and let stand 1 hour.

• Heat grill or grill pan to medium-high (alternately, you can use a large nonstick skillet). Toss bulgur with tomatoes, cucumber, feta, mint and parsley.

• In a small bowl, whisk lemon juice and zest, garlic, honey, ¼ teaspoon of the salt and ⅛ teaspoon of the pepper. While whisking, add oil in a stream.

• Toss turkey with 2 tablespoons of the dressing and season with remaining ¼ teaspoon salt and ⅛ teaspoon pepper. Coat cutlets with a spritz of nonstick cooking spray. Grill cutlets for 3 to 4 minutes, turning once (or sauté over medium-high heat).

• Toss bulgur mixture with remaining dressing. Serve turkey cutlets over tabbouleh.

PER SERVING 429 **CAL**; 18 g **FAT** (4 g **SAT**); 35 g **PRO**; 35 g **CARB**; 8 g **FIBER**; 709 mg **SODIUM**; 58 mg **CHOL**

SALMON SKEWERS OVER
ROASTED VEGETABLES

Salmon Skewers over Roasted Vegetables

MAKES 4 servings PREP 20 minutes ROAST at 425° for 40 minutes BROIL 5 minutes

2	tablespoons red wine vinegar
1	teaspoon Dijon mustard
½	teaspoon smoked or traditional paprika, plus more for sprinkling
¾	teaspoon salt
½	teaspoon black pepper
2	tablespoons plus 2 teaspoons olive oil
1½	pounds red-skinned potatoes, cut into 1½-inch pieces
½	red onion
1	pound asparagus, tough ends discarded, or green beans
1	pound skinless salmon fillet, cut into 1½-inch cubes
16	cherry tomatoes

• Heat oven to 425°.

• In a small bowl, whisk together vinegar, mustard, paprika, ¼ teaspoon of the salt and ⅛ teaspoon of the pepper. While whisking, add the oil in a stream.

• Toss potatoes with 2 tablespoons of the dressing and spread onto a rimmed baking sheet. Sprinkle paprika on cut side of onion and add to pan, cut side up. Roast at 425° for 20 minutes.

• Stir potatoes and push to one side of the pan. Remove onion to a cutting board. Toss asparagus with 1 tablespoon of the remaining dressing and add to pan. Continue to roast at 425° for 20 minutes.

• Meanwhile, toss salmon with remaining 2 tablespoons dressing. Cut onion into 4 wedges, then cut wedges in half. Thread eight 6- to 8-inch skewers with salmon, onion and cherry tomatoes. Season with ¼ teaspoon salt and ⅛ teaspoon pepper.

• Remove potatoes and asparagus from oven. Season with remaining ¼ teaspoon salt and ¼ teaspoon pepper. Turn oven temperature up to broil.

• Broil skewers, 4 inches from heat, for 5 minutes, turning once. Serve skewers over roasted vegetables.

PER SERVING 433 CAL; 18 g FAT (3 g SAT); 32 g PRO; 38 g CARB; 7 g FIBER; 538 mg SODIUM; 72 mg CHOL

Spinach, Orange and Chicken Salad

MAKES 6 servings PREP 25 minutes
MICROWAVE 40 seconds MARINATE 15 minutes
GRILL 14 minutes

6	small juice oranges
2	tablespoons red wine vinegar
1	teaspoon grainy mustard
½	teaspoon sugar
½	teaspoon salt
¼	teaspoon black pepper
⅛	teaspoon ground cumin
⅓	cup olive oil
1½	pounds boneless, skinless chicken breasts
1	package (5 ounces) baby spinach
1	head green leaf lettuce, trimmed, cleaned and torn into bite-size pieces
½	red onion, thinly sliced
1	package (3.5 ounces) crumbled goat cheese

• Cut off peel and slice sections from 5 of the oranges. Place in a bowl. Juice remaining orange (you will need ¼ cup juice).

• In a small bowl, whisk orange juice, vinegar, mustard, sugar, ¼ teaspoon of the salt and ⅛ teaspoon of the pepper. Microwave cumin in a small bowl for 40 seconds or until fragrant. Whisk into orange juice mixture. While whisking, add oil in a thin stream.

• Place chicken in a resealable plastic bag and add ⅓ cup of the dressing. Marinate 15 minutes.

• Meanwhile, heat grill or grill pan. Remove chicken from marinade and discard any remaining marinade. Grill for 14 minutes, turning once, or until chicken registers 160° on an instant-read thermometer.

• In a very large bowl, toss spinach, lettuce, orange sections (and any juice in bowl), red onion slices, goat cheese and remaining dressing. Slice chicken and fan over top of salad. Sprinkle with remaining ¼ teaspoon salt and ⅛ teaspoon pepper and serve.

PER SERVING 528 CAL; 16 g FAT (4 g SAT); 29 g PRO; 65 g CARB; 4 g FIBER; 661 mg SODIUM; 72 mg CHOL

SPINACH, ORANGE AND
CHICKEN SALAD

GET CRACKING

Our Top 10 egg recipes can't be beat (we just couldn't resist!).

SPRING EGGS
BENEDICT, PAGE 107

MINI KEY LIME MERINGUE PIES,
PAGE 111

SHRIMP PAD THAI

Shrimp Pad Thai

MAKES 4 servings **PREP** 15 minutes
SOAK 30 minutes **COOK** 9 minutes, 30 seconds

- ½ **package (16 ounces) rice noodles (8 ounces total)**
- 3 **tablespoons packed light brown sugar**
- 2 **tablespoons plus 1 teaspoon fish sauce**
- 1 **tablespoon balsamic vinegar**
- ¼ **teaspoon cayenne pepper**
- 2 **tablespoons canola oil**
- 3 **cloves garlic, chopped**
- ¾ **pound raw peeled and deveined shrimp**
- 3 **eggs**
- 1 **cup bean sprouts**
- 1 **cup sliced scallions**
- ⅓ **cup chopped roasted unsalted peanuts, plus more for garnish**
- 1 **lime, cut into wedges**
  Fresh cilantro (optional)

• Soak noodles in water for 30 minutes or according to package directions. Drain; set aside.

• In a small bowl, stir together brown sugar, fish sauce, vinegar and cayenne; set aside. Heat oil in a large nonstick skillet on medium-high heat. Add garlic; sauté 30 seconds. Stir in shrimp; sauté 2 minutes, flipping once. Move garlic and shrimp to side of pan closest to handle. Tilt skillet so that empty side is closest to burner; add noodles and ½ cup water. Stir noodles for 3 to 4 minutes, until almost all the water is absorbed, keeping skillet tilted and shrimp untouched. Return entire pan to burner. Pour in fish sauce-brown sugar mixture and stir, combining shrimp and noodles. Make a well in the center. Add 1 egg; when white starts to set (it takes about 1 minute), break yolk with a rubber spatula, scramble and mix into shrimp-noodle mixture. Repeat with remaining 2 eggs, making a well each time. Stir in bean sprouts, ¾ cup of the scallions and the peanuts.

• Serve immediately. Garnish with remaining ¼ cup scallions and, if desired, chopped peanuts, a squirt of lime and fresh cilantro.

PER SERVING 498 **CAL**; 18 g **FAT** (3 g **SAT**); 26 g **PRO**; 59 g **CARB**; 3 g **FIBER**; 1,020 mg **SODIUM**; 285 mg **CHOL**

EGG DROP SOUP

Egg Drop Soup

MAKES 6 servings **PREP** 10 minutes **COOK** 2 minutes

- 1 **tablespoon soy sauce**
- 1 **tablespoon cornstarch**
- 4 **cups chicken broth**
- ¼ **teaspoon salt**
- ⅛ **teaspoon white or black pepper**
- 8 **ounces cubed super-firm tofu**
- 1 **cup sliced scallions**
- 3 **eggs, beaten**

• In a small bowl, stir together soy sauce and cornstarch until smooth. In a medium lidded pot, bring broth, salt and pepper to a boil. Slowly pour in soy sauce mixture; stir and reduce heat to a low boil. Stir in tofu and ½ cup of the scallions. Simmer for 2 minutes.

• Slowly pour beaten eggs into soup in a thin stream while stirring in a circular motion. Serve immediately, garnishing with remaining ½ cup scallions.

PER SERVING 150 **CAL**; 8 g **FAT** (2 g **SAT**); 14 g **PRO**; 5 g **CARB**; 1 g **FIBER**; 899 mg **SODIUM**; 212 mg **CHOL**

ITALIAN BAKED EGGS

The Mexican casserole called Chilaquiles was created as a thrifty and tasty way to use up leftover tortillas.

Chilaquiles

MAKES 6 servings **PREP** 15 minutes
COOK 8 minutes

1	**cup canola oil**
8	**corn tortillas, cut into ¾-inch strips**
¼	**plus ⅛ teaspoon salt**
6	**eggs, beaten**
2	**cups shredded cooked chicken**
1	**cup salsa verde** **Shredded queso fresco, sliced scallions and chopped cilantro (optional)**

• Heat oil in a large heavy-bottom skillet over medium-high heat until shimmering, about 350° to 375° on a deep-fry thermometer. Fry tortilla strips in 3 batches until golden brown, 1 to 2 minutes each, gently moving around in oil with a slotted spoon. Remove with spoon to a paper-towel-lined plate. Season strips with ¼ teaspoon of the salt.

• Carefully discard all but 1 tablespoon of the oil. Add eggs and cook over medium heat until scrambled, about 2 minutes. Season with remaining ⅛ teaspoon salt. Meanwhile, heat the shredded chicken and salsa verde in a medium pan.

• Arrange tortilla strips on a large platter. Spoon chicken mixture on top, then scatter eggs on the chicken. Garnish with shredded queso fresco, sliced scallions and chopped cilantro, if desired.

PER SERVING 320 **CAL**; 17 g **FAT** (3 g **SAT**); 23 g **PRO**; 19 g **CARB**; 2 g **FIBER**; 392 mg **SODIUM**; 251 mg **CHOL**

Italian Baked Eggs

MAKES 4 servings **PREP** 10 minutes **COOK** 11 minutes **BAKE** at 400° for 8 minutes

1	**tablespoon olive oil**
1	**small onion, diced**
3	**garlic cloves, chopped**
1	**can (28 ounces) crushed tomatoes**
½	**cup chopped fresh basil**
¼	**teaspoon salt**
⅛	**teaspoon pepper**
4	**eggs**
4	**ounces smoked or regular fresh mozzarella, sliced** **Crusty bread**

• Heat oven to 400°. In a large oven-safe skillet (not nonstick), heat olive oil over medium heat. Stir in onion; cook 3 to 5 minutes until softened. Stir in garlic; cook 1 minute until softened. Pour in tomatoes, ¼ cup of the basil, the salt and pepper. Reduce heat to medium-low and simmer 5 minutes.

• Remove skillet from heat. Crack eggs into sauce, spacing evenly apart. Distribute cheese around skillet. Bake at 400° on top rack until egg whites are set, about 8 minutes.

• Carefully remove skillet from oven. Scatter remaining ¼ cup basil on top and serve immediately with crusty bread.

PER SERVING 267 **CAL**; 16 g **FAT** (7 g **SAT**); 16 g **PRO**; 19 g **CARB**; 4 g **FIBER**; 679 mg **SODIUM**; 232 mg **CHOL**

CORNED BEEF HASH

Corned Beef Hash

MAKES 6 servings **PREP** 10 minutes
COOK 30 minutes

- **1** **pound deli corned beef, cut into ½-inch-thick slices**
- **5** **tablespoons unsalted butter**
- **4** **cups frozen unsalted potato cubes or shredded potatoes**
- **1** **medium onion, diced**
- **1** **sweet red pepper, diced**
- **3** **cloves garlic, chopped**
- **1** **teaspoon chopped fresh thyme**
- **¾** **teaspoon salt**
- **¼** **teaspoon freshly cracked pepper, plus more for serving (optional)**
- **6** **eggs**
  Chopped fresh parsley (optional)

• Slice corned beef into ½-inch cubes; set aside. Over medium heat, melt 3 tablespoons of the butter in a 9- or 10-inch cast-iron skillet. Stir in potatoes, onion, red pepper, garlic, thyme, ½ teaspoon of the salt and the pepper. Mix well and press down with a spatula. Cook 10 minutes. Stir, scraping brown bits from bottom. Press down and cook another 10 minutes. Stir in corned beef, again scraping brown bits from bottom. Press down and cook 10 more minutes.

• Meanwhile, during the final 10 minutes of cooking time, fry eggs: Heat 1 tablespoon of the butter in a large nonstick skillet over medium heat. Crack 3 eggs into skillet, spacing evenly apart. Fry for 3 minutes until whites are set. Repeat with remaining 1 tablespoon butter and remaining 3 eggs. Season all of the eggs evenly with the remaining ¼ teaspoon salt.

• Serve eggs over hash and, if desired, season with more pepper and chopped fresh parsley.

PER SERVING 309 **CAL**; 17 g **FAT** (9 g **SAT**); 22 g **PRO**; 17 g **CARB**; 2 g **FIBER**; 916 mg **SODIUM**; 277 mg **CHOL**

SPRING EGGS BENEDICT

Spring Eggs Benedict

MAKES 4 servings **PREP** 25 minutes **BAKE** at 400° for 12 minutes **COOK** 10 minutes
MICROWAVE 1 minute

- **1** **sheet puff pastry (from a 17.3-ounce box), thawed**
- **9** **eggs plus 1 yolk**
- **8** **ounces asparagus, trimmed**
- **1** **tablespoon fresh lemon juice**
- **¼** **teaspoon plus ⅛ teaspoon salt**
  Pinch cayenne pepper
- **5** **tablespoons unsalted butter**
  Chopped parsley (optional)
  Freshly cracked pepper (optional)

• Heat oven to 400°. Roll out thawed puff pastry to 11 x 9½ inches. Using a 3-inch round cutter, remove 8 rounds. Separate 1 egg; beat white and reserve yolk. Transfer rounds to a parchment-lined baking sheet and brush with egg white. Bake at 400° for 12 minutes or until puffed and golden.

• Fill a large, straight-sided skillet three-fourths full with water. Bring to a boil. Add asparagus and cook 1 to 2 minutes, until crisp-tender. Remove with a slotted spoon and toss in 1 teaspoon of the lemon juice. Season with ⅛ teaspoon of the salt and set aside.

• In the same skillet, reduce heat until water is barely simmering. Crack 4 eggs into separate cups. Pour into water one by one. Poach eggs 3 to 4 minutes or until whites are set. Remove with a slotted spoon to a paper-towel-lined plate. Repeat with 4 more eggs.

• Meanwhile, place 2 egg yolks (including the 1 reserved), remaining 2 teaspoons lemon juice, ⅛ teaspoon of the salt and the cayenne in a blender; process until combined. Melt butter in a bowl in microwave for 1 minute, covering to avoid splatter. Slowly stream melted butter into blender while running; hollandaise should thicken immediately.

• To serve, place 2 puff pastry rounds on a plate. Place 2 asparagus spears and 1 poached egg on each round. Season eggs with remaining ⅛ teaspoon salt and pour a bit of hollandaise over each egg. Garnish with chopped parsley and freshly cracked pepper, if desired.

PER SERVING 452 **CAL**; 35 g **FAT** (15 g **SAT**); 19 g **PRO**; 16 g **CARB**; 2 g **FIBER**; 556 mg **SODIUM**; 531 mg **CHOL**

SMOKED SALMON AND CHIVE DEVILED EGGS

Spinach-Artichoke Strata

MAKES 8 servings **PREP** 10 minutes
COOK 7 minutes **REFRIGERATE** overnight
BAKE at 350° for 1 hour **LET REST** 10 minutes

1	tablespoon olive oil
1	box (9 ounces) frozen artichoke hearts
2	bags (6 ounces each) fresh baby spinach
8	eggs
2½	cups 2% milk
¾	teaspoon salt
¼	teaspoon pepper
7	ounces feta cheese, crumbled
⅓	cup pitted Kalamata olives, chopped
1	oval loaf Italian bread, cut into 1-inch cubes (about 1 pound)

• Spray a 13 x 9-inch baking dish with nonstick cooking spray. Heat oil in a large sauté pan over medium-high heat. Add artichoke hearts; cook 3 to 5 minutes or until thawed and browned. Stir in spinach; cook until wilted, about 1 to 2 minutes. Remove to a mesh strainer and gently press to release some liquid from spinach. Set vegetables aside.

• In a large bowl, whisk eggs. Whisk in milk, salt and pepper until combined. Stir in feta, olives and cooked vegetables. Gently stir in bread cubes, tossing to coat evenly in egg mixture. Transfer to baking dish, cover with aluminum foil and refrigerate overnight.

• Remove strata from refrigerator 30 minutes before baking. Heat oven to 350°. Bake, covered, for 25 minutes. Remove foil and bake another 35 minutes. Let rest 10 minutes before serving.

PER SERVING 350 **CAL**; 18 g **FAT** (7 g **SAT**); 19 g **PRO**; 41 g **CARB**; 6 g **FIBER**; 1,070 mg **SODIUM**; 240 mg **CHOL**

Smoked Salmon and Chive Deviled Eggs

MAKES 12 servings **PREP** 5 minutes **LET STAND** 10 minutes

12	eggs
⅓	cup mayonnaise
¼	cup cream cheese, at room temperature
2	teaspoons Dijon mustard
⅓	cup chopped chives, plus extra for garnish
2	ounces smoked salmon, finely chopped

• Place eggs in a lidded pot and add enough water to cover eggs by 1 inch; cover. Bring to a boil. Turn off heat and let stand 10 minutes. Remove to a bowl filled with ice water; cool completely.

• Peel eggs; discard shells. Halve eggs lengthwise. Remove yolks to a bowl. Place whites cut side up on a large platter.

• Beat yolks, mayonnaise, cream cheese and Dijon mustard with a hand mixer until smooth. Stir in chives and salmon. Spoon some of the mixture into each egg white half. Garnish with chives.

PER SERVING 149 **CAL**; 12 g **FAT** (3 g **SAT**); 9 g **PRO**; 1 g **CARB**; 0 g **FIBER**; 185 mg **SODIUM**; 226 mg **CHOL**

SPINACH-ARTICHOKE
STRATA

DARK CHOCOLATE SOUFFLÉ

Dark Chocolate Soufflé

MAKES 6 servings **PREP** 10 minutes
BAKE at 375° for 17 minutes

	Butter for coating ramekins
¼	**cup granulated sugar, plus extra for coating ramekins**
7	**ounces bittersweet dark chocolate, roughly chopped**
¼	**cup heavy cream**
3	**egg yolks**
¼	**teaspoon vanilla**
6	**egg whites**
	Pinch salt
	Confectioners' sugar (optional)

• Heat oven to 375°. Butter and sugar six 6-ounce ramekins. Fill a small pot with 1 inch of water and bring to a simmer. In a metal bowl large enough to rest on the pot, combine chocolate and heavy cream. Stir until melted. Remove from heat and whisk in egg yolks one at a time, being careful not to scramble. Stir in vanilla.

• In a large bowl (or a stand mixer fitted with whisk attachment), whisk egg whites on high until soft peaks form. While whisking, add sugar and salt; whisk on high until stiff peaks form.

• Gently fold chocolate mixture into whipped egg whites until no streaks remain. (Do not overmix or the soufflés won't rise to the maximum level.) Carefully spoon mixture evenly among ramekins. Bake at 375° for 17 minutes, or until puffed and a cake tester inserted in the middle comes out clean. Dust with confectioners' sugar, if desired, and serve immediately.

PER SERVING 265 **CAL**; 20 g **FAT** (10 g **SAT**); 8 g **PRO**; 23 g **CARB**; 2 g **FIBER**; 67 mg **SODIUM**; 119 mg **CHOL**

MINI KEY LIME MERINGUE PIES

Mini Key Lime Meringue Pies

MAKES 6 servings **PREP** 15 minutes **COOK** 8 minutes **BAKE** at 375° for 7 minutes
REFRIGERATE 2 hours **BROIL** 1 minute

3	**whole eggs, beaten**
1	**cup plus 3 tablespoons sugar**
⅔	**cup Key lime juice**
4	**tablespoons unsalted butter**
4	**egg whites**
1	**package mini graham cracker piecrusts (6)**
⅛	**teaspoon cream of tartar**

• In a small heavy-bottomed pot, combine whole eggs, 1 cup of the sugar, the Key lime juice and butter over medium heat. Cook, stirring constantly, until mixture reaches 175° and coats the back of a spoon, about 8 minutes. Be careful not to heat mixture above that temperature or it will curdle. Pour into a bowl through a mesh strainer. Cool completely, cover with plastic wrap and refrigerate until using.

• Heat oven to 375°. Beat 1 of the egg whites. Place pie shells on a baking sheet and brush with egg white. Bake at 375° for 5 to 7 minutes or until golden brown. Cool completely on a baking rack.

• Fill cooled piecrusts with cooled lime curd. Cover gently with plastic wrap and refrigerate for 2 hours.

• Heat broiler to HIGH. With a hand mixer or a stand mixer fitted with whisk attachment, combine remaining 3 egg whites and the cream of tartar. Beat on high until soft peaks form. With machine running, pour in remaining 3 tablespoons sugar and beat on high until stiff peaks form. Do not overbeat. Spoon meringue onto pies, using back of spoon to create texture. (Alternately, pipe meringue in a continuous spiral around curd.) Broil on HIGH for 30 seconds to 1 minute, about 7 inches from the top, until meringue is golden.

PER SERVING 326 **CAL**; 15 g **FAT** (7 g **SAT**); 7 g **PRO**; 46 g **CARB**; 0 g **FIBER**; 199 mg **SODIUM**; 126 mg **CHOL**

COME FOR DINNER

This casually elegant menu celebrates all things spring.

ROAST CHICKEN WITH
THYME-SCENTED GRAVY

SPRING
VEGETABLE
SAUTÉ

SCALLOPED POTATOES
WITH LEEKS AND
MANCHEGO CHEESE

Roast Chicken with Thyme-Scented Gravy

MAKES 8 servings **PREP** 20 minutes
ROAST at 450° for 30 minutes, then at 400° for 45 minutes **COOK** 4 minutes

- **1** large chicken (about 8 pounds)
- **½** lemon, sliced
- **4** cloves garlic, sliced
- **6** sprigs fresh herbs, such as thyme, sage and oregano
- **2** tablespoons unsalted butter, softened
- **½** teaspoon salt
- **¼** teaspoon black pepper

GRAVY

- **2** tablespoons all-purpose flour
- **2** cups reduced-sodium chicken broth
- **½** cup dry white wine
- **1** teaspoon fresh thyme leaves

• Heat oven to 450°. Place a rack in a large roasting pan.

• Place chicken in prepared roasting pan. Gently lift up breast skin and place lemon, garlic and herbs under skin. Rub softened butter over outside of chicken and season with salt and pepper, inside cavity and out. Tie legs with cotton twine.

• Roast at 450° for 30 minutes; reduce oven temperature to 400° and roast for an additional 45 minutes or until internal temperature in thigh reaches 170°. Remove to a cutting board and allow to rest while preparing gravy.

• **Gravy:** Remove rack from roasting pan and skim off fat. Pour out drippings, reserving ¼ cup. Place roasting pan with reserved drippings over medium heat and whisk in flour. Cook for 1 minute; gradually whisk in broth and wine; stir in thyme. Simmer, stirring continuously, for 3 minutes until slightly thickened. Strain if necessary.

• Carve chicken and serve with gravy.

PER SERVING 511 **CAL**; 30 g **FAT** (9 g **SAT**); 50 g **PRO**; 3 **CARB**; 0 g **FIBER**; 447 mg **SODIUM**; 165 mg **CHOL**

Scalloped Potatoes with Leeks and Manchego Cheese

MAKES 8 servings **PREP** 25 minutes
COOK 5 minutes **BAKE** at 375° for 60 minutes

- **2** cups half-and-half
- **⅛** teaspoon nutmeg
- **⅛** teaspoon cayenne
- **3** pounds large baking potatoes, peeled and cut into slices about ⅛ inch thick
- **2** tablespoons unsalted butter
- **2** large leeks, rinsed, halved lengthwise and sliced
- **3** scallions, sliced
- **½** teaspoon salt
- **2** tablespoons flour
- **3** cups shredded Manchego cheese

• Heat oven to 375°. Lightly coat a 3-quart baking dish with nonstick cooking spray.

• Combine half-and-half, nutmeg and cayenne in a large pot; add potatoes and bring to a boil. Lower heat and simmer for 5 minutes. Drain potatoes over a large bowl, reserving half-and-half.

• Meanwhile, melt butter in a large skillet over medium heat; add leeks and scallions. Cook for 5 minutes, stirring occasionally.

• Layer one-third of the potatoes in prepared baking dish, overlapping as necessary. Sprinkle with ¼ teaspoon of the salt, 1 tablespoon of the flour, half the leek mixture and 1 cup of the cheese. Repeat layering. Top with remaining third of the potatoes and 1 cup cheese.

• Pour half-and-half over potatoes; tilt dish from side to side to evenly distribute. Cover and bake at 375° for 30 minutes; uncover and bake for an additional 30 minutes or until potatoes are tender and top of casserole is lightly browned.

• Cool slightly before serving.

PER SERVING 401 **CAL** 20 g **FAT** (12 g **SAT**); 14 g **PRO**; 41 **CARB**; 3 g **FIBER**; 763 mg **SODIUM**; 60 mg **CHOL**

Spring Vegetable Sauté

MAKES 8 servings **PREP** 15 minutes
COOK 9 minutes

- **1** pound Broccolini or broccoli florets
- **¾** pound haricots verts
- **½** pound fresh or frozen green peas
- **2** sweet red peppers, seeded, cored and sliced
- **3** tablespoons olive oil
- **4** cloves garlic, chopped
- **¼** teaspoon red pepper flakes
- **½** teaspoon salt
  Grilled lemon slices (optional)

• Bring a large pot of lightly salted water to a boil. Add Broccolini, haricots verts, peas and red peppers. Return to a boil and cook for 3 minutes; drain.

• In a large skillet, heat oil over medium-high heat; add garlic and red pepper flakes. Cook for 30 seconds; add vegetables and cook, stirring frequently, for 4 to 5 minutes or until vegetables are tender. Season with salt.

• Serve with grilled lemon slices, if desired.

PER SERVING 111 **CAL**; 6 g **FAT** (1 g **SAT**); 4 g **PRO**; 13 **CARB**; 5 g **FIBER**; 186 mg **SODIUM**; 0 mg **CHOL**

Swap sweet potatoes for baking potatoes, or use a combination of the two.

SCALLOPED POTATOES WITH LEEKS AND MANCHEGO CHEESE

WARM CRAB DIP

HERB AND ASIAGO POPOVERS

• Remove pan from oven and generously coat all over with nonstick cooking spray. Divide batter among 12 popover cups, about ⅓ cup in each (you will have some batter left over). Top with cheese.

• Bake at 400° in middle of oven, placing a tray on lower shelf, for 30 minutes or until popovers are golden brown and risen. Remove from pan and serve immediately.

PER SERVING 171 **CAL**; 7 g **FAT** (3 g **SAT**); 8 g **PRO**; 18 g **CARB**; 1 g **FIBER**; 249 mg **SODIUM**; 85 mg **CHOL**

Coconut-Strawberry Napoleons

MAKES 8 servings **PREP** 25 minutes
BAKE at 400° for 14 minutes

1	sheet frozen puff pastry, thawed, from a 17.3-ounce package
1	package (2.75 ounces) cook-and-serve vanilla pudding
1	can (13.5 ounces) light coconut milk
¼	teaspoon coconut extract
½	cup shredded coconut
1	pound strawberries, cored and sliced, plus more for garnish Confectioners' sugar for dusting

• Heat oven to 400°. Coat a baking sheet with nonstick cooking spray.

• On a lightly floured surface, unroll pastry sheet. Cut into 3 equal pieces along folds. Transfer to baking sheet and bake at 400° for 14 minutes or until golden brown. Remove pastry to a wire rack. Cool completely.

• Prepare pudding following package directions, replacing milk with coconut milk; allow to cool. Stir in coconut extract and shredded coconut.

• Slice each pastry in half horizontally for a total of 6 pieces. Spread a quarter of the pudding over cut side of each of 2 bottom pieces; fan a quarter of the strawberries on each. Repeat layering once more. Top each stack with remaining 2 pieces of pastry. Chill until serving.

• With a serrated knife, cut each pastry into 4 equal pieces, using a sawing motion. Dust tops with confectioners' sugar and garnish with additional sliced strawberries.

PER SERVING 148 **CAL**; 7 g **FAT** (4 g **SAT**); 1 g **PRO**; 20 **CARB**; 2 g **FIBER**; 127 mg **SODIUM**; 0 mg **CHOL**

Warm Crab Dip

MAKES 12 servings **PREP** 15 minutes
COOK 20 minutes **BAKE** at 350° for 30 minutes

2	tablespoons unsalted butter
1	large onion, thinly sliced
2	sprigs fresh thyme
2	packages (8 ounces each) reduced-fat cream cheese, at room temperature
1	container (8 ounces) sour cream
¼	cup milk
2	teaspoons Worcestershire sauce
¼	teaspoon garlic powder
3	scallions, chopped
8	ounces crab claw meat Crackers and celery sticks, for dipping

• Heat oven to 350°.

• Melt butter in a medium skillet over medium heat; add onion and thyme. Cook 15 to 20 minutes, stirring occasionally, until browned. Discard thyme sprigs.

• In a large bowl, combine cream cheese, sour cream, milk, Worcestershire sauce, garlic powder and sautéed onion. Reserve 3 tablespoons of the scallions; stir in remainder. Gently fold in crab and turn out into an 11 x 7-inch baking dish. Bake at 350° for 30 minutes until bubbly around edges.

• Garnish with reserved scallions; serve with crackers and celery sticks.

PER SERVING 178 **CAL**; 14 g **FAT** (9 g **SAT**); 9 g **PRO**; 3 **CARB**; 0 g **FIBER**; 251 mg **SODIUM**; 58 mg **CHOL**

Herb and Asiago Popovers

MAKES 12 popovers **PREP** 15 minutes
BAKE at 400° for 30 minutes

4	eggs, at room temperature
3	tablespoons fresh chopped herbs, such as thyme, chives and oregano
½	teaspoon salt Pinch of cayenne Pinch of nutmeg
2	cups warm milk
2	cups all-purpose flour
1¼	cups shredded Asiago cheese

• Heat oven to 400°. Place one 12-cup popover pan in preheated oven.

• In a large bowl, whisk together eggs, herbs, salt, cayenne and nutmeg. Whisk in warm milk gradually so that eggs do not cook. Gradually whisk in flour until smooth.

COCONUT-STRAWBERRY
NAPOLEONS

BATTER UP

Start with vanilla or chocolate base, add mix-ins, then bake; frost and decorate as directed.

Basic Vanilla Cupcake Recipe

MAKES 36 mini cupcakes **PREP** 15 minutes
BAKE at 325° for 18 minutes

2	**cups all-purpose flour**
1½	**teaspoons baking powder**
¼	**teaspoon salt**
10	**tablespoons (1¼ sticks) unsalted butter, softened**
1	**cup sugar**
3	**large egg whites**
1	**teaspoon vanilla extract**

• Heat oven to 325°. Place paper liners in cups of mini muffin pans (36 total).

• In a small bowl, whisk together flour, baking powder and salt. In a large bowl, beat butter until smooth. Add sugar and beat until fluffy, about 2 minutes. Add egg whites, one at a time, beating well after each. Beat in vanilla. On low, beat in half the flour mixture, then ¾ cup water. Beat in remaining flour mixture.

• Divide batter evenly among prepared cups. Bake at 325° for 18 minutes. Frost and decorate as desired.

PER SERVING 76 **CAL**; 3 g **FAT** (2 g **SAT**); 1 g **PRO**; 11 g **CARB**; 0 g **FIBER**; 38 mg **SODIUM**; 8 mg **CHOL**

Basic Chocolate Cupcake Recipe

MAKES 36 mini cupcakes **PREP** 15 minutes
BAKE at 325° for 19 minutes

1½	**cups all-purpose flour**
½	**cup unsweetened cocoa powder**
1	**teaspoon baking powder**
¼	**teaspoon baking soda**
¼	**teaspoon salt**
½	**cup (1 stick) unsalted butter, softened**
1	**cup sugar**
2	**large eggs**
¼	**cup plain yogurt or sour cream**

• Heat oven to 325°. Place paper liners in cups of mini muffin pans (36 total).

• In a small bowl, whisk together flour, cocoa, baking powder, baking soda and salt.

• In a large bowl, beat together butter and sugar. Beat in eggs, one at a time, beating well after each addition. Beat in yogurt. On low, beat in half the flour mixture. Pour in ⅔ cup water and beat on low until blended. Scrape down side of bowl. On low, beat in remaining flour mixture.

• Divide batter among prepared cups. Bake at 325° for 19 minutes. Cool completely. Frost and decorate as desired.

PER SERVING 73 **CAL**; 3 g **FAT** (2 g **SAT**); 1 g **PRO**; 10 g **CARB**; 1 g **FIBER**; 41 mg **SODIUM**; 20 mg **CHOL**

Vanilla Cupcake Variations

Banana Split (2) Mash 2 **ripe bananas** and finely chop 4 **strawberries**. Fold fruit into batter, along with ½ teaspoon **banana extract**. To frost: Whip 1¼ cups **heavy cream** with 3 tablespoons **confectioners' sugar**. Transfer to a pastry bag fitted with a large star tip. Pipe whipped cream onto cupcakes. Sprinkle with finely chopped **walnuts** and top each with a **maraschino cherry**.

Apple Cobbler (5) Toss 1 peeled, cored and diced **Gala apple** with 2 teaspoons **cornstarch**. Melt 1 tablespoon **butter** in a skillet over medium heat. Add apple, 2 tablespoons packed **light brown sugar**, 2 tablespoons **water** and a pinch of **salt**. Cook 5 to 7 minutes. Cool and fold into batter with ⅛ teaspoon **pumpkin pie spice**. To frost: Beat 1 stick (½ cup) softened **unsalted butter** with 2 cups **confectioners' sugar**, 2 tablespoons **milk** and ¾ teaspoon **pumpkin pie spice**. Spread over cupcakes. Crumble 4 **shortbread cookies** and toss with ½ teaspoon **pumpkin pie spice**. Garnish cupcakes with cookie crumbs.

Red Velvet (8) Prepare batter, adding ¼ cup **cocoa powder** to flour mixture and 2 tablespoons **red food coloring** with vanilla. To frost: After baking, trim 6 tops from tallest cupcakes and crumble trimmings. In a small bowl, beat 1 package (8 ounces) **cream cheese**, ⅔ cup **confectioners' sugar** and 2 tablespoons **milk**. Spread over cupcakes and sprinkle with cake crumbs.

Strawberry Shortcake (11) Combine ¾ cup (about 5 or 6) trimmed **strawberries** with 2 teaspoons **sugar** in a mini chopper. Pulse until chopped; fold into batter. To fill and frost: Beat 1¼ cups **heavy cream**, 3 tablespoons **sugar** and ½ teaspoon **vanilla extract** in a bowl to stiff peaks. Transfer to a piping bag fitted with a wide round tip. Press frosting tip into cupcake and apply gentle pressure to squeeze frosting into cupcake. Dollop frosting onto top of cake and top with a thin **strawberry slice** (you'll need 6 strawberries for all the cupcakes). Repeat with remaining cupcakes, frosting and strawberry slices.

Peanut Butter Cup (7) Combine ¼ cup each **peanuts** and **mini chocolate chips** in a mini chopper and pulse until chopped. Fold into vanilla batter. To frost: Beat together ¼ cup **peanut butter**, ¼ cup (½ stick) softened **unsalted butter**, 2 cups **confectioners' sugar**, 3 tablespoons **milk** and ⅛ teaspoon **salt**. Spread over cupcakes and garnish with 12 **mini Reese's peanut butter cups**, unwrapped and chopped.

Dulce de Leche (12) Combine 25 unwrapped **Werther's Original chewy caramel candies** (5.5-ounce package) and ¼ cup **water** in a small saucepan. Heat over medium heat until melted. Set aside to cool. Prepare vanilla batter, replacing ½ cup of the sugar with packed **light brown sugar** and remaining ½ cup sugar with ½ cup of the melted caramels. Add ¼ teaspoon **ground cinnamon**. To frost: Beat 1 package (8 ounces) **Philadelphia Indulgence dulce de leche caramel** and 4 ounces **cream cheese**. Spread onto cupcakes; drizzle with remaining melted caramels.

Chocolate Cupcake Variations

Cookies 'n' Creme (1) Finely chop ⅓ cup **mini Oreo cookies** (about 10); fold into batter. To frost: Beat ½ cup (1 stick) softened **unsalted butter**, 2 cups **confectioners' sugar** and 2 tablespoons **milk**. Crush 8 **mini Oreos** and fold into frosting. Spread frosting over cupcakes and top each with a **mini Oreo**.

Chocolate-Covered Pretzel (3) Chop 12 small **chocolate-covered pretzels** (½ cup chopped). Fold into batter. To frost: Melt 3 ounces coarsely chopped **semisweet chocolate** in microwave for 1½ minutes. Stir until smooth. Cool slightly. Beat ½ cup (1 stick) softened **unsalted butter** with 2 cups **confectioners' sugar** and 2 tablespoons **milk**. Beat in 1 heaping tablespoon of the melted chocolate. Transfer remaining chocolate to a resealable plastic bag. Spread frosting over cupcakes. Snip a small corner from bag and drizzle chocolate over cupcakes (reheat if needed). Top with ½ cup chopped **chocolate-covered pretzels**.

Mochaccino (4) Blend 2 teaspoons **instant espresso powder** with 2 tablespoons **warm water**. Fold into batter, along with two .375-ounce squares **Ghirardelli dark chocolate**, grated. To frost: Combine 1 cup **heavy cream**, 3 tablespoons **sugar** and 1 teaspoon **coffee extract** in a bowl. Beat on medium to high speed with an electric mixer until stiff peaks form. Spread over cupcakes and garnish with additional grated chocolate (1 square **Ghirardelli dark chocolate**).

Coconut (6) Finely chop ½ cup **sweetened flake coconut**. Fold into batter along with ½ teaspoon **coconut extract**. To frost: Combine 1 **egg white**, ¼ cup **sugar**, 2 teaspoons **water** and a pinch of **salt** in a double boiler set over simmering water. Cook, whisking constantly, until mixture is foamy and registers 160° on an instant-read thermometer. Remove top of double boiler and beat with an electric mixer until stiff peaks form. Beat in ½ teaspoon **coconut extract**. Spread in a thin layer over cupcakes and top with 1⅓ cups **sweetened flake coconut**.

Grasshopper Mint (10) Unwrap and chop 12 **Andes mints** (about ⅓ cup) and fold into batter. To frost: Combine 1 stick (½ cup) softened unsalted **butter** with 2 cups **confectioners' sugar**, 2 tablespoons **milk**, ½ teaspoon **peppermint extract** and 2 drops **green food coloring** in a bowl. Beat on medium speed until smooth. Spread over cupcakes and roll edges in 16 unwrapped and finely chopped **Andes mints**.

S'mores (9) Chop ¾ cup **honey graham sticks** and fold into batter. To frost: Melt four 1.55-ounce **milk chocolate bars** in microwave for 1 minute, stirring halfway. Stir until melted and smooth. Crush ½ cup **honey graham sticks**. Dip top of each cupcake in milk chocolate. Roll edge of cupcake in crushed grahams. Top each cupcake with 4 or 5 **mini marshmallows**. Broil, 4 inches from heat, 1 minute, or until golden brown.

SOCIAL SUPPERS

For family or for friends—these slow cooker dinners are ready when you are.

Lamb Curry

MAKES 6 servings **PREP** 20 minutes **SLOW COOK** on LOW for 10 hours and HIGH for 15 minutes

- **2** pounds boneless lamb shoulder, cut into 2-inch pieces
- **1** teaspoon garam masala
- **1** teaspoon ground coriander
- **1** teaspoon salt
- **1** teaspoon black pepper
- **½** teaspoon turmeric
- **1** large onion, chopped
- **2** tablespoons chopped ginger
- **2** cloves garlic, chopped
- **1** can (15 ounces) diced tomatoes
- **1** cup vegetable broth
- **1** green bell pepper, cored, seeded and cut into 1-inch pieces
- **1** red sweet pepper, cored, seeded and cut into 1-inch pieces
- **½** cup cilantro leaves
- **½** cup plain yogurt
- Basmati rice and naan (optional)

• Coat slow cooker bowl with nonstick cooking spray. Place lamb in slow cooker.

• In a small bowl, combine garam masala, coriander, ½ teaspoon of the salt, ½ teaspoon of the pepper and the turmeric. Season meat with spice mixture. Scatter onion, ginger and garlic over lamb.

• Pour tomatoes and broth over top. Cover and cook on LOW for 10 hours.

• Stir in green and red peppers and remaining ½ teaspoon each salt and pepper. Cook on HIGH for 15 minutes.

• Stir in cilantro. Serve with yogurt and, if desired, basmati rice and naan.

PER SERVING 363 **CAL**; 21 g **FAT** (9 g **SAT**); 31 g **PRO**; 11 g **CARB**; 2 g **FIBER**; 817 mg **SODIUM**; 110 mg **CHOL**

CHICKEN WITH FIGS AND BLUE CHEESE

Pork and Sauerkraut

MAKES 8 servings **PREP** 15 minutes
SLOW COOK on LOW for 10 hours
LET REST 10 minutes **MICROWAVE** 1 minute

1   boneless pork shoulder roast (3¼ to 4 pounds), excess fat trimmed
½   teaspoon salt
¼   teaspoon black pepper
1   onion, thinly sliced
1   bag (2 pounds) refrigerated sauerkraut
1   apple, peeled, cored and diced
1   bottle (12 ounces) full-bodied beer
1   tablespoon brown sugar
1   tablespoon red wine vinegar
1   teaspoon caraway seeds
1   can (14 ounces) whole-berry cranberry sauce
    Cooked spaetzle (optional)

• Coat slow cooker bowl with nonstick cooking spray. Season pork with salt and pepper. If desired, brown in a skillet on all sides, about 5 minutes. Place in slow cooker.

• Add onion, sauerkraut and apple. Blend beer, brown sugar, vinegar and caraway seeds. Pour over pork. Cover and cook on LOW for 10 hours. Remove pork; let rest 10 minutes. Transfer vegetables to a platter with a slotted spoon. Strain liquid into a bowl and skim excess fat.

• Microwave cranberry sauce in a glass bowl 1 minute. Slice pork and serve over sauerkraut, drizzling with some of the cooking liquid. Top with cranberry sauce. Serve with spaetzle, if desired.

PER SERVING 367 **CAL**; 10 g **FAT** (3 g **SAT**); 34 g **PRO**; 31 g **CARB**; 4 g **FIBER**; 868 mg **SODIUM**; 102 mg **CHOL**

Chicken with Figs and Blue Cheese

MAKES 6 servings **PREP** 20 minutes **COOK** 13 minutes **SLOW COOK** on LOW for 5 hours

1½   cups low-sodium chicken broth
¼   cup balsamic vinegar
1   tablespoon grated orange zest
¾   teaspoon salt
½   teaspoon black pepper
1   package (8 ounces) dried Mission figs, stems removed
2   tablespoons vegetable oil
2   pounds boneless, skinless chicken thighs
1   large onion, thinly sliced
2   tablespoons flour
1   tube (16 ounces) prepared polenta
⅔   cup crumbled blue cheese

• In a small bowl, stir together broth, vinegar, orange zest and ¼ teaspoon each salt and pepper; set aside. Coarsely chop figs.

• Heat oil in a large nonstick skillet over medium-high heat. Add chicken to skillet and cook 5 minutes per side or until browned. Remove chicken to slow cooker and add onion to skillet. Sprinkle with ¼ teaspoon each salt and pepper and cook, stirring often, for 2 minutes. Stir in flour and cook for 1 minute. Pour in broth mixture and bring to a boil. Pour skillet contents into slow cooker and add figs.

• Cover and cook on LOW for 5 hours.

• Meanwhile, prepare polenta following package directions. Sprinkle remaining ¼ teaspoon salt into chicken mixture. Serve polenta with chicken and fig mixture; divide blue cheese among servings.

PER SERVING 459 **CAL**; 17 g **FAT** (5 g **SAT**); 37 g **PRO**; 42 g **CARB**; 5 g **FIBER**; 997 mg **SODIUM**; 160 mg **CHOL**

BBQ BEEF BRISKET,
PAGE 142

PULLED-PORK CEMITA,
PAGE 143

SHREDDED CHICKEN,
PAGE 145

MAY

126   131   138

SLIM PICKINGS

Light takes on all your favorite comfort foods—including mac and cheese!

BACON-WRAPPED
MEATLOAF AND
SMASHED POTATOES,
PAGE 129

FETTUCCINE ALFREDO,
PAGE 126

PRETZEL-COATED "FRIED"
CHICKEN WITH GRAVY

Pretzel-Coated "Fried" Chicken with Gravy

MAKES 6 servings **PREP** 25 minutes
BAKE at 475° for 15 minutes **COOK** 2 minutes

½	**pound unsalted pretzels, finely crushed**
3	**egg whites, lightly beaten**
1	**tablespoon brown mustard**
½	**cup all-purpose flour**
1	**tablespoon paprika**
1	**teaspoon garlic powder**
1	**teaspoon salt**
½	**teaspoon black pepper**
2	**pounds uncooked chicken tenders**
2	**tablespoons unsalted butter**
1	**cup reduced-sodium chicken broth**
1	**cup 2% milk**

• Heat oven to 475°. Fit a baking sheet with a rack and lightly coat with nonstick cooking spray.

• Place pretzels in a shallow dish. Whisk together egg whites and mustard in another shallow dish. In a third shallow dish, combine flour, paprika, garlic powder, ½ teaspoon of the salt and the black pepper. Reserve 3 tablespoons of the flour mixture for gravy.

• Dredge chicken in flour, then dip in egg, allowing excess to drip off, and coat with pretzel crumbs. Place chicken on prepared rack. Bake at 475° for 15 minutes or until internal temperature registers 160°.

• In a small saucepan, melt butter over medium heat; stir in reserved flour mixture and cook 30 seconds. Whisk in broth and milk and bring to a boil. Reduce heat; simmer 1 minute or until thickened.

• Sprinkle remaining ½ teaspoon salt over chicken. Serve with gravy and, if desired, Collards with Turkey Bacon.

PER SERVING 398 **CAL**; 12 g **FAT** (6 g **SAT**); 39 g **PRO**; 32 g **CARB**; 1 g **FIBER**; 733 mg **SODIUM**; 103 mg **CHOL**

Collards with Turkey Bacon In a large saucepan, heat 1 tablespoon olive oil over medium-high heat. Add 6 slices turkey bacon cut into thin ribbons and 3 cloves chopped garlic. Cook 1 minute, until bacon just starts to crisp. Add a large bunch of rinsed collard greens that have been cut into 1-inch strips and ¼ teaspoon salt. Reduce heat to medium. Cook, covered, 30 minutes or until tender, stirring occasionally.

CHICKEN CORDON BLEU

Chicken Cordon Bleu

MAKES 4 servings **PREP** 20 minutes **BAKE** at 375° for 30 minutes

4	**boneless, skinless chicken breasts (about 4 ounces each)**
⅛	**teaspoon salt**
⅛	**teaspoon black pepper**
8	**thin slices (about 4 ounces) reduced-fat Swiss cheese**
4	**thin slices (about 4 ounces) reduced-sodium smoked ham**
2	**egg whites, lightly beaten**
1	**tablespoon Dijon mustard**
1	**cup seasoned panko**
1	**envelope (.9 ounce) hollandaise sauce**
1	**cup 2% milk**
2	**tablespoons Brummel & Brown yogurt spread**

• Heat oven to 375°. Place a rack in a baking pan; coat rack with nonstick cooking spray.

• On a flat work surface, place chicken between sheets of plastic wrap and pound to ¼-inch thickness. Remove top sheet of plastic wrap and season top of chicken with salt and pepper. Place an equal amount of cheese and ham on chicken and roll up tightly from a short end.

• Place egg whites and mustard in a shallow dish and whisk to combine. Place panko in a second shallow dish. Roll chicken in egg mixture and then in panko, covering all sides. Place on prepared rack, seam side down, and spritz with nonstick cooking spray. Bake at 375° for 30 minutes or until chicken is cooked through.

• Prepare hollandaise mix following package directions, using 2% milk and yogurt spread in place of butter.

• Serve chicken with sauce and, if desired, Orzo and Broccoli Pilaf.

PER SERVING 471 **CAL**; 16 g **FAT** (7 g **SAT**); 42 g **PRO**; 38 g **CARB**; 1 g **FIBER**; 781 mg **SODIUM**; 104 mg **CHOL**

Orzo and Broccoli Pilaf In a saucepan, cook ½ small chopped onion in 1 tablespoon olive oil for 2 minutes. Stir in 1 cup RiceSelect whole wheat orzo, 2 cups reduced-sodium chicken stock and ¼ teaspoon salt; simmer, covered, about 8 minutes or until broth is absorbed. Stir in 2 cups steamed broccoli florets.

FETTUCCINE ALFREDO

Eggplant Parmesan

MAKES 6 servings PREP 25 minutes
BAKE at 375° for 75 minutes

- ⅓ cup all-purpose flour
- 4 egg whites, lightly beaten
- 1½ cups panko
- 1¾ pounds eggplant, cut into twelve ½-inch slices
- 3 cups marinara sauce, plus more for pasta (if desired)
- ¼ teaspoon salt
- ¼ teaspoon black pepper
- 2 cups reduced-fat shredded mozzarella
- 12 large basil leaves
- ½ cup grated Parmesan cheese
- 1 package (14.5 ounces) Barilla Plus spaghetti, cooked following package directions

• Heat oven to 375°. Fit a baking sheet with a rack and coat with nonstick cooking spray.

• Place flour, egg whites and panko in separate shallow dishes. Dredge eggplant slices in flour, dip in egg whites and coat with panko. Place on prepared rack. Bake at 375° for 45 minutes or until tender.

• Spread 1 cup of the sauce over the bottom of a 13 x 9-inch baking dish. Place half the eggplant slices over sauce and season with ⅛ teaspoon each of the salt and pepper. Layer with 1 cup of the sauce, 1 cup of the mozzarella and the basil. Repeat layering with remaining eggplant, salt, pepper, sauce and mozzarella.

• Sprinkle ¼ cup of the Parmesan over top and loosely tent with nonstick foil. Bake at 375° for 30 minutes or until bubbly.

• Serve with cooked spaghetti, remaining Parmesan and, if desired, additional sauce.

PER SERVING 500 CAL; 9 g FAT (5 g SAT); 29 g PRO; 84 g CARB; 13 g FIBER; 798 mg SODIUM; 28 mg CHOL

Fettuccine Alfredo

MAKES 6 servings PREP 10 minutes COOK 10 minutes

- 1 pound fettuccine
- 1 cup frozen peas, thawed
- 1 small sweet red pepper, cored, seeded and thinly sliced
- ½ cup fat-free half-and-half
- ⅓ cup heavy cream
- 2 tablespoons unsalted butter
- 1 teaspoon garlic powder
- ¾ teaspoon salt
- ¼ teaspoon black pepper
- 4 tablespoons reduced-fat cream cheese
- ¾ cup grated Parmesan cheese
- ¼ cup parsley, chopped

• Cook fettuccine following package directions, about 10 minutes. Add peas and red pepper during last minute of cooking. Drain.

• Meanwhile, in a medium saucepan, combine half-and-half, cream, butter, garlic powder, salt and black pepper. Bring to a simmer; gradually whisk in cream cheese and take off heat. Stir in ½ cup of the Parmesan.

• Place drained pasta mixture in a large bowl and toss with sauce. Sprinkle with remaining ¼ cup Parmesan and the chopped parsley. Serve immediately.

PER SERVING 412 CAL; 18 g FAT (11 g SAT); 18 g PRO; 47 g CARB; 3 g FIBER; 655 mg SODIUM; 96 mg CHOL

EGGPLANT PARMESAN

MEXICAN WAGON WHEELS
AND CHEESE

Mexican Wagon Wheels and Cheese

MAKES 8 servings **PREP** 20 minutes
COOK 8 minutes **BAKE** at 350° for 30 minutes

1	sweet red pepper, cored, seeded and chopped
1	green bell pepper, cored, seeded and chopped
4	scallions, thinly sliced
3	cloves garlic, chopped
3	tablespoons unsalted butter
¼	cup all-purpose flour
1	quart 2% milk
1	teaspoon salt
½	teaspoon chili powder
2	cups reduced-fat Mexican cheese blend
2	cups reduced-fat shredded mozzarella
1	pound wagon wheel pasta, cooked following package directions

• Heat oven to 350°. Coat a 13 x 9-inch baking pan with nonstick cooking spray.

• Heat a large nonstick skillet over medium-high heat; coat with nonstick cooking spray and add red and green peppers, scallions and garlic. Cook for 5 minutes, stirring frequently, until peppers soften. Set aside.

• In a large saucepan, melt butter over medium-high heat. Whisk in flour and cook 1 minute; gradually whisk in milk and bring to a boil. Cook 2 minutes or until thickened. Turn off heat and stir in salt, chili powder and 1¾ cups of each of the cheeses until smooth. Add cooked pasta and pepper mixture and stir until combined.

• Turn out mixture into prepared pan and scatter remaining ¼ cup of each of the cheeses over top. Bake at 350° for 30 minutes, until bubbly and lightly browned.

PER SERVING 465 **CAL**; 16 g **FAT** (9 g **SAT**); 28 g **PRO**; 54 g **CARB**; 3 g **FIBER**; 785 mg **SODIUM**; 51 mg **CHOL**

BACON-WRAPPED MEATLOAF AND SMASHED POTATOES

Bacon-Wrapped Meatloaf and Smashed Potatoes

MAKES 6 servings **PREP** 20 minutes **BAKE** at 375° for 60 minutes **COOK** 15 minutes

2	pounds extra-lean ground beef
½	pound white mushrooms, grated
½	cup old-fashioned oats (not quick cooking)
3	egg whites, lightly beaten
¾	teaspoon onion salt
½	teaspoon dried oregano
½	teaspoon black pepper
¼	cup ketchup
1	tablespoon brown sugar
6	slices turkey bacon
2	pounds unpeeled Yukon gold potatoes, scrubbed and cut into 1-inch chunks
¾	cup reduced-sodium chicken broth
2	tablespoons olive oil
¼	teaspoon salt
⅛	teaspoon nutmeg
¼	cup parsley, chopped

• Heat oven to 375°. Fit a baking sheet with a rack and coat lightly with nonstick cooking spray.

• In a large bowl, combine ground beef, mushrooms, oats, egg whites, onion salt, oregano and ¼ teaspoon of the pepper. Form into a loaf and place on prepared pan. Combine ketchup and brown sugar and spread half on top of meatloaf. Arrange bacon over meatloaf in a crisscross pattern. Bake at 375° for 45 minutes; spread on remaining ketchup mixture and bake for an additional 15 minutes or until internal temperature registers 160°.

• Meanwhile, place potatoes in a pot and cover with lightly salted water. Bring to a boil; lower heat and simmer, partially covered, for 15 minutes or until fork-tender. Drain and add broth, olive oil, salt, remaining ¼ teaspoon black pepper and the nutmeg. Mash to desired consistency; stir in parsley. Serve with meatloaf.

PER SERVING 414 **CAL**; 14 g **FAT** (4 g **SAT**); 38 g **PRO**; 36 g **CARB**; 3 g **FIBER**; 794 mg **SODIUM**; 95 mg **CHOL**

GLOBAL KITCHEN

Travel around the world in 10 delicious dishes.

WIENER
SCHNITZEL,
PAGE 137

Ceviche (Peru)

MAKES 4 servings   **PREP** 15 minutes   **REFRIGERATE** 20 minutes

1	**pound salmon, skin removed, diced into ½-inch cubes**
½	**cup fresh lime juice**
1	**avocado, diced into ½-inch cubes**
½	**cup red onion, finely diced**
1	**jalapeño, seeded and finely diced**
½	**cup cilantro, chopped, plus more for garnish (optional)**
½	**teaspoon salt**

• Combine salmon and lime juice in a bowl, making sure fish is submerged. Cover with plastic wrap and refrigerate for 20 minutes.

• Pour off all but 1 tablespoon of the lime juice. Gently mix in avocado, onion, jalapeño, cilantro and salt. Garnish with more cilantro, if desired.

PER SERVING 276 **CAL**; 16 g **FAT** (2 g **SAT**); 27 g **PRO**; 7 g **CARB**; 4 g **FIBER**; 353 mg **SODIUM**; 72 mg **CHOL**

Arepas (Venezuela)

MAKES 8 arepas **PREP** 10 minutes
LET REST 15 minutes **COOK** 26 minutes
BAKE at 350° for 15 minutes

- **1¾ cups masa harina corn flour**
- **½ teaspoon salt**
- **1 tablespoon unsalted butter, melted**
- **2 tablespoons canola oil**
- **2 links (3 ounces each) fully cooked chorizo**
- **½ avocado, peeled, pitted and sliced**
- **2 ounces Cotija cheese or queso fresco, sliced**
  Tomatillo salsa (optional)

• Heat oven to 350°. In a bowl, combine masa harina and salt. Pour 2 cups boiling water over masa harina; stir well. Mix in melted butter. Cover dough with plastic wrap and let rest for 15 minutes.

• Shape dough into 8 balls. Place each ball between 2 pieces of plastic wrap and carefully flatten with a pan to form disks measuring 3 inches wide and ½ inch thick. Mend any cracked edges with your fingers. Place arepas on a baking sheet; cover with plastic wrap.

• Heat 1 tablespoon of the oil in a cast-iron skillet or sauté pan over medium heat. Add 4 arepas to skillet. Cook 5 minutes on each side, until golden brown. Transfer back to baking sheet. Add remaining 1 tablespoon oil to skillet and repeat cooking with last 4 arepas. Place baking sheet with all 8 arepas in oven and bake at 350° for 15 minutes.

• Meanwhile, slice chorizo lengthwise, then cut each of those pieces in half on the bias (there should be a total of 8 pieces). In the same skillet, cook chorizo over medium heat until hot and browned, about 6 minutes.

• Slice hot arepas lengthwise about three-fourths of the way through. Fill each with a piece of chorizo, avocado and cheese. If desired, drizzle with tomatillo salsa. Serve immediately.

PER SERVING 226 **CAL**; 13 g **FAT** (4 g **SAT**); 7 g **PRO**; 21 g **CARB**; 4 g **FIBER**; 291 mg **SODIUM**; 20 mg **CHOL**

BABA GANOUSH

Baba Ganoush (Lebanon)

MAKES 2 cups **PREP** 10 minutes **ROAST** at 450° for 30 minutes

- **2 eggplants (2 pounds total)**
- **1 teaspoon salt**
- **3 tablespoons olive oil, plus more for drizzling (optional)**
- **⅓ cup tahini**
- **1 tablespoon lemon juice**
- **½ teaspoon lemon zest**
- **⅛ teaspoon cayenne pepper**
  Fresh parsley, chopped
  Pitas

• Heat oven to 450°. Trim eggplants and slice in half lengthwise. Sprinkle cut sides with ¼ teaspoon of the salt and 1 tablespoon of the oil. Place cut sides down on a foil-lined baking sheet. Roast at 450° for 30 minutes, or until eggplant flesh is soft and skin has begun to collapse. Cool slightly. Scoop out flesh and break into bite-size pieces with a fork; discard skins.

• Stir in tahini, lemon juice, lemon zest, cayenne, remaining oil and remaining ¾ teaspoon salt. Garnish with fresh chopped parsley and, if desired, drizzle with olive oil. Serve with pitas, grilled, if desired, and cut into wedges.

PER ¼ CUP 131 **CAL**; 11 g **FAT** (1 g **SAT**); 3 g **PRO**; 9 g **CARB**; 4 g **FIBER**; 297 mg **SODIUM**; 0 mg **CHOL**

PORK PHO

Massaman Curry (India)

MAKES 4 servings **PREP** 15 minutes
COOK 29 minutes

- **1**   **cup jasmine rice**
- **¾**   **teaspoon salt**
- **2**   **tablespoons canola oil**
- **1**   **medium onion, diced**
- **1¼**   **pounds boneless, skinless chicken breasts, cut into ¼-inch bias slices**
- **1**   **tablespoon chopped fresh ginger**
- **2**   **cloves garlic, chopped**
- **½**   **teaspoon ground cumin**
- **1**   **teaspoon ground turmeric (optional)**
- **¼**   **to ½ teaspoon cayenne pepper**
- **¼**   **teaspoon ground cardamom**
- **¼**   **teaspoon ground cloves**
- **1**   **tablespoon balsamic vinegar**
- **1**   **can (13.5 ounces) light or regular coconut milk**
- **2**   **tablespoons packed brown sugar**
- **1**   **extra-large baking potato, peeled and diced into ¾-inch cubes**
- **¼**   **cup roasted unsalted peanuts**
- **1**   **cinnamon stick**
       Fresh cilantro, chopped (optional)

● In a small, lidded pot, bring rice, ¼ teaspoon of the salt and 2 cups water to a boil. Reduce heat to a simmer and cook 20 minutes or per package directions. Remove from heat and keep covered.

● Meanwhile, heat oil in a large sauté pan over medium heat. Add onion and cook 5 to 7 minutes, until translucent. Add chicken, ginger, garlic, cumin, turmeric (if desired), cayenne, cardamom and cloves; cook 2 minutes, stirring frequently. Stir in vinegar, scraping bottom of pan. Add in coconut milk, brown sugar, potato, peanuts and cinnamon stick; bring to a boil. Reduce heat and simmer, uncovered, 15 to 20 minutes, until potato is cooked. Stir in remaining ½ teaspoon salt.

● To serve, ladle curry over rice. Garnish with chopped cilantro, if desired.

PER SERVING 513 **CAL**; 24 g **FAT** (7 g **SAT**); 34 g **PRO**; 39 g **CARB**; 2 g **FIBER**; 521 mg **SODIUM**; 78 mg **CHOL**

Pork Pho (Vietnam)

MAKES 6 servings **PREP** 20 minutes **SLOW COOK** on HIGH for 6 hours or LOW for 8 hours
COOK 5 minutes

- **2**   **pounds spareribs**
- **1**   **small onion, peeled and halved**
- **⅓**   **cup peeled and sliced ginger**
- **2**   **cloves garlic, smashed**
- **1**   **tablespoon coriander seeds**
- **5**   **whole cloves**
- **2**   **whole star anise**
- **6**   **cups low-sodium chicken broth**
- **2**   **tablespoons fish sauce**
- **2**   **tablespoons packed brown sugar**
- **¼**   **teaspoon salt**
- **1**   **box (8 ounces) rice noodles**
       Lime wedges, fresh cilantro, sliced scallions, bean sprouts, fresh sliced bird's-eye or habañero chile peppers, and sriracha sauce (optional)

● Place spareribs, onion, ginger, garlic, coriander, cloves and star anise in bottom of slow cooker. Pour chicken broth on top. In a bowl, mix together 3 cups water, the fish sauce and brown sugar; pour into slow cooker. Cover and cook on HIGH for 6 hours or LOW for 8 hours.

● Remove spareribs. Shred meat, discarding bones, tendons and fat. Cover and set aside. Carefully pour remaining slow cooker contents through a strainer over a lidded pot; skim. Stir in salt. Cover and bring to a boil. Add rice noodles and cook 4 to 5 minutes, until softened.

● Ladle some of the broth and noodles into bowls. Top with shredded meat and, if desired, lime wedges, cilantro, scallions, bean sprouts, chile peppers and sriracha sauce.

PER SERVING 425 **CAL**; 22 g **FAT** (8 g **SAT**); 24 g **PRO**; 32 g **CARB**; 1 g **FIBER**; 1,077 mg **SODIUM**; 85 mg **CHOL**

MASSAMAN CURRY

FIDEUÀ

Put on music appropriate to the country of origin for the dish you are cooking (polka from Austria or flamenco from Spain) and your "passport dinner" is complete.

WIENER SCHNITZEL

Fideuà (Spain)

MAKES 4 servings **PREP** 10 minutes
COOK 15 minutes

- ¼   cup olive oil
- 1   bag (12 ounces) fine egg noodles
- 3   cloves garlic, sliced
- 2   teaspoon smoked paprika
- ½   teaspoon salt
- ¼   teaspoon saffron (optional)
- 2   cups seafood stock
- 1   pound peeled and deveined shrimp
- ⅓   cup fresh parsley, chopped, plus more for garnish

• In a large, heavy-bottomed pot, heat oil on medium-high. Add noodles and stir with tongs until golden brown, about 2 minutes. Add garlic, smoked paprika, salt and, if desired, saffron. Cook 1 minute. Pour in 1½ cups of the seafood stock. Bring to a simmer, then reduce heat to medium and cook 4 minutes. Add shrimp and cook, stirring frequently, for 6 to 8 minutes or until shrimp are cooked and pasta is tender. (If noodles seem too dry, add remaining ½ cup seafood stock.) Stir in chopped parsley.

• Serve immediately, garnishing with additional parsley.

PER SERVING 578 **CAL**; 19 g **FAT** (3 g **SAT**); 37 g **PRO**; 59 g **CARB**; 2 g **FIBER**; 744 mg **SODIUM**; 320 mg **CHOL**

Wiener Schnitzel (Austria)

MAKES 4 servings **PREP** 20 minutes **COOK** 12 minutes

- 1   tablespoon fresh lemon juice
- 1   tablespoon olive oil
- 1   teaspoon salt
- 4   cups frisée, roughly chopped
- ⅔   cup all-purpose flour
- ¼   teaspoon pepper
- 2   eggs
- 1   cup bread crumbs
- 1   pound thinly sliced veal cutlets
- 4   tablespoons unsalted butter
- 4   lemon wedges

• Heat oven to 200°. In a large bowl, whisk together lemon juice, oil and ¼ teaspoon of the salt. Add frisée to bowl and gently toss. Set aside in refrigerator.

• In a shallow dish, combine flour with remaining ¾ teaspoon salt and the pepper. Beat eggs in a separate dish with 1 tablespoon water. Pour bread crumbs into another dish. Coat a veal cutlet in flour, then dip into egg mixture, allowing excess to drip off. Finally, coat cutlet in bread crumbs. Set aside on a plate. Repeat with remaining veal cutlets.

• Heat 2 tablespoons of the butter in a large nonstick skillet over medium-high heat. Add a few of the veal cutlets, being sure not to crowd skillet. (Cooking should be done in 3 batches.) Cook 2 minutes; flip and cook another 2 minutes, until veal is golden brown. Transfer to a baking sheet and place in 200° oven. Repeat with remaining cutlets 2 more times, adding 1 tablespoon of the butter for each remaining batch.

• Serve frisée over cutlets. Garnish with lemon wedges.

PER SERVING 468 **CAL**; 27 g **FAT** (12 g **SAT**); 32 g **PRO**; 27 g **CARB**; 8 g **FIBER**; 600 mg **SODIUM**; 229 mg **CHOL**

PROFITEROLES

Spanakopita (Greece)

MAKES 12 servings **PREP** 25 minutes
COOK 10 minutes **BAKE** at 350° for 45 minutes
LET STAND 10 minutes

8	ounces (20 sheets or half a 16-ounce package) phyllo dough
1	tablespoon olive oil
1	large onion, diced
2½	pounds fresh spinach, trimmed and washed
2	eggs, beaten
8	ounces feta cheese, crumbled
1	cup fresh mint, roughly chopped
¼	cup fresh oregano, roughly chopped
¼	teaspoon nutmeg
¾	teaspoon salt
½	teaspoon pepper
6	tablespoons unsalted butter, melted

• Bring phyllo dough to room temperature (keep in package). Unroll and place a damp paper towel on top of sheets. Heat oven to 350°.

• Meanwhile, heat oil in a large sauté pan over medium heat. Add onion and cook 5 minutes. Add spinach (in batches, if necessary). Cook 5 minutes or until just wilted. Transfer to a bowl to cool slightly. Drain excess liquid by gently pressing mixture. Roughly chop and return to bowl. Stir in eggs, cheese, mint, oregano, nutmeg, salt and pepper. Set aside.

• Brush a 13 x 9-inch pan with a bit of the melted butter. Place a phyllo sheet on bottom of pan; brush with more melted butter. Continue layering sheets, brushing each with butter, until there is a stack of 10. Spread spinach mixture evenly on top (drain before doing so if more liquid has accumulated). Layer the remaining 10 sheets, brushing each with butter. Score spanakopita into 12 squares. Bake at 350° for 45 minutes or until golden. Let stand 10 minutes, then slice into squares along scored lines.

PER SERVING 212 **CAL**; 13 g **FAT** (7 g **SAT**); 8 g **PRO**; 17 g **CARB**; 4 g **FIBER**; 537 mg **SODIUM**; 65 mg **CHOL**

Profiteroles (France)

MAKES 12 pastries **PREP** 10 minutes **COOL** 5 minutes **BAKE** at 425° for 10 minutes, 350° for 15 minutes

4	tablespoons unsalted butter
1	teaspoon sugar
	Pinch salt
½	cup all-purpose flour
2	eggs
2¼	cups ice cream (vanilla or chocolate or both)
	Chocolate sauce (optional)

• Heat oven to 425°. In a small pot, bring ½ cup water, the butter, sugar and salt to a boil. Reduce heat to medium. Add flour and stir quickly until a ball of dough forms, about 1 minute. Remove to a bowl. Cool 5 minutes. Stir in eggs one at a time, until dough is smooth.

• Transfer dough to a piping bag or resealable plastic bag with the corner snipped. Pipe twelve 1½-inch mounds, spaced 2 inches apart, onto a parchment-lined baking sheet. Smooth out tops with a wet finger.

• Bake at 425° for 10 minutes. Reduce heat to 350° and bake another 10 to 15 minutes, or until golden brown. Cool completely.

• Slice each profiterole in half crosswise. Place a small scoop (about 3 tablespoons) ice cream into bottom of each profiterole, then replace tops. Drizzle with chocolate sauce, if desired.

Per pastry 115 **CAL**; 7 g **FAT** (4 g **SAT**); 2 g **PRO**; 10 g **CARB**; 0 g **FIBER**; 32 mg **SODIUM**; 56 mg **CHOL**

SPANAKOPITA

Potica (Slovenia and Croatia)

MAKES 2 loaves (28 servings) PREP 15 minutes LET STAND 5 minutes KNEAD 10 minutes LET RISE 2 hours BAKE at 350° for 25 minutes, 325° for 20 minutes

DOUGH

½	cup milk
¼	cup sugar
2	packages (.25 ounce each) active dry yeast
4	cups all-purpose flour
½	teaspoon salt
4	tablespoons unsalted butter, at room temperature
1	egg plus 1 yolk, beaten
⅔	cup sour cream, at room temperature

FILLING

¼	cup half-and-half
8	ounces walnuts (about 2 cups), finely ground in food processor
2	tablespoons unsalted butter, cut into small cubes
¼	cup honey
¼	cup sugar
2	teaspoons orange zest
1	teaspoon cinnamon
½	teaspoon vanilla extract
1	egg yolk, beaten
3	egg whites
⅔	cup golden raisins

• **Dough.** Heat oven to 170° for 10 minutes; turn off. Heat milk in a small pot to approximately 110°. Stir in 1 tablespoon of the sugar. Gently stir in yeast; let stand 5 minutes.

• In a large bowl, stir together flour, remaining 3 tablespoons sugar and the salt. Stir in softened butter, beaten egg plus yolk, and sour cream. Make a well in the center and pour in yeast mixture; mix well. Knead dough 10 minutes, until soft. Dough should spring back slowly when touched. Divide into 2 pieces and place in separate greased bowls. Cover each with plastic wrap and a clean kitchen towel; set aside in warm oven to rise for 1 hour.

• **Filling.** Meanwhile, heat half-and-half in a small pot. Pour over ground walnuts and cubed butter in a medium bowl. Stir in honey, 3 tablespoons of the sugar, the orange zest, cinnamon, vanilla and beaten egg yolk. In a separate bowl, whisk 2 of the egg whites with remaining 1 tablespoon sugar to stiff peaks with a hand mixer. Fold into walnut mixture.

• Roll out one mound of dough on a lightly floured surface to a 16 x 10-inch oval. Spread a heaping cup of the filling on oval, leaving a 2-inch border on one of the short ends and a 1-inch border around remaining edges. Sprinkle ⅓ cup of the raisins over filling. Roll dough, starting from short end with 1-inch border and finishing at 2-inch border. Pinch to seal seam and ends. Place on a greased baking sheet seam side down; cover with plastic wrap and kitchen towel. Repeat with second mound of dough and another heaping cup of filling and raisins (there will be filling left over). Place on a separate baking sheet. Allow loaves to rise for 1 hour. Heat oven to 350°.

• Beat remaining egg white. Brush onto each loaf. Place on middle racks of oven and bake at 350° for 25 minutes. Reduce heat to 325° and rotate loaves. Bake another 20 minutes, until golden brown. Cool before slicing.

PER SERVING 193 CAL; 10 g FAT (3 g SAT); 4 g PRO; 24 g CARB; 1 g FIBER; 56 mg SODIUM; 27 mg CHOL

SANDWICH GENERATION

You have dinner in hand with these 5 slow cooker suppers.

BBQ Beef Brisket

MAKES 8 servings **PREP** 10 minutes **SLOW COOK** on HIGH for 6 hours or LOW for 8 hours **COOK** 3 minutes **LET STAND** 15 minutes

2	**tablespoons packed dark brown sugar**
1	**tablespoon Italian seasoning**
1	**teaspoon onion powder**
¼	**teaspoon salt**
¼	**teaspoon black pepper**
3	**pounds natural beef brisket**
2½	**cups beef broth**
3	**tablespoons molasses**
2	**tablespoons Worcestershire sauce**
3	**dashes liquid smoke (optional)**
3	**tablespoons cornstarch**
1	**tablespoon white vinegar**
8	**onion rolls**
2	**cups prepared creamy coleslaw**

• In small bowl, combine brown sugar, Italian seasoning, onion powder, salt and pepper. Rub onto brisket and place in slow cooker.

• In a bowl, whisk broth, molasses, Worcestershire and, if desired, liquid smoke. Add to slow cooker. Slow cook on HIGH for 6 hours or LOW for 8 hours.

• Carefully remove brisket from slow cooker and shred with 2 forks. In a small bowl, combine ¼ cup water, cornstarch and vinegar. Strain liquid in slow cooker into a saucepan and add cornstarch mixture. Bring to a boil over medium-high heat and cook 3 minutes, until thickened and clear. Combine 5 cups of the sauce with brisket in a large bowl. Let stand, covered, for 15 minutes.

• Split onion rolls and fill with brisket and coleslaw. Serve immediately.

PER SERVING 427 **CAL**; 11 g **FAT** (3 g **SAT**); 43 g **PRO**; 37 g **CARB**; 2 g **FIBER**; 711 mg **SODIUM**; 77 mg **CHOL**

PULLED-PORK CEMITA

Turkey Sloppy Joes

MAKES 12 servings PREP 15 minutes
SLOW COOK on HIGH for 3 hours or LOW for
6 hours

1	package (20.8 ounces) ground turkey
2	carrots, peeled and finely chopped
1	medium onion, finely chopped
1	rib celery, finely chopped
1	garlic clove, minced
1	can (6 ounces) tomato paste
2	tablespoons cider vinegar
2	tablespoons light brown sugar
1	teaspoon Worcestershire sauce
¾	teaspoon paprika
½	teaspoon dry mustard
½	teaspoon salt
12	hamburger buns

• In slow cooker bowl, stir together
ground turkey, carrots, onion, celery,
garlic, tomato paste, vinegar, brown
sugar, Worcestershire sauce, paprika
and dry mustard. Cover and cook on
HIGH for 3 hours or LOW for 6 hours,
stirring turkey mixture halfway through
cooking time.

• Stir in salt. Spoon ⅓ cup of the turkey
mixture on each bun and serve
immediately.

PER SERVING 226 CAL; 6 g FAT (2 g SAT);
14 g PRO; 29 g CARB; 2 g FIBER; 383 mg SODIUM;
39 mg CHOL

Pulled-Pork Cemita

MAKES 8 servings PREP 10 minutes COOK 6 minutes SLOW COOK on HIGH for 6 hours or LOW for 8 hours

1	bone-in pork loin roast (about 3 pounds)
¼	teaspoon salt
¼	teaspoon black pepper
2	tablespoons oil
1	medium onion, sliced
1	can (10 ounces) enchilada sauce
3	tablespoons lime juice
2	teaspoons chili powder
8	sesame seed rolls, split
¾	cup jarred black bean spread
¾	cup prepared guacamole or smashed ripe avocado
1	large tomato, sliced
4	ounces goat cheese, crumbled Cilantro leaves

• Place pork on a cutting board; season
with salt and pepper. Heat oil in a large
stainless skillet over high heat. Brown
pork on all sides, about 6 minutes total.
Remove from heat.

• Place onion in bottom of slow cooker.
Whisk in enchilada sauce, ½ cup water,
lime juice and chili powder. Add pork to
slow cooker; cover and cook on HIGH
for 6 hours or LOW for 8 hours.

• Remove pork to a clean cutting board.
Cool slightly. When cool enough to
handle, separate and discard bones, fat
and connective tissue from meat,
leaving pork in pieces as large as
possible. Place pork on a platter and
drizzle with about 1 cup of the liquid
from slow cooker.

• Assemble sandwiches: Spread bottom
cut side of rolls with an equal amount of
bean spread (about 2 tablespoons each),
and remaining halves with guacamole.
Top bean spread with pork, tomato
slices, goat cheese and cilantro.

PER SERVING 418 CAL; 20 g FAT (8 g SAT); 33 g
PRO; 29 g CARB; 2 g FIBER; 883 mg SODIUM;
76 mg CHOL

TURKEY SLOPPY JOES

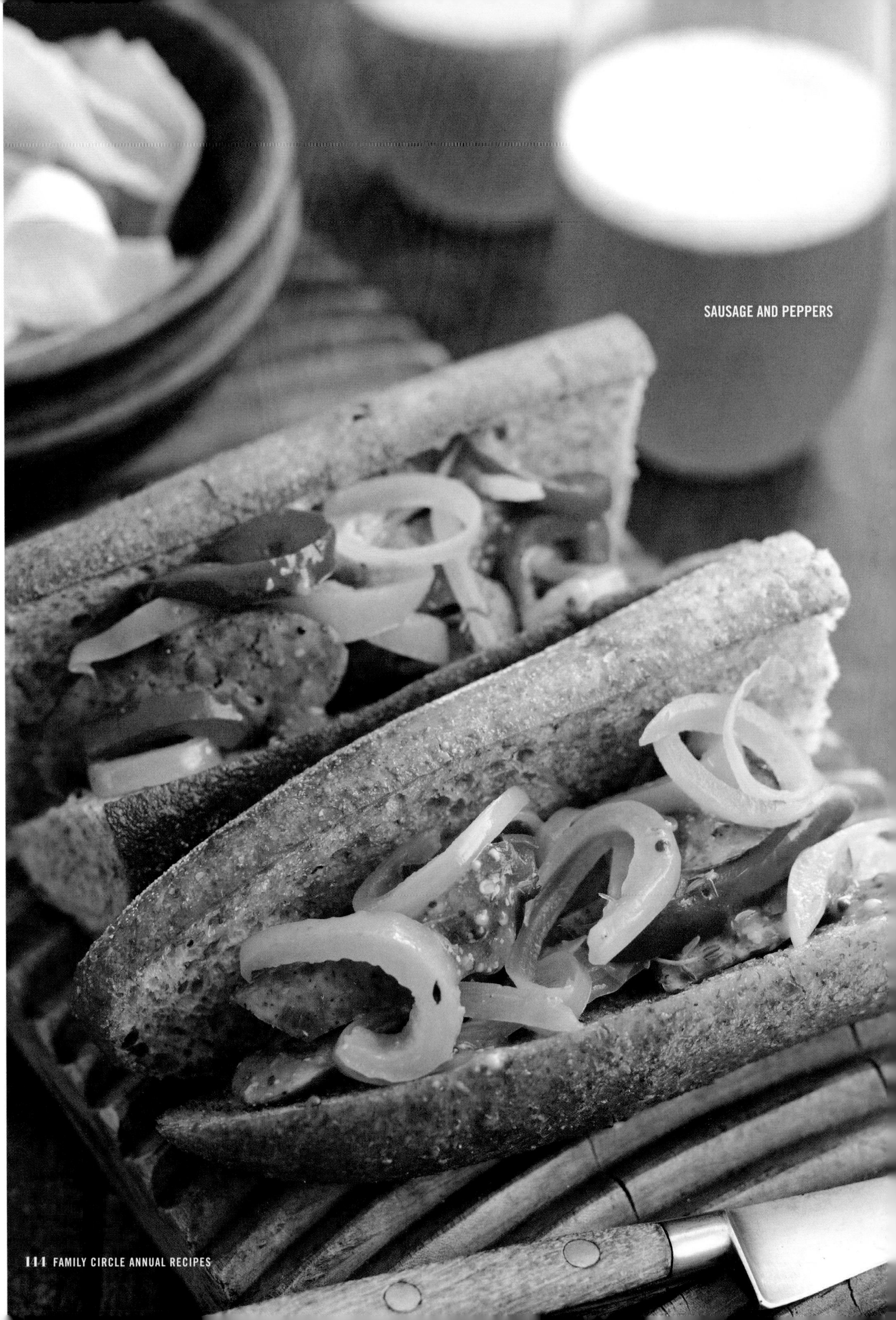
SAUSAGE AND PEPPERS

SHREDDED CHICKEN

Sausage and Peppers

MAKES 6 servings **PREP** 10 minutes
SLOW COOK on HIGH for 3 hours or LOW for
6 hours **COOK** 1 minute **BROIL** 2 minutes

2	**large sweet red peppers, seeded and sliced**
1	**large green bell pepper, seeded and sliced**
1	**large sweet yellow pepper, seeded and sliced**
1	**large onion, cut into wedges**
1	**package (20 ounces) hot or sweet Italian turkey sausages**
¼	**cup red wine vinegar**
½	**teaspoon dried thyme**
½	**teaspoon black pepper**
1½	**tablespoons cornstarch mixed with 2 tablespoons water**
1	**tablespoon grainy mustard**
6	**small multigrain submarine or hoagie rolls (2 to 3 ounces each)**

• Combine peppers, onion, sausages, vinegar, thyme and black pepper in a 5- to 6-quart slow cooker.

• Cook on HIGH for 3 hours or LOW for 6 hours. Use a slotted spoon to remove peppers and sausages from slow cooker; set aside and keep warm.

• Heat broiler. Pour liquid from slow cooker into a small saucepan. Whisk in cornstarch mixture and mustard. Bring to a boil; boil for 1 minute or until thickened.

• Meanwhile, slice rolls almost all the way through lengthwise. Place on a baking sheet, cut side up, on top rack under broiler for 1 to 2 minutes or until toasted. Cut sausages diagonally into ½-inch-thick slices and stir back into pepper mixture. Place a scant 1 cup of the sausage mixture on each roll. Drizzle each sandwich with a generous 2 tablespoons of the sauce, reserving remaining sauce for dipping. Serve immediately.

PER SERVING 386 **CAL**; 14 g **FAT** (1 g **SAT**); 23 g **PRO**; 47 g **CARB**; 8 g **FIBER**; 945 mg **SODIUM**; 56 mg **CHOL**

Shredded Chicken

MAKES 8 sandwiches **PREP** 5 minutes **SLOW COOK** on HIGH for 6 hours or LOW for 8 hours
COOK 3 minutes **LET STAND** 10 minutes **BAKE** at 350° for 3 minutes

1½	**pounds boneless, skinless chicken breasts**
1½	**pounds boneless, skinless chicken thighs, trimmed of excess fat**
1	**teaspoon dried oregano**
½	**teaspoon ground cumin**
1	**cup Dr Pepper soda**
1	**can (8 ounces) tomato sauce**
2	**chipotle peppers in adobo, seeded and diced**
¼	**cup sugar**
2	**tablespoons cornstarch**
½	**teaspoon salt**
3	**tablespoons balsamic vinegar**
8	**slices white cheddar or pepper Jack**
8	**soft egg buns**
	Pickle slices
	Sliced red onion (optional)

• Place chicken in a 4- to 5-quart slow cooker. Season with oregano and cumin. In a bowl, stir together soda, tomato sauce and chipotles. Pour into slow cooker, cover and cook on HIGH for 6 hours or LOW for 8 hours.

• Heat oven to 350°. Remove chicken to a bowl and pour liquid from slow cooker into a saucepan. In a small bowl, blend sugar, cornstarch and salt. Stir into a saucepan along with vinegar. Place over medium-high heat and bring to a boil.

• Reduce heat to medium and simmer 3 minutes, until thickened and clear. Shred chicken with 2 forks. Pour sauce over chicken and stir to combine. Let stand, covered, for 10 minutes.

• Make sandwiches: Place a slice of cheese on each roll. Bake at 350° for 2 to 3 minutes or until cheese melts. Divide chicken among rolls. Add pickle slices and, if desired, red onion.

PER SERVING 474 **CAL**; 15 g **FAT** (6 g **SAT**); 46 g **PRO**; 38 g **CARB**; 2 g **FIBER**; 858 mg **SODIUM**; 152 mg **CHOL**

TRIPLE MELON
SALAD, PAGE 164

JUNE

151   157   169

FAST, FILLING 400-CALORIE DINNERS

Quick and healthy are not mutually exclusive—and here's the proof.

SLICED STEAK WITH GERMAN POTATO SALAD, PAGE 155

GRILLED CITRUS
CHICKEN RICE BOWL,
PAGE 152

GRILLED HOISIN-GLAZED
HALIBUT AND BOK CHOY

Grilled Hoisin-Glazed Halibut and Bok Choy

MAKES 4 servings **PREP** 15 minutes
COOK 7 minutes **GRILL** 8 minutes

¼	cup reduced-sodium vegetable broth
2	tablespoons reduced-sodium soy sauce
2	tablespoons hoisin sauce
1	tablespoon lime juice
1	tablespoon chopped fresh ginger
1	tablespoon rice vinegar
½	teaspoon Asian chili paste
4	halibut or mahi mahi fillets (about 6 ounces each)
½	pound baby bok choy, trimmed and separated into pieces
⅛	teaspoon salt
6	ounces whole wheat or whole grain angel hair pasta or thin spaghetti
½	red sweet pepper, cored, seeded and cut into thin strips
4	scallions, thinly sliced
1	lime, cut into wedges

• In a small bowl, combine broth, soy sauce, hoisin sauce, lime juice, ginger, rice vinegar and chili paste. Reserve 3 tablespoons of the sauce for noodles.

• Heat a gas or stovetop grill to medium-high or the coals in a charcoal grill to medium-hot. Lightly oil grill grates. Drizzle sauce on both sides of fish and brush to coat. Grill for 4 minutes on flesh side. Turn and drizzle and brush generously again with sauce; grill for an additional 4 minutes on skin side or until fish flakes easily. Drizzle any remaining sauce over top. Gently remove from grill with a large spatula.

• While fish is grilling, lightly spritz bok choy with nonstick cooking spray and season with salt. Grill for 3 minutes per side or until lightly charred and tender.

• Meanwhile, cook pasta following package directions, about 7 minutes. Drain; stir in red pepper, half the scallions and the reserved 3 tablespoons sauce.

• Serve fish immediately with noodles and bok choy. Squeeze lime wedges over each portion and sprinkle remaining scallions on top.

PER SERVING 394 **CAL**; 4 g **FAT** (1 g **SAT**); 35 g **PRO**; 53 g **CARB**; 5 g **FIBER**; 800 mg **SODIUM**; 45 mg **CHOL**

SHRIMP TOSTADAS

Shrimp Tostadas

MAKES 4 servings **PREP** 20 minutes **BAKE** at 450° for 7 minutes **BROIL** 4 minutes

½	cup reduced-fat mayonnaise
1	tablespoon lime juice
1	teaspoon brown sugar
¼	teaspoon chipotle chile powder
8	white corn tortillas
1	pound large shrimp, shells removed, deveined
¼	teaspoon salt
⅛	teaspoon black pepper
4	cups shredded iceberg lettuce
2	plum tomatoes, cored and diced
1	small red onion, chopped
½	cucumber, peeled and cut into thin matchsticks
½	cup cilantro leaves
1	lime, cut into wedges
½	cup prepared tomato salsa
	Sour cream (optional)

• In a small bowl, whisk together mayonnaise, lime juice, brown sugar and chile powder. Refrigerate.

• Heat oven to 450°. Place 2 racks on each of 2 baking sheets. Place tortillas on racks and lightly spritz both sides with nonstick cooking spray. Bake at 450° for 5 to 7 minutes or until crisp. Remove tortillas from oven and reserve.

• Heat broiler. Coat broiler pan with nonstick cooking spray. Season shrimp with salt and pepper and place on broiler pan. Broil for 2 minutes per side or until cooked through. Remove shrimp to a plate.

• Spread top of each tortilla with about 1 tablespoon of mayonnaise mixture. Top with equal amounts shrimp, lettuce, tomatoes, onion, cucumber and cilantro. Squeeze a wedge of lime over each. Serve with salsa and, if desired, sour cream on the side.

PER SERVING 329 **CAL**; 13 g **FAT** (2 g **SAT**); 22 g **PRO**; 31 g **CARB**; 4 g **FIBER**; 741 mg **SODIUM**; 179 mg **CHOL**

GRILLED CITRUS CHICKEN RICE BOWL

Oven Sweet-and-Sour Chicken with Red Quinoa

MAKES 4 servings **PREP** 20 minutes
BAKE at 400° for 25 minutes **COOK** 15 minutes

3	tablespoons apricot preserves
2	tablespoons ketchup
1	tablespoon reduced-sodium soy sauce
1	tablespoon rice vinegar
½	teaspoon ground ginger
1	pound boneless, skinless chicken breasts, cut into 2-inch pieces
1	large green bell pepper, cored, seeded and cut into 1-inch pieces
1	large red sweet pepper, cored, seeded and cut into 1-inch pieces
1	large carrot, peeled and cut into thick coins
6	scallions, trimmed and cut into 2-inch pieces
1	cup red quinoa
1	can (14.5 ounces) reduced-sodium chicken broth
⅛	teaspoon salt
⅛	teaspoon black pepper
½	pound Brussels sprouts, trimmed and shredded
2	tablespoons sliced almonds

• Heat oven to 400°. Coat a 13 x 9 x 2-inch baking dish with nonstick cooking spray.

• In a medium bowl, whisk apricot preserves, ketchup, soy sauce, vinegar, ginger and 1 tablespoon water. Toss chicken with 3 tablespoons of the apricot mixture and place in prepared baking dish. Toss peppers, carrot and scallions with remaining mixture and spoon over chicken. Loosely tent with foil, venting at one end.

• Bake at 400° for 25 minutes or until chicken reaches 160° and vegetables are tender.

• Meanwhile, place quinoa, broth, salt and pepper in a medium saucepan. Bring to a boil over high heat; reduce heat to medium-low and simmer, covered, for 15 minutes or until tender. Stir in Brussels sprouts during last minute of cooking.

• Sprinkle almonds over quinoa. Serve with chicken and vegetables.

PER SERVING 395 **CAL**; 7 g **FAT** (1 g **SAT**); 32 g **PRO**; 51 g **CARB**; 6 g **FIBER**; 790 mg **SODIUM**; 63 mg **CHOL**

Grilled Citrus Chicken Rice Bowl

MAKES 4 servings **PREP** 20 minutes **MARINATE** 2 to 4 hours **GRILL** 16 minutes

¼	cup orange juice
3	tablespoons olive oil
2	tablespoons lemon juice
1	tablespoon white wine vinegar
1	teaspoon orange zest
1	teaspoon salt
½	teaspoon sugar
¼	teaspoon black pepper
2	scallions, finely chopped
1	pound boneless, skinless chicken breasts
3	cups cooked brown rice
1	cup baby arugula
1	cup carrot matchsticks
½	cup cucumber matchsticks
2	tablespoons chopped mint

• In a medium bowl, whisk together orange juice, olive oil, lemon juice, vinegar, orange zest, ¾ teaspoon of the salt, the sugar, pepper and scallions.

• Place chicken in a resealable plastic bag and add 3 tablespoons of the citrus dressing. Seal bag and shake to coat chicken with dressing. Marinate in refrigerator for 2 to 4 hours.

• Heat a gas or stovetop grill to medium-high or the coals in a charcoal grill to medium-hot. Remove chicken from marinade and discard marinade. Grill chicken 7 to 8 minutes per side or until internal temperature reaches 160°. Slice chicken thinly on the bias.

• In a large salad bowl, combine rice, arugula, carrot, cucumber and mint. Toss with 4 tablespoons of the citrus dressing and season with remaining ¼ teaspoon salt.

• Serve rice salad with sliced chicken and drizzle with remaining dressing.

PER SERVING 399 **CAL**; 14 g **FAT** (2 g **SAT**); 27 g **PRO**; 40 g **CARB**; 4 g **FIBER**; 519 mg **SODIUM**; 63 mg **CHOL**

OVEN SWEET-AND-
SOUR CHICKEN
WITH RED QUINOA

SMOKY PORK TENDERLOIN WITH
PINEAPPLE-MANGO SALSA

Smoky Pork Tenderloin with Pineapple-Mango Salsa

MAKES 4 servings **PREP** 15 minutes
ROAST at 450° for 20 minutes **LET REST** 10 minutes

SALSA

2	cups cubed pineapple
2	cups cubed mango (about 1 large)
½	cup chopped red onion
2	scallions, thinly sliced
¼	cup cilantro leaves, chopped
1	jalapeño pepper, seeded and chopped
2	tablespoons canola oil
¼	teaspoon salt

PORK

1	pork tenderloin (about 1¼ pounds)
1	tablespoon canola oil
1	teaspoon smoked paprika
½	teaspoon salt
⅛	teaspoon black pepper

• **Salsa.** In a large bowl, combine pineapple, mango, red onion, scallions, cilantro, jalapeño, canola oil and salt. Cover and refrigerate until serving.

• **Pork.** Heat oven to 450°. Rub tenderloin with canola oil and season all sides with smoked paprika, salt and black pepper. Place in a roasting pan on a rack and roast at 450° for 20 minutes or until internal temperature reaches 145°. (Alternately, grill on an oiled grate over medium-high heat, turning several times, 14 to 18 minutes.) Tent with foil and allow to rest 10 minutes before slicing thinly.

• Serve pork with salsa and, if desired, Citrus-Chili Sweet Potatoes (recipe below).

PER SERVING 378 **CAL**; 16 g **FAT** (3 g **SAT**); 31 g **PRO**; 30 g **CARB**; 4 g **FIBER**; 512 mg **SODIUM**; 92 mg **CHOL**

Citrus-Chili Sweet Potatoes Bake 2 pounds sweet potatoes (about 3 large) at 450° for 45 minutes until fork-tender. Spoon flesh into a large bowl; add ¼ cup orange juice, 1 tablespoon brown sugar, ¼ teaspoon each cinnamon and chili powder and ⅛ teaspoon salt. Mash to desired consistency.

SLICED STEAK WITH GERMAN POTATO SALAD

Sliced Steak with German Potato Salad

MAKES 4 servings **PREP** 15 minutes **COOK** 20 minutes **BROIL** 6 minutes **LET REST** 5 minutes

1¼	pounds red, white and blue-skinned small potatoes
2	ribs celery, sliced
½	red onion, chopped
2	scallions, sliced
3	tablespoons canola oil
3	tablespoons white vinegar
1	teaspoon sugar
½	teaspoon salt
¼	teaspoon black pepper
1¾	teaspoons beau monde seasoning
1	pound flank steak

• Place potatoes in a medium saucepan and cover with lightly salted water. Bring to a boil; simmer for 15 to 20 minutes or until tender. Drain and quarter potatoes; place in a large bowl. Stir in celery, red onion and scallions.

• In a small bowl, whisk together oil, vinegar, sugar, salt and pepper. Gently fold into potato mixture and cover with plastic wrap.

• Heat broiler. Rub beau monde seasoning on both sides of steak. Broil for 3 minutes per side or until internal temperature reaches 135°. Allow to rest 5 minutes before thinly slicing against the grain.

• Serve sliced steak with warm potato salad.

PER SERVING 356 **CAL**; 17 g **FAT** (3 g **SAT**); 28 g **PRO**; 21 g **CARB**; 3 g **FIBER**; 799 mg **SODIUM**; 37 mg **CHOL**

SUMMER STARTS HERE

Fantastic burgers, sangria and 8 more hot-weather essentials make the living easy.

GUACAMOLE WITH
GRILLED QUESADILLAS,
PAGE 164

Spicy Chipotle Burgers

MAKES 8 servings **PREP** 15 minutes **GRILL** 10 minutes

- 2   pounds ground beef
- 3   chipotles in adobo, seeded and chopped, plus 2 teaspoons adobo
- ½   cup fresh cilantro, chopped, plus more for garnish
- ⅓   cup finely grated onion
- 2   cloves garlic, finely grated
- 1   teaspoon salt
- 8   ounces smoked mozzarella, thinly sliced
- 8   potato hamburger buns
- 1   large tomato, cut into 8 slices

• Heat a grill or grill pan to medium-high heat. In a large bowl, combine beef, chipotles, adobo, cilantro, onion, garlic and salt. Form into 8 patties. Grill 4 minutes; flip and distribute cheese among burgers. Grill another 3 to 4 minutes for medium, or to desired doneness. Remove to a plate. Grill buns on cut side 1 to 2 minutes until lightly charred.

• Place burgers on buns and garnish with tomato slices, cilantro and, if desired, Chipotle Sour Cream (recipe below).

PER SERVING 400 **CAL**; 19 g **FAT** (9 g **SAT**); 32 g **PRO**; 25 g **CARB**; 2 g **FIBER**; 1,059 mg **SODIUM**; 89 mg **CHOL**

Chipotle Sour Cream In a small bowl, combine 1 cup sour cream, 1 seeded and diced chipotle in adobo, 1 teaspoon adobo and ¼ teaspoon salt.

FRIED GREEN TOMATOES
WITH RED PEPPER AIOLI

Fried Green Tomatoes with Red Pepper Aioli

MAKES 9 servings **PREP** 25 minutes
COOK 4 minutes per batch
KEEP WARM in 200° oven

RED PEPPER AIOLI

½	cup light mayonnaise
¼	cup roasted red peppers, drained
1	large clove garlic, coarsely chopped

TOMATOES

2	pounds firm green tomatoes
½	teaspoon salt
⅓	cup all-purpose flour
2	large eggs
⅔	cup yellow cornmeal
2	tablespoons grated Parmesan cheese
⅛	teaspoon black pepper
	Pinch cayenne pepper
7	tablespoons vegetable or canola oil, for frying

• **Aioli.** Combine mayonnaise, red peppers and garlic in a mini chopper. Process until well combined and fairly smooth, scraping down sides of chopper halfway through. Transfer to a small bowl. Refrigerate until serving.

• **Tomatoes.** Core tomatoes and cut a thin slice from top and bottom of each. Cut each tomato into three or four ¼-inch-thick slices and dry slightly on paper towels. Sprinkle with ⅛ teaspoon of the salt.

• Combine flour and ⅛ teaspoon of the salt in a shallow dish. Lightly beat eggs in a second shallow dish; whisk together cornmeal, Parmesan, remaining ¼ teaspoon salt, the black pepper and cayenne in a third shallow dish.

• Coat 6 of the tomato slices in seasoned flour, followed by egg, then cornmeal mixture. Heat oven to 200°.

• Heat 3 tablespoons of the oil in a large nonstick skillet over medium-high heat. Add the 6 coated tomato slices and fry for 2 minutes. Carefully flip over slices and fry an additional 2 minutes. Transfer to a baking sheet fitted with a wire rack and keep warm in oven. Repeat, coating all tomato slices with seasoned flour, egg and cornmeal mixture.

• Add 2 tablespoons of the oil to skillet before frying each consecutive batch (you should have 2 more batches to fry). Serve tomatoes warm with aioli on the side.

PER SERVING 216 **CAL**; 17 g **FAT** (2 g **SAT**); 4 g **PRO**; 13 g **CARB**; 1 g **FIBER**; 299 mg **SODIUM**; 53 mg **CHOL**

Grilled Panzanella Salad

MAKES 8 servings **PREP** 15 minutes
GRILL 14 minutes **LET STAND** 30 minutes

¼	cup extra-virgin olive oil, plus more for brushing
¼	cup red wine vinegar
1	teaspoon Dijon mustard
¾	teaspoon salt
¼	teaspoon pepper
1	loaf (14 ounces) Italian bread
1	small red onion, peeled and quartered
4	medium tomatoes (1½ pounds total), diced into 1-inch pieces
1	large seedless cucumber, diced into ½-inch pieces
1	large garlic clove, minced
1	cup packed basil leaves, roughly chopped

• Heat a grill or grill pan to medium-high heat. In a large bowl, whisk together olive oil, vinegar, mustard, salt and pepper. Set aside.

• Cut bread loaf in half crosswise, then cut each half lengthwise into four 1-inch-thick slices, for a total of 8 slices. Brush slices lightly with olive oil. Grill 2 minutes per side; set aside. Lightly brush onion quarters with olive oil. Grill 5 minutes; rotate and grill another 5 minutes.

• Cut bread slices into 1-inch cubes. Cut onion quarters into thin slices. Toss bread, onion, tomatoes, cucumber, garlic and basil in dressing. Cover and let stand for 30 minutes to allow flavors to combine.

PER SERVING 238 **CAL**; 10 g **FAT** (2 g **SAT**); 6 g **PRO**; 31 g **CARB**; 3 g **FIBER**; 529 mg **SODIUM**; 0 mg **CHOL**

GRILLED PANZANELLA SALAD

GAZPACHO

Shrimp Po' Boy

MAKES 6 servings **PREP** 20 minutes
COOK 2 minutes per batch
KEEP WARM in 200° oven

6	cups vegetable oil
1	cup plain bread crumbs
4	teaspoons Cajun seasoning
⅛	teaspoon salt
1½	pounds cleaned raw 21-30 count shrimp (thawed, if frozen)
2	large egg whites, lightly beaten
6	hoagie rolls or 3 small loaves Italian bread, trimmed, halved and split
6	tablespoons tartar sauce
1½	cups arugula
1	large tomato, sliced

• Heat oil in a saucepan (not more than half full) over medium-high heat to 365° on a deep-fat fry thermometer. Adjust temperature under pot to maintain 365°.

• In a large bowl, whisk together the bread crumbs, Cajun seasoning and salt. Heat oven to 200°. Line a large baking sheet with a double layer of paper towels.

• Toss ⅓ of the shrimp with egg whites. With tongs or a slotted spoon, transfer shrimp to bread crumb mixture and toss to coat. Fry in 365° oil for 2 minutes. Remove with a slotted spoon to paper-towel-lined sheet and keep warm in 200° oven. Repeat twice more with remaining shrimp, egg whites and bread crumb mixture (you will have egg white and bread crumbs left over).

• Fry shrimp in 2 more batches, letting oil return to 360° to 365° before adding next batch.

• Meanwhile, spread 1 tablespoon tartar sauce on each hoagie roll or Italian bread section. Top each with ¼ cup arugula leaves, about 8 shrimp and 2 tomato slices. Sandwich and serve.

PER SERVING 501 **CAL**; 23 g **FAT** (4 g **SAT**); 33 g **PRO**; 42 g **CARB**; 3 g **FIBER**; 809 mg **SODIUM**; 175 mg **CHOL**

Gazpacho

MAKES 6 servings **PREP** 15 minutes **LET STAND** 15 minutes **CHILL** 1 hour

3	slices white bread
2	pounds tomatoes, stemmed and roughly chopped
1	sweet red pepper, cored, seeded and roughly chopped
1¼	cups diced cucumber
1	cup diced white onion
1	large clove garlic
⅓	cup extra-virgin olive oil, plus more for drizzling (optional)
3	tablespoons sherry vinegar, plus more for drizzling (optional)
1¼	teaspoons salt
¼	teaspoon pepper

• In a bowl, cover bread slices with cold water; let stand 15 minutes. Drain and squeeze water from bread.

• In a food processor, combine tomatoes, sweet red pepper, 1 cup of the cucumber, the onion, garlic and ½ cup cold water. Process until very finely chopped. Add bread, oil, vinegar, salt and pepper. Process until smooth.

• Transfer to a resealable container and chill for 1 hour. Garnish gazpacho with remaining ¼ cup cucumber and, if desired, drizzle with additional olive oil and vinegar.

PER SERVING 194 **CAL**; 13 g **FAT** (2 g **SAT**); 3 g **PRO**; 19 g **CARB**; 3 g **FIBER**; 597 mg **SODIUM**; 0 mg **CHOL**

SHRIMP PO' BOY

CHIMICHURRI
VEGETABLE SKEWERS

BALSAMIC-GLAZED
KIELBASA SKEWERS

MEDITERRANEAN
MEATBALL SKEWERS

FIVE-SPICE
CHICKEN SKEWERS

Balsamic-Glazed Kielbasa Skewers

MAKES 6 servings   **PREP** 20 minutes
GRILL 10 minutes

3	tablespoons balsamic vinegar
3	tablespoons olive oil
2	tablespoons honey
¼	teaspoon salt
¼	teaspoon pepper
1	package (13 ounces) light kielbasa, cut into ½-inch-thick bias slices
1	pound cremini mushrooms
2	green bell peppers, cored, seeded and cut into 1½-inch pieces
1	medium white onion, trimmed, peeled and cut into 1-inch wedges

• Heat grill to medium-high heat. In a bowl, whisk together vinegar, oil, honey, salt and pepper until well combined.

• Thread kielbasa, mushrooms, green peppers and onion on twelve 10-inch skewers. Brush generously with dressing. Grill on medium-high 5 minutes, flip, and grill another 5 minutes.

PER SERVING 368 **CAL**; 24 g **FAT** (6 g **SAT**); 19 g **PRO**; 22 g **CARB**; 3 g **FIBER**; 1,064 mg **SODIUM**; 58 mg **CHOL**

Chimichurri Vegetable Skewers

MAKES 4 servings   **PREP** 20 minutes
COOK 10 minutes   **REFRIGERATE** 1 hour
GRILL 12 minutes

16	small red potatoes, about 1½ inches around (about 1 pound)
⅓	cup olive oil
¼	cup red wine vinegar
½	teaspoon salt
3	large cloves garlic, finely chopped
1	cup parsley, chopped
¼	cup cilantro, chopped
2	medium zucchini, sliced into 1-inch-thick pieces
2	medium yellow squash, sliced into 1-inch-thick pieces
1	small red onion, trimmed, peeled and cut into 1-inch wedges

• In a sided skillet, cover potatoes with 1 inch of cold water. Bring to a boil. Reduce heat to a simmer and cook 10 minutes, until fork-tender. Drain and rinse under cold water until cooled.

• In a bowl, whisk together oil, vinegar and salt until well combined. Stir in garlic, parsley and cilantro. In a resealable plastic bag, toss vegetables with ¾ of the chimichurri. Refrigerate 30 minutes to 1 hour.

• Heat grill to medium-high heat. Thread vegetables on eight 10-inch skewers. Grill on medium-high heat for 6 minutes, flip, and cook another 6 minutes. Serve with remaining chimichurri on the side.

PER SERVING 312 **CAL**; 21 g **FAT** (3 g **SAT**); 5 g **PRO**; 29 g **CARB**; 6 g **FIBER**; 315 mg **SODIUM**; 0 mg **CHOL**

Mediterranean Meatball Skewers

MAKES 4 servings   **PREP** 25 minutes
GRILL 12 minutes

3	tablespoons white wine vinegar
3	tablespoons olive oil
2	cloves garlic, chopped
1	tablespoon chopped fresh thyme
2	teaspoons Dijon mustard
½	teaspoon plus ⅛ teaspoon salt
¼	teaspoon plus ⅛ teaspoon pepper
1	pound lean ground beef
1	egg, beaten
¾	cup shredded Parmesan
½	cup bread crumbs
8	fresh baby artichokes
16	cherry tomatoes

• Heat grill to medium-high heat. In a bowl, whisk together vinegar, oil, garlic, thyme, mustard, ⅛ teaspoon of the salt and ⅛ teaspoon of the pepper until well blended. Set aside.

• In another bowl, mix together beef, beaten egg, Parmesan, bread crumbs, remaining ½ teaspoon salt and remaining ¼ teaspoon pepper until well combined. Form into 24 meatballs, about 1½ inches in diameter.

• Slice off stem and top third of each artichoke; discard. Peel and discard the few top layers of leaves until artichokes are light green. Slice in half.

• Thread the meatballs, artichokes and tomatoes on eight 10-inch skewers. Brush generously with the dressing. Grill on medium-high 12 minutes, rotating a few times, until meatballs are cooked through.

PER SERVING 519 **CAL**; 28 g **FAT** (9 g **SAT**); 38 g **PRO**; 32 g **CARB**; 10 g **FIBER**; 1,024 mg **SODIUM**; 137 mg **CHOL**

Five-Spice Chicken Skewers

MAKES 4 servings   **PREP** 20 minutes
REFRIGERATE 2 hours   **GRILL** 14 minutes

¼	cup rice wine vinegar
¼	cup canola oil
3	tablespoons soy sauce
2	teaspoons Chinese five-spice powder
1	teaspoon sesame oil
½	cup sliced scallions
2	tablespoons chopped fresh ginger
1¼	pounds boneless skinless chicken breasts, cut into 1½-inch chunks
2	orange sweet peppers, cored, seeded and cut into 1½-inch pieces
16	large scallions, trimmed, and bottom third (root end) of each sliced into two 2½-inch pieces

• In a bowl, whisk together vinegar, canola oil, soy sauce, five-spice powder and sesame oil. Stir in the scallions and the ginger.

• In a resealable plastic bag, toss chicken and peppers with ¾ of the marinade. Refrigerate 1 to 2 hours.

• Heat grill to medium-high heat. Thread marinated chicken and peppers, as well as large sliced scallions, on eight 10-inch skewers. Brush skewers with remaining marinade. Grill on medium-high heat for 7 minutes, flip and grill another 7 minutes or until chicken is cooked through.

PER SERVING 333 **CAL**; 17 g **FAT** (2 g **SAT**); 36 g **PRO**; 8 g **CARB**; 2 g **FIBER**; 792 mg **SODIUM**; 82 mg **CHOL**

Triple Melon Salad

MAKES 8 servings **PREP** 15 minutes
COOK 3 minutes

- ½ **small seedless watermelon, rind removed, diced (4 cups)**
- ½ **honeydew melon, seeded, rind removed, diced (2 cups)**
- ½ **cantaloupe, seeded, rind removed, diced (2 cups)**
- 3 **ounces prosciutto, torn or cut into strips**
- 3 **tablespoons packed fresh mint leaves, chopped**
- ⅛ **teaspoon salt**
  Pinch cayenne pepper

SYRUP

- ⅓ **cup sugar**
- ¼ **cup fresh lime juice**
- 2 **jalapeños, seeded and minced**

• Combine watermelon, honeydew and cantaloupe in a large bowl. Set aside.

• **Syrup.** In a medium saucepan, combine sugar, fresh lime juice, jalapeños and 2 tablespoons water. Bring to a simmer over medium-high heat and cook for 3 minutes. Remove from heat, strain out jalapeño pieces and cool completely.

• While syrup cools, add prosciutto, mint, salt and cayenne to melon in bowl. Pour the syrup over salad and stir gently to combine.

PER SERVING 110 **CAL**; 2 g **FAT** (1 g **SAT**); 4 g **PRO**; 23 g **CARB**; 1 g **FIBER**; 312 mg **SODIUM**; 7 mg **CHOL**

Guacamole with Grilled Quesadillas

MAKES 6 servings **PREP** 20 minutes **COOK** 10 minutes **GRILL** 2 minutes per batch

GUACAMOLE

- 3 **ripe avocados, peeled and pitted**
- 2 **tablespoons fresh lime juice**
- ¼ **teaspoon salt**
- ⅛ **teaspoon black pepper**
- 1 **plum tomato, seeded and finely diced**
- ¼ **cup cilantro leaves, chopped**
- 1 **jalapeño, seeded and finely chopped**
- 2 **large cloves garlic, chopped**

GRILLED QUESADILLAS

- 1 **tablespoon unsalted butter**
- 1 **sweet onion, thinly sliced**
- ¼ **teaspoon salt**
- 6 **large tortillas (wraps)**
- 12 **ounces Manchego cheese, grated (3 cups)**

• **Guacamole.** Cut avocados into large chunks and place in a medium bowl. Add lime juice, salt and pepper and mash to desired consistency. Stir in tomato, cilantro, jalapeño and garlic. Set aside.

• **Quesadillas.** Heat grill to medium-high heat. Melt butter in a cast-iron skillet set on grill rack. Add onion and salt and cook 10 minutes, stirring frequently. Carefully remove pan from grill.

• Place 2 tortillas on grill and spread half of each with some of the onion. Grill 30 seconds. Sprinkle ½ cup of the cheese over each tortilla and fold to enclose filling. Grill 1 minute, then flip over and grill 30 more seconds. Repeat with remaining tortillas, onion and cheese. Cut each quesadilla into wedges and serve with guacamole.

PER ⅓ CUP GUACAMOLE 166 **CAL**; 15 g **FAT** (2 g **SAT**); 2 g **PRO**; 10 g **CARB**; 7 g **FIBER**; 105 mg **SODIUM**; 0 mg **CHOL**

PER QUESADILLA 465 **CAL**; 25 g **FAT** (13 g **SAT**); 23 g **PRO**; 36 g **CARB**; 8 g **FIBER**; 940 mg **SODIUM**; 64 mg **CHOL**

TRIPLE MELON SALAD

CHERRY GALETTE

Cherry Galette

MAKES 8 servings **PREP** 30 minutes
REFRIGERATE 1 hour **BAKE** at 375° for 55 minutes

DOUGH

1¼	cups all-purpose flour
1	stick (½ cup) cold unsalted butter, cubed
1	tablespoon sugar
¼	teaspoon salt

FILLING

1½	pounds sweet cherries, stemmed, pitted and halved
⅓	cup granulated sugar
1	tablespoon cornstarch
1	tablespoon lemon juice
¼	teaspoon almond extract
⅛	teaspoon salt
	Cream or half-and-half, for brushing
2	tablespoons turbinado or raw sugar

• **Dough.** In a food processor, combine flour, butter, sugar and salt. Pulse until butter resembles coarse crumbs (a few larger pieces are okay). With machine running, stream in 2 tablespoons ice water, about 20 seconds. Check to see if dough has come together. If it seems dry, add ice water 1 tablespoon at a time with machine running, being careful not to make dough too wet. Do not overmix. Transfer dough onto a work surface, form into a disk, wrap in plastic and refrigerate for 1 hour.

• **Filling.** Heat oven to 375°. In a bowl, combine cherries, sugar, cornstarch, lemon juice, almond extract and salt. Set aside.

• On a lightly floured surface, roll out chilled dough to a 13-inch circle. Transfer dough to a baking sheet lined with parchment paper. Pour filling into middle of dough, leaving a 2-inch border around edges. Fold edges over filling (galette should be 9 inches wide when complete). Brush border with cream and sprinkle with sugar. Bake at 375° for 50 to 55 minutes, until crust is golden brown. Cool on a wire rack before slicing.

PER SERVING 528 CAL; 16 g FAT (4 g SAT); 29 g PRO; 65 g CARB; 4 g FIBER; 661 mg SODIUM; 72 mg CHOL

CHERRY-BERRY SANGRIA

Cherry-Berry Sangria

MAKES 8 servings **PREP** 5 minutes **REFRIGERATE** 2 hours

1	bottle (750 ml) dry red wine
2	cups cherry-pomegranate juice or cranberry juice
½	cup brandy
½	pound cherries (fresh or frozen), pitted and halved
1	cup quartered strawberries
¾	cup blueberries
2	tablespoons superfine sugar (optional)
1	can (12 ounces) cold lemon-lime soda

• In a large pitcher, combine wine, juice, brandy, cherries, strawberries, blueberries and, if desired, sugar. Refrigerate at least 2 hours.

• Just before serving, stir mixture and add lemon-lime soda. Serve over ice.

PER SERVING 197 CAL; 0 g FAT (0 g SAT); 1 g PRO; 24 g CARB; 1 g FIBER; 22 mg SODIUM; 0 mg CHOL

SWEET SOMETHINGS

Delicious slow-cooked desserts keep the kitchen cool.

Summary Fruit Compote

Summer Fruit Compote

MAKES 8 servings **PREP** 15 minutes
SLOW COOK on HIGH for 3¾ hours or LOW for 5¾ hours

3	cups fresh pineapple chunks
2	medium pears, peeled, cored and cut into ½-inch chunks (about 2 cups)
2	cups frozen sliced peaches
1	cup frozen pitted cherries
¾	cup dried apricots, quartered
⅔	cup frozen orange juice concentrate, thawed
1	tablespoon packed dark brown sugar
1	teaspoon vanilla extract
2	tablespoons cornstarch
½	cup sliced almonds, toasted
	Vanilla ice cream (optional)

• Combine pineapple, pears, peaches, cherries, apricots, orange juice, brown sugar and vanilla in slow cooker. Cover and cook on HIGH for 3½ hours or LOW for 5½ hours.

• Uncover and remove 2 tablespoons of the liquid. In a small bowl, stir together liquid and cornstarch. Stir cornstarch mixture back into slow cooker; cook 15 minutes more or until thickened. Sprinkle with almonds. Serve warm with vanilla ice cream, if desired.

PER SERVING 139 **CAL**; 2 g **FAT** (0 g **SAT**); 2 g **PRO**; 29 g **CARB**; 3 g **FIBER**; 3 mg **SODIUM**; 0 mg **CHOL**

Sour Cherry Rice Pudding

MAKES 4 servings PREP 5 minutes
SLOW COOK on LOW for 4 hours, 50 minutes
LET STAND 10 minutes COOL 30 minutes

- ¾ **cup arborio rice, rinsed and drained**
- 1 **can (12 ounces) evaporated milk**
- ⅔ **cup sugar**
- ½ **cup milk**
   Pinch of salt
- ½ **cup cherry juice**
- 1 **cup dried cherries**
- ⅛ **teaspoon ground cinnamon**
   Pinch ground nutmeg

• Combine 1 cup water, rice and evaporated milk in a 2- to 3-quart round slow cooker.

• In a small saucepan, cook sugar and milk over medium-high heat for 1 minute or until bubbles appear around edges and sugar has dissolved. Stir into slow cooker with salt. Cover and cook on LOW for 4½ hours.

• While rice is cooking, bring cherry juice to a boil and pour over cherries in a small bowl; let stand 10 minutes. Drain, reserving juice.

• Stir cherries, 3 tablespoons of the warm juice, the cinnamon and nutmeg into slow cooker; cover and cook on LOW for 20 minutes more.

• Turn off slow cooker and allow pudding to cool, partially covered, for 30 minutes.

PER SERVING 408 CAL; 1 g FAT (1 g SAT); 11 g PRO; 87 g CARB; 3 g FIBER; 202 mg SODIUM; 7 mg CHOL

Ricotta Vanilla Bread Pudding

MAKES 6 servings PREP 10 minutes COOK 15 minutes SLOW COOK 2½ hours on HIGH COOL 20 minutes

- 2 **tablespoons unsalted butter, melted**
- 6 **slices challah bread, each 1¼ inches thick, cut into ½-inch cubes**
- ½ **cup golden raisins**
- 1 **cup milk**
- 1 **container (15 ounces) ricotta cheese**
- ½ **cup sugar**
- 2 **eggs**
- 1 **cup sour cream**
- 1 **teaspoon grated lemon zest**
- 1 **teaspoon vanilla extract**
- ¼ **teaspoon ground cinnamon**

• Coat a 1½-quart soufflé dish with 1 tablespoon of the melted butter. Add bread and raisins to dish. Pour milk over top; stir to combine. Set aside.

• Combine ricotta, sugar, eggs, sour cream, lemon zest and vanilla. Pour ricotta mixture over bread; mix lightly. Drizzle remaining 1 tablespoon butter over bread and sprinkle with cinnamon. Cover dish with aluminum foil; place in slow cooker. Fill slow cooker with boiling water to reach 1 inch up the side of soufflé dish.

• Cover top of slow cooker with a dish towel; top with lid. Slow cook on HIGH for 2½ hours or until internal temperature of pudding registers 140°. Cool at least 20 minutes.

PER SERVING 448 CAL; 21 g FAT (12 g SAT); 16 g PRO; 48 g CARB; 1 g FIBER; 274 mg SODIUM; 163 mg CHOL

STRAWBERRY CORNMEAL
SHORTCAKE, PAGE 201

JULY

185   189   197

WE LOVE SUMMER

Dive into the perfect party menu.

WILD RICE AND CORN SALAD

NEW-WAVE SURF AND TURF WITH AVOCADO-ORANGE SALSA

New-Wave Surf and Turf with Avocado-Orange Salsa

MAKES 8 servings **PREP** 20 minutes **MARINATE** 4 hours (steak), 30 minutes (fish)
GRILL 13 minutes **REST** 5 minutes

4	tablespoons vegetable oil
8	cloves garlic, chopped
3	tablespoons Worcestershire sauce
	Juice and zest of 2 limes
4	tablespoons chopped cilantro
2	pounds flatiron steak
2	pounds tuna steaks (4 steaks, about 8 ounces each, 1 inch thick), cut in half vertically
¼	teaspoon salt

SALSA

3	ripe avocados, diced
⅓	cup chopped red onion
1	jalapeño pepper, seeds removed, diced
3	tablespoons orange juice
1	tablespoon olive oil
¼	teaspoon garlic salt
2	oranges, peeled and cut into segments, each segment cut into 3 pieces
2	tablespoons chopped cilantro

• In a large bowl, combine oil, garlic, Worcestershire sauce, lime juice, zest and cilantro. Divide marinade evenly between 2 large resealable plastic bags. Place steak in one bag, seal and marinate in refrigerator 4 hours. Thirty minutes before grilling, add tuna to second bag, reseal and refrigerate.

• **Salsa.** In a medium bowl, combine avocados, onion, jalapeño, orange juice, olive oil and garlic salt. Fold in oranges and cilantro. Place plastic wrap directly on surface; refrigerate 2 hours.

• Heat a gas grill to medium-high or the coals in a charcoal grill to medium-hot. Lightly grease grates. Grill steaks 3 to 4 minutes per side, turning once, for medium-rare. Remove to a platter and allow to rest 5 minutes before slicing against the grain. Sprinkle with salt.

• Grill tuna 3 minutes, turn and grill an additional 2 minutes for medium-rare.

• Serve sliced steak and tuna with salsa.

PER SERVING 509 CAL; 27 g FAT (6 g SAT); 52 g PRO; 16 g CARB; 7 g FIBER; 277 mg SODIUM; 91 mg CHOL

Wild Rice and Corn Salad

MAKES 8 servings **PREP** 20 minutes
COOK 15 minutes

1½	cups white, brown, wild and red rice blend
3	cups fresh corn kernels (about 4 ears)
½	red onion, chopped
2	ribs celery, thinly sliced
½	cup dried cherries, chopped
½	cup dark cherry balsamic vinegar
¼	cup extra-virgin olive oil
¾	teaspoon salt
½	teaspoon black pepper

• Cook rice following package directions. Spread out on a baking sheet to cool.

• In a large bowl, combine rice, corn, onion, celery and dried cherries.

• In a small bowl, whisk together vinegar, oil, salt and pepper. Toss with rice and corn mixture. Cover and refrigerate until serving.

PER SERVING 258 CAL; 8 g FAT (1 g SAT); 4 g PRO; 47 g CARB; 3 g FIBER; 227 mg SODIUM; 0 mg CHOL

VIETNAMESE VEGETABLE
PINWHEELS

These light and fresh nibbles are based on peak-of-season produce.

Vietnamese Vegetable Pinwheels

MAKES 24 pieces **PREP** 20 minutes
REFRIGERATE 2 to 4 hours

4	burrito-size flour tortillas
4	large leaves red leaf lettuce, tough ribs removed
4	tablespoons sesame-soy salad dressing, plus more for dipping (optional)
1⅓	cups shredded cabbage
½	cup shredded carrot
1	cucumber, peeled, cut into 2-inch matchsticks
4	teaspoons rice vinegar
1	cup cilantro leaves
1	cup mint leaves

• Place a tortilla on a flat work surface. On one side place a lettuce leaf and drizzle with 1 tablespoon of the dressing. Layer with ⅓ cup cabbage, 2 tablespoons carrot and 12 cucumber sticks. Drizzle with 1 teaspoon vinegar and top with some of the cilantro and mint. Roll up tightly and wrap in plastic wrap. Twist ends of wrap to secure tightly. Repeat with remaining ingredients. Refrigerate 2 to 4 hours.

• To serve, unwrap rolls and cut each on the bias into 6 pieces. Serve with additional dressing for dipping, if desired.

PER PIECE 36 **CAL**; 1 g **FAT** (0 g **SAT**); 0 g **PRO**; 7 g **CARB**; 1 g **FIBER**; 85 mg **SODIUM**; 0 mg **CHOL**

GRILLED BRUSCHETTA CAPRESE

Grilled Bruschetta Caprese

MAKES 16 pieces **PREP** 15 minutes **GRILL** 2 minutes

1	loaf sourdough bread (about 1 pound), cut into ½-inch-thick slices
4	garlic cloves, peeled
2	tablespoons olive oil
2	teaspoons sea salt
16	large fresh basil leaves
1	pound fresh mozzarella, thinly sliced
2	heirloom tomatoes, thinly sliced White balsamic vinegar

• Heat a gas grill to medium-high or the coals in a charcoal grill to medium-hot.

• Grill bread slices 1 minute per side, until toasted.

• Rub one side of each slice with garlic, lightly brush with olive oil and sprinkle with a pinch of sea salt.

• On each bruschetta, place a basil leaf, a slice of cheese and a tomato slice. Drizzle with balsamic vinegar and sprinkle with additional sea salt, if desired.

PER PIECE 192 **CAL**; 9 g **FAT** (5 g **SAT**); 10 g **PRO**; 18 g **CARB**; 1 g **FIBER**; 531 mg **SODIUM**; 20 mg **CHOL**

BABY LETTUCE AND
ARUGULA SALAD WITH
SUMMER TOMATO DRESSING

Berry Margarita Cheesecake Squares

MAKES 20 squares **PREP** 15 minutes
BAKE at 350° for 35 minutes **REFRIGERATE** 1 hour

CRUST

¾	cup (1½ sticks) unsalted butter, at room temperature
⅓	cup packed dark brown sugar
⅓	cup granulated sugar
2	cups all-purpose flour
1	cup pecans, chopped

CHEESECAKE TOPPING

2	packages (8 ounces each) cream cheese, at room temperature
½	cup granulated sugar
2	eggs
1	teaspoon vanilla extract
2	tablespoons tequila
1	tablespoon lime juice
1	tablespoon lime zest
1	tablespoon cornstarch
1	cup each blueberries, raspberries, sliced strawberries and blackberries

• Heat oven to 350°.

• **Crust.** In a large bowl, beat butter 1 minute; add sugars and beat 3 minutes. Beat in flour on low speed until just incorporated. Beat in pecans.

• Press mixture evenly over bottom of a 13 x 9 x 2-inch nonstick baking pan. Bake at 350° for 10 minutes. Cool slightly.

• **Cheesecake Topping.** In a large bowl, beat cream cheese and sugar 3 minutes. Add eggs and vanilla and beat 2 minutes; beat in tequila, lime juice and zest. Beat in cornstarch.

• Pour topping over crust. Bake at 350° for 20 to 25 minutes, until set. Cool slightly; refrigerate 1 hour.

• Cut into 20 squares and refrigerate until serving. To serve, trim off browned edges and top with berries.

PER SQUARE 286 **CAL**; 20 g **FAT** (10 g **SAT**); 5 g **PRO**; 24 g **CARB**; 2 g **FIBER**; 77 mg **SODIUM**; 64 mg **CHOL**

Baby Lettuce and Arugula Salad with Summer Tomato Dressing

MAKES 8 servings **PREP** 10 minutes **COOK** 3 minutes

½	pound green beans, trimmed
¼	cup extra-virgin olive oil
2	tablespoons red wine vinegar
¼	teaspoon salt
⅛	teaspoon black pepper
1	large shallot, finely chopped
1	large beefsteak tomato
8	cups mixed baby lettuces
2	cups baby arugula

• Bring a medium saucepan of lightly salted water to a boil. Add green beans and cook 3 minutes, until crisp-tender. Drain; run under cold water.

• In a medium bowl, whisk together olive oil, vinegar, salt and pepper. Add shallot; grate tomato over bowl.

• In a large bowl, combine lettuces, arugula and string beans. Toss with dressing and serve immediately.

PER SERVING 89 **CAL**; 7 g **FAT** (1 g **SAT**); 2 g **PRO**; 6 g **CARB**; 3 g **FIBER**; 96 mg **SODIUM**; 0 mg **CHOL**

BERRY MARGARITA
CHEESECAKE
SQUARES

CHOPPED!

These refreshing, protein-packed salads have staying power to keep you satisfied.

POACHED SALMON
SALAD, PAGE 185

BOMBAY CHICKEN
SALAD, PAGE 182

SESAME STEAK
SALAD

Sesame Steak Salad

MAKES 4 servings   PREP 15 minutes
MARINATE 15 minutes   BROIL OR GRILL 6 minutes
LET REST 5 minutes

3	tablespoons rice vinegar
2	tablespoons low-sodium soy sauce
2	tablespoons packed brown sugar
1	tablespoon minced fresh ginger
1	teaspoon yellow mustard
1	tablespoon dark sesame oil
1¼	pounds skirt steak
8	cups watercress (2 bunches), tough stems removed
1	sweet red pepper, cored, seeded and thinly sliced
1	cup shredded carrots
3	scallions, trimmed and sliced
2	ribs celery, sliced on the diagonal
1	tablespoon toasted sesame seeds
¼	teaspoon salt

• In a small bowl, combine vinegar, soy sauce, brown sugar, ginger and mustard. While whisking, add oil.

• Place steak in a resealable plastic bag and add 3 tablespoons of the dressing. Marinate at room temperature for 15 minutes. Heat broiler or gas grill to medium-high heat.

• Remove steak from bag; discard bag with remaining marinade. Broil or grill steak for 2 to 3 minutes per side, turning once, or until desired doneness. Let rest 5 minutes.

• Combine watercress, red pepper, carrots, scallions and celery in a large bowl. Thinly slice steak across the grain and add to salad. Toss with remaining dressing. Sprinkle with sesame seeds and salt and gently toss again.

PER SERVING 350 CAL; 18 g FAT (11 g SAT); 32 g PRO; 16 g CARB; 3 g FIBER; 535 mg SODIUM; 69 mg CHOL

PEANUT PORK AND NOODLES

Peanut Pork and Noodles

MAKES 4 servings   PREP 25 minutes   MARINATE 15 minutes   COOK 3 minutes   GRILL 4 minutes

DRESSING

¼	cup rice vinegar
¼	cup creamy peanut butter
3	tablespoons low-sodium soy sauce
2	tablespoons honey
1	tablespoon minced garlic
1	tablespoon minced ginger
1	teaspoon garlic-chili paste

SALAD

8	ounces thinly sliced boneless pork chops
2	packages (3 ounces each) ramen noodles, flavor packets discarded
8	ounces snow peas, tough strings removed, sliced
8	ounces baby bok choy, trimmed, cleaned and sliced crosswise
1	sweet red pepper, cored seeded and thinly sliced
⅛	teaspoon salt
3	tablespoons dry-roasted unsalted peanuts

• In a small bowl, combine vinegar, peanut butter, 3 tablespoons water, the soy sauce, honey, garlic, ginger and chili paste. Whisk until smooth; set aside.

• Heat grill or grill pan to medium-high heat. Combine pork chops and ⅓ cup of the dressing in a resealable plastic bag. Marinate at least 15 minutes.

• Meanwhile, bring a large pot of water to a boil. Break up ramen noodles, stir into pot and cook 2 minutes. Add snow peas and bok choy. Return to a boil, cook 1 minute, then drain and rinse in cold water. Drain and place mixture in a large bowl with sliced red pepper.

• Remove pork from marinade; discard marinade. Grill for 3 to 4 minutes, turning halfway through. Transfer to a cutting board.

• Toss noodle mixture with remaining dressing and the salt. Slice pork into thin strips and scatter over salad. Sprinkle with peanuts and serve immediately.

PER SERVING 438 CAL; 14 g FAT (3 g SAT); 26 g PRO; 53 g CARB; 7 g FIBER; 800 mg SODIUM; 31 mg CHOL

BOMBAY
CHICKEN
SALAD

Bombay Chicken Salad

MAKES 4 servings PREP 20 minutes COOK 9 minutes GRILL 12 minutes

SALAD

1½	teaspoons curry powder
½	teaspoon salt
¼	teaspoon sugar
¼	teaspoon ground cumin
⅛	teaspoon black pepper
1	pound boneless, skinless chicken breasts, pounded to an even thickness
1	cup pearl couscous
1	mango, peeled, pitted and diced
½	cup golden raisins
3	scallions, trimmed and sliced
¼	cup sliced almonds, toasted

DRESSING

2	tablespoons lemon juice
1	teaspoon honey
¼	teaspoon salt
⅛	teaspoon curry powder
⅛	teaspoon black pepper
3	tablespoons olive oil

• **Salad.** In a small bowl, combine curry powder, salt, sugar, ground cumin and black pepper. Rub onto chicken. Heat grill to medium-high heat.

• Meanwhile, bring a medium saucepan of lightly salted water to a boil. Add couscous and cook for 9 minutes. Drain and rinse with cool water.

• Grill chicken for 5 to 6 minutes per side, depending on thickness. Remove to a cutting board and cut into ½-inch pieces.

• **Dressing.** In a small bowl, whisk together lemon juice, honey, salt, curry powder and pepper. While whisking, add oil in a thin stream.

• Place couscous in a large bowl. Add mango, raisins, scallions, almonds and cubed chicken. Drizzle with dressing and toss to coat. Refrigerate unless serving immediately.

PER SERVING 482 CAL; 15 g FAT (2 g SAT); 33 g PRO; 56 g CARB; 5 g FIBER; 516 mg SODIUM; 66 mg CHOL

Veggie Bowl

MAKES 4 servings SOAK overnight
PREP 15 minutes COOK 40 minutes

1½	cups kamut (khorasan wheat) berries (such as Bob's Red Mill)
½	pound broccoli crowns, cut into bite-size pieces
1	cup shelled edamame
½	cup light mayonnaise
⅓	cup 2% Greek yogurt
¼	cup parsley, chopped
2	tablespoons chopped dill
2	tablespoons fresh lemon juice
2	tablespoons olive oil
1	tablespoon snipped chives
2	teaspoons country Dijon mustard
1	teaspoon sugar
1	teaspoon garlic salt
1	bag (6 ounces) baby spinach
½	cup crunchy sprouts (pea, adzuki and lentil blend; optional)

• Combine kamut berries and 4 cups water in a bowl. Soak overnight.

• Drain kamut and transfer to a large shallow pot. Add 4½ cups lightly salted water and bring to a boil over high heat. Cover and reduce heat to medium. Simmer 35 minutes.

• Add broccoli and edamame to pot with kamut. Cover and cook 5 minutes. Drain and rinse with cool water.

• Meanwhile, whisk together mayonnaise, yogurt, parsley, dill, lemon juice, olive oil, chives, mustard, sugar and ½ teaspoon of the garlic salt.

• In a large bowl, combine spinach, kamut mixture, ¾ cup of the dressing and the sprouts, if desired. Gently toss. Season with remaining ½ teaspoon garlic salt and toss again. Refrigerate any leftover dressing for another use.

PER SERVING 448 CAL; 17 g FAT (2 g SAT); 19 g PRO; 68 g CARB; 13 g FIBER; 533 mg SODIUM; 9 mg CHOL

VEGGIE BOWL

SANTORINI
SHRIMP SALAD

Santorini Shrimp Salad

MAKES 4 servings **PREP** 15 minutes
COOK 4 minutes **GRILL OR BROIL** 5 minutes

DRESSING

¼	cup red wine vinegar
3	tablespoons chopped fresh parsley
2	teaspoons honey mustard
¼	teaspoon salt
¼	teaspoon black pepper
¼	teaspoon red pepper flakes
⅓	cup olive oil

SALAD

½	pound green beans, trimmed
1¼	pounds cleaned shrimp
1	cup cherry tomatoes, halved
½	cup (2 ounces) feta cheese cubes or crumbles
1	bag (5 ounces) arugula
½	red onion, thinly sliced
¼	teaspoon salt

• **Dressing.** In a medium bowl, whisk together vinegar, parsley, mustard, salt, pepper and red pepper flakes. While whisking, add oil in a thin stream. Set aside.

• **Salad.** Bring a saucepan of water to a boil. Add beans; cook for 3 to 4 minutes. Drain and rinse with cool water.

• Place shrimp in a resealable plastic bag or glass dish. Add ¼ cup of the dressing and toss to combine. Marinate at least 10 minutes while heating grill or broiler. Thread shrimp onto skewers or place on broiler pan. Grill or broil for 5 minutes, turning, until cooked through.

• In a medium bowl, toss green beans, tomatoes and feta cheese with 1 tablespoon of the remaining dressing. Place arugula and red onion on a serving platter or in a large bowl. Top with shrimp and season with salt. Drizzle with 2 tablespoons of the dressing and add green bean mixture. Serve remaining dressing on the side, if desired.

PER SERVING 339 **CAL**; 18 g **FAT** (4 g **SAT**); 33 g **PRO**; 12 g **CARB**; 3 g **FIBER**; 634 mg **SODIUM**; 228 mg **CHOL**

POACHED SALMON SALAD

Poached Salmon Salad

MAKES 6 servings **PREP** 20 minutes **COOK** 10 minutes **REFRIGERATE** at least 1 hour

SALMON

3	cups low-sodium vegetable broth
1	small onion, halved
3	cloves garlic, sliced
10	whole peppercorns
½	teaspoon red pepper flakes
1¼	pounds salmon fillets, thawed if frozen
⅛	teaspoon salt

DRESSING AND SALAD

¼	cup orange juice
2	tablespoons red wine vinegar
2	teaspoons spicy brown mustard
¾	teaspoon salt
½	teaspoon hot sauce
2	tablespoons olive oil
12	ounces fresh kale leaves (8 packed cups), tough stems removed, chopped
1½	cups seedless red grapes, halved if large
¼	cup roasted, salted sunflower seeds

• **Salmon.** Combine broth, onion, garlic, peppercorns and red pepper flakes in a straight-sided sauté pan. Cover and bring to a boil, then reduce heat to medium. Simmer 5 minutes. Season salmon with salt and add to pan. Cover and cook at very low simmer for 5 minutes. Remove fish to a plate with a large spatula and refrigerate at least 1 hour.

• **Dressing and Salad.** In a small bowl, whisk together orange juice, vinegar, mustard, ½ teaspoon of the salt and the hot sauce. While whisking, add olive oil in a thin stream.

• Combine the kale, grapes and sunflower seeds in large bowl. Remove salmon skin. Flake salmon into bite-size pieces and add to bowl. Pour dressing over salad and season with remaining ¼ teaspoon salt. Gently salad toss to combine.

PER SERVING 339 **CAL**; 18 g **FAT** (3 g **SAT**); 23 g **PRO**; 22 g **CARB**; 3 g **FIBER**; 751 mg **SODIUM**; 56 mg **CHOL**

VEGGING OUT

New ideas for corn, tomatoes, squash and all the season's best!

CARIBBEAN-STYLE GRILLED
CORN, PAGE 194

Tomato and Goat Cheese Stacks

MAKES 4 servings **PREP** 20 minutes

- 8 ounces fresh goat cheese, room temperature
- ¼ cup heavy cream
- ⅓ cup chopped fresh chives
- ⅛ teaspoon pepper
- 4 heirloom tomatoes (8 ounces each), sliced into thirds horizontally
- ¼ teaspoon salt
- ⅓ cup shelled pistachios, roughly chopped

Extra-virgin olive oil and balsamic glaze (such as Colavita), for drizzling

• Using a hand mixer, beat goat cheese and heavy cream in a bowl until well combined, about 1 minute. Beat in chives and pepper.

• Place the 4 tomato bottoms on a plate and sprinkle with ⅛ teaspoon of the salt. Spread 2 tablespoons of the goat cheese mixture on each tomato bottom. Sprinkle about 2 teaspoons of the pistachios over each, then drizzle lightly with olive oil and balsamic glaze. Place middle tomato slice on top of each and repeat with remaining ⅛ teaspoon salt, goat cheese, pistachios, oil and glaze. Place tops on tomatoes.

PER SERVING 351 **CAL**; 27 g **FAT** (13 g **SAT**); 15 g **PRO**; 14 g **CARB**; 4 g **FIBER**; 415 mg **SODIUM**; 46 mg **CHOL**

GRILLED PEPPERS,
SHRIMP AND CHORIZO

Grilled Peppers, Shrimp and Chorizo

MAKES 8 appetizer servings PREP 20 minutes
GRILL 28 minutes

2	tablespoons olive oil, plus more for coating peppers
1	tablespoon white wine vinegar
½	teaspoon smoked paprika
¼	teaspoon garlic powder
¼	teaspoon plus ⅛ teaspoon salt
½	pound large peeled and deveined shrimp
4	sweet peppers (combination of red, orange and yellow)
2	fully cooked chorizo sausages (3 ounces each), split lengthwise
	Fresh parsley, chopped (optional)

• Heat grill or grill pan to medium-high heat. In a bowl, whisk together oil, vinegar, paprika, garlic powder and salt. Toss 2 teaspoons of the vinaigrette with shrimp. Thread shrimp onto 2 skewers. Set aside remaining vinaigrette.

• Lightly coat peppers with oil. Grill on medium-high heat for 20 minutes, turning every 5 minutes. Transfer to a bowl and cover with plastic wrap to cool slightly. Peel and discard skins (it's okay to leave a little on). Quarter peeled peppers, discarding stems and cores. Toss with remaining vinaigrette.

• Grill the 4 chorizo halves 3 to 4 minutes per side. Slice into half-moons. Grill shrimp skewers 2 minutes per side, until cooked through.

• Arrange pepper quarters on a large platter. Scatter chorizo and shrimp on top, and drizzle with any residual vinaigrette. Garnish with chopped parsley, if desired.

PER SERVING 139 CAL; 9 g FAT (2 g SAT); 9 g PRO; 6 g CARB; 2 g FIBER; 295 mg SODIUM; 56 mg CHOL

CUCUMBER-LIME AGUA FRESCA

Cucumber-Lime Agua Fresca

MAKES 8 servings PREP 10 minutes

1	pound cucumbers, cut into large chunks, plus slices for garnish
⅓	cup fresh lime juice, plus wedges for garnish
3	tablespoons sugar
⅛	teaspoon salt

• In a blender, combine cucumbers, lime juice, sugar, salt and 4 cups cold water. Blend until smooth. Pour mixture into a mesh strainer placed over a pitcher, pressing pulp to release as much liquid as possible. Discard pulp. Add enough ice to fill pitcher. Garnish agua fresca and glasses with cucumber slices and lime wedges.

PER SERVING 16 CAL; 0 g FAT (0 g SAT); 0 g PRO; 5 g CARB; 0 g FIBER; 37 mg SODIUM; 0 mg CHOL

BEANS AND GREENS WITH SHERRY-SHALLOT VINAIGRETTE

Moroccan Eggplant

MAKES 6 servings
PREP 15 minutes **GRILL** 10 minutes

¼	cup olive oil
¼	cup lemon juice
2	tablespoons honey
1	teaspoon ground cumin
½	teaspoon cinnamon
½	teaspoon turmeric
½	teaspoon salt
¼	teaspoon ground cayenne
½	cup chopped cilantro, plus more for garnish
2	cloves garlic, minced
1	large eggplant or 2 medium eggplants (about 1½ pounds total)
2	peaches or 3 apricots
8	ounces halloumi or bread cheese
3	tablespoons roughly chopped almonds

• Heat grill or grill pan to medium-high heat. In a small bowl, whisk together olive oil, lemon juice, honey, cumin, cinnamon, turmeric, salt and cayenne until well combined. Stir in cilantro and garlic. Set aside.

• Trim eggplant and slice lengthwise into ½-inch-thick planks. Halve and pit peaches; slice each half into 3 wedges. Slice cheese into four ½-inch-thick planks. Brush eggplant, fruit and cheese generously with dressing.

• Grill eggplant and fruit on medium-high for 2 to 3 minutes per side, until eggplant is cooked and fruit has grill marks. Grill cheese 2 minutes per side.

• Arrange eggplant, fruit and cheese on a platter. Garnish with almonds and cilantro. Cube cheese before serving.

PER SERVING 295 **CAL**; 22 g **FAT** (8 g **SAT**); 11 g **PRO**; 18 g **CARB**; 5 g **FIBER**; 598 mg **SODIUM**; 27 mg **CHOL**

Beans and Greens with Sherry-Shallot Vinaigrette

MAKES 6 servings **PREP** 10 minutes **COOK** 4 minutes

½	pound fresh green beans
½	pound fresh wax beans
2	tablespoons olive oil
2	tablespoons sherry vinegar
1	teaspoon Dijon mustard
½	teaspoon salt
¼	teaspoon pepper
¼	cup finely diced shallots
10	cups roughly chopped escarole

• Bring a pot of salted water to a boil. Add beans; return to a boil and cook 3 to 4 minutes, until crisp-tender. Drain beans and run under cold water until cool. Set aside.

• In a large bowl, whisk together oil, vinegar, mustard, salt and pepper. Stir in shallots. Toss dressing with beans and escarole.

PER SERVING 87 **CAL**; 5 g **FAT** (1 g **SAT**); 3 g **PRO**; 10 g **CARB**; 5 g **FIBER**; 137 mg **SODIUM**; 0 mg **CHOL**

MOROCCAN
EGGPLANT

MIDDLE EASTERN
CHOPPED SALAD
(FATTOUSH)

Middle Eastern Chopped Salad (Fattoush)

MAKES 6 servings **PREP** 20 minutes
GRILL 4 minutes

2	large pitas, brushed with olive oil
¼	cup olive oil
2	tablespoons lemon juice
2	teaspoons lemon zest
2	tablespoons white wine vinegar
1	clove garlic, minced
¾	teaspoon salt
¼	teaspoon pepper
6	cups chopped romaine
3	cups cherry tomatoes, halved
1	large English cucumber, halved and sliced into half-moons
1	cup sliced scallions
1	cup fresh parsley, chopped
¾	cup fresh mint, chopped

• Heat grill or grill pan to medium-high heat. Grill pitas on medium-high heat for 1 to 2 minutes per side, until lightly charred. Set aside to cool.

• In a large bowl, whisk together olive oil, lemon juice, zest, vinegar, garlic, ¼ teaspoon of the salt and the pepper. Toss dressing with romaine, tomatoes, cucumber, scallions, parsley, mint and remaining ½ teaspoon salt. Tear cooled pitas into bite-size pieces and toss with rest of salad.

PER SERVING 178 **CAL**; 10 g **FAT** (1 g **SAT**); 4 g **PRO**; 21 g **CARB**; 4 g **FIBER**; 415 mg **SODIUM**; 0 mg **CHOL**

SNAP PEAS AND RADISHES

Snap Peas and Radishes

MAKES 4 servings **PREP** 10 minutes **COOK** 2 minutes

1	pound snap peas
2	tablespoons olive oil
2	tablespoons tarragon vinegar
1	to 2 tablespoons chopped fresh tarragon
½	teaspoon salt
6	medium radishes, washed, trimmed and thinly sliced
	Freshly cracked pepper

• Bring a pot of lightly salted water to a boil. Add snap peas; cook 1 to 2 minutes, until crisp-tender. Drain snap peas; run under cold water until cool.

• In a large bowl, whisk together oil, vinegar, tarragon and salt until well combined. Toss snap peas and radishes in dressing. Season with freshly cracked pepper. Serve at room temperature or chilled.

PER SERVING 107 **CAL**; 7 g **FAT** (1 g **SAT**); 4 g **PRO**; 8 g **CARB**; 3 g **FIBER**; 298 mg **SODIUM**; 0 mg **CHOL**

SMOKY BLTS

Smoky BLTs

MAKES 4 servings PREP 10 minutes BAKE at 400° for 20 minutes GRILL 8 minutes

8	slices double-smoked bacon
1	large tomato, sliced into four ½-inch-thick slices
4	leaves romaine lettuce
1	avocado, halved and pitted (optional)
8	slices country white bread
¼	cup chipotle mayonnaise

• Heat oven to 400°. Place bacon strips on a rimmed baking sheet fitted with a wire rack. Bake bacon at 400° for 20 minutes, until crisp.

• Heat grill or grill pan to medium-high heat. Coat grill lightly with nonstick cooking spray. Grill tomato slices 1 to 2 minutes per side, until grill marks appear. Grill romaine leaves 1 minute per side. (If using avocado, grill 2 minutes on cut side, then peel and slice.) Grill bread 30 seconds to 1 minute per side.

• Spread 1 tablespoon chipotle mayonnaise on 4 of the bread slices. Place 2 bacon slices on top of each, along with a slice of grilled tomato, half a romaine leaf and, if desired, an avocado slice. Top with remaining 4 bread slices.

PER SERVING 408 CAL; 20 g FAT (6 g SAT); 12 g PRO; 44 g CARB; 5 g FIBER; 793 mg SODIUM; 23 mg CHOL

Zucchini-Carrot Ribbons with Farfalle

MAKES 6 servings PREP 20 minutes COOK 9 minutes

2	cups packed basil leaves
½	cup walnuts, toasted
1	clove garlic
1	tablespoon lemon juice
½	cup olive oil
½	cup grated Pecorino Romano cheese
½	teaspoon salt
¼	teaspoon pepper
2	medium carrots, peeled
2	medium zucchini, ends trimmed
1	box (12 ounces) veggie farfalle

• In a food processor, combine basil, ¼ cup of the walnuts, the garlic and lemon juice. While processing, slowly stream in olive oil until smooth. Transfer mixture to a bowl and stir in Pecorino Romano, salt and pepper. Set aside.

• Using a vegetable peeler, create long strips of carrots and zucchini. Chop remaining ¼ cup walnuts. Set aside.

• Bring a pot of salted water to a boil. Add farfalle and cook 9 minutes. Drain and rinse under cold water until cool. Stir in pesto, carrot and zucchini strips, and remaining walnuts.

PER SERVING 478 CAL; 28 g FAT (5 g SAT); 15 g PRO; 48 g CARB; 4 g FIBER; 401 mg SODIUM; 10 mg CHOL

Caribbean-Style Grilled Corn

MAKES 4 servings PREP 10 minutes GRILL 20 minutes

4	ears corn with husks
½	cup light or regular mayonnaise
1	tablespoon jerk seasoning
1	cup sweetened coconut flakes
4	lime wedges

• Heat grill or grill pan to medium-high heat. Carefully pull back corn husks, leaving them attached at the base. Remove silk and discard. Re-cover corn with husks. Grill corn on medium-high heat for 20 minutes, rotating every 5 minutes. (Husks will char.)

• In a small bowl, combine mayonnaise and jerk seasoning. Pull back husks and liberally spread mayonnaise mixture on grilled corn, about 2 tablespoons per ear.

• Scatter coconut on a large plate. Roll mayonnaise-coated corn in coconut. Serve warm with lime wedges.

PER SERVING 275 CAL; 18 g FAT (6 g SAT); 5 g PRO; 30 g CARB; 4 g FIBER; 502 mg SODIUM; 11 mg CHOL

ZUCCHINI-CARROT RIBBONS
WITH FARFALLE

SUMMER-FRESH SIDES

Pair simple grilled meats, poultry or fish with these inspiring sides.

MEDITERRANEAN PASTA

TRICOLOR
COLESLAW

BACON
POTATO
SALAD

Mediterranean Pasta

MAKES 8 servings **PREP** 10 minutes
COOK 6 minutes

12	ounces dumpling egg noodles or mafalda (such as Creamette), or your favorite shape pasta
8	ounces snow peas, halved
1	pint cherry tomatoes, halved
1	sweet orange pepper, cored, seeded and cut into 1 x ¼-inch strips
1	cup crumbled feta cheese
½	medium red onion, thinly sliced
½	cup fresh basil leaves, thinly sliced

VINAIGRETTE

¼	cup distilled white vinegar
2	teaspoons Dijon mustard
1	teaspoon sugar
¾	teaspoon salt
¼	teaspoon black pepper
⅓	cup extra-virgin olive oil

• Bring a large pot of lightly salted water to a boil. Add noodles and cook 6 minutes (or to al dente, if using different shape). Add snow peas during last minute. Drain and rinse well in cold water. Drain again.

• Meanwhile, place tomatoes, pepper strips, feta and onion in a large bowl.

• **Vinaigrette.** Whisk together vinegar, mustard, sugar, salt and pepper. Add oil in a thin stream until blended. Add pasta with snow peas and vinaigrette to bowl and toss to combine. Scatter sliced basil over salad and gently stir. Refrigerate until serving.

PER SERVING 326 **CAL**; 14 g **FAT** (4 g **SAT**); 10 g **PRO**; 39 g **CARB**; 4 g **FIBER**; 465 mg **SODIUM**; 17 mg **CHOL**

Bacon Potato Salad

MAKES 6 servings **PREP** 15 minutes
COOK 12 minutes

2¼	pounds small red potatoes, larger ones halved
1½	teaspoons salt
6	slices bacon
2	ribs celery, diced
3	scallions, trimmed and sliced
¼	cup light mayonnaise
¼	cup low-fat buttermilk
2	teaspoons country Dijon mustard
½	teaspoon sugar
¼	teaspoon black pepper

• Place potatoes in a large pot. Add enough cold water to cover by 1 inch. Bring to a boil; add 1 teaspoon of the salt. Cook 10 to 12 minutes, until just tender. Drain; rinse with cool water. Cut into 1-inch pieces.

• Meanwhile, cook bacon in a skillet over medium heat until crisp, about 8 minutes, turning. Remove to a paper towel.

• Transfer potatoes to a serving bowl; add celery and scallions. In a small bowl, whisk together mayonnaise, buttermilk, 2 tablespoons water, the mustard, sugar, remaining ½ teaspoon salt and the pepper. Crumble bacon over potatoes; toss with dressing. Refrigerate until serving.

PER SERVING 197 **CAL**; 6 g **FAT** (1 g **SAT**); 6 g **PRO**; 30 g **CARB**; 3 g **FIBER**; 686 mg **SODIUM**; 11 mg **CHOL**

Tricolor Coleslaw

MAKES 8 servings **PREP** 15 minutes
REFRIGERATE 30 minutes

½	cup light mayonnaise
¼	cup sour cream
3	tablespoons to ¼ cup milk
2	tablespoons lemon juice
1	tablespoon sugar
1	tablespoon chopped fresh dill
¾	teaspoon salt
¼	teaspoon black pepper
1	package (16 ounces) old-fashioned coleslaw mix (with extra carrots)
1	cup shredded red cabbage
3	scallions, chopped

• Whisk together mayonnaise, sour cream, milk, lemon juice, sugar, dill, salt and pepper in a large glass or plastic bowl.

• Stir in coleslaw mix, red cabbage and scallions until all vegetables are coated with dressing. Refrigerate at least 30 minutes before serving.

PER SERVING 96 **CAL**; 6 g **FAT** (2 g **SAT**); 1 g **PRO**; 8 g **CARB**; 2 g **FIBER**; 362 mg **SODIUM**; 11 mg **CHOL**

GREAT OUTDOORS

Break out the lounge chairs, big cushy pillows and pretty lanterns!

Peach Bellini

MAKES 12 servings **PREP** 10 minutes

- 3   **ripe peaches (or 1 pound frozen peaches, thawed), peeled, pitted and cut into wedges**
- 1   **tablespoon sugar**
- 2   **bottles chilled Prosecco**
      Thin peach slices for garnish

• Blend peaches and sugar in a blender.

• For each Bellini, spoon 2 tablespoons of the peach puree into the bottom of a champagne flute. Carefully pour in 4 ounces Prosecco. Stir gently. Garnish with a thin peach slice. Serve immediately.

PER SERVING 117 **CAL**; 0 g **FAT** (0 g **SAT**); 0 g **PRO**; 7 g **CARB**; 0 g **FIBER**; 0 mg **SODIUM**; 0 mg **CHOL**

Warm Fingerling Potato Salad

MAKES 8 servings   **PREP** 15 minutes
COOK 20 minutes

3	pounds fingerling potatoes, cut into 1-inch pieces
6	tablespoons extra-virgin olive oil
2	large leeks, cleaned, dark green parts removed, sliced
2	shallots, chopped
2	cloves garlic, chopped
3	tablespoons red wine vinegar
2	tablespoons coarse Dijon mustard
¾	teaspoon salt
¼	teaspoon black pepper
½	cup parsley, chopped

• Place potatoes in a large saucepan and cover with cold water. Lightly salt and bring to a boil. Reduce heat to medium; cook 15 to 20 minutes, until fork-tender. Drain and place in a serving bowl.

• Meanwhile, heat 2 tablespoons of the olive oil in a large skillet over medium heat. Add leeks, shallots and garlic; cook 10 minutes, until leeks are tender. Stir occasionally.

• Toss potatoes with leek mixture. Whisk together remaining 4 tablespoons olive oil, the vinegar, mustard, salt and pepper. Fold into potatoes; gently stir in parsley. Serve warm or at room temperature.

PER SERVING 245 **CAL**; 11 g **FAT** (1 g **SAT**); 4 g **PRO**; 35 g **CARB**; 3 g **FIBER**; 316 mg **SODIUM**; 0 mg **CHOL**

WARM FINGERLING POTATO SALAD

SALMON SLIDERS WITH CHIPOTLE MAYONNAISE

Salmon Sliders with Chipotle Mayonnaise

MAKES 16 sliders   **PREP** 15 minutes   **COOK** 6 minutes

½	cup plus 2 tablespoons reduced-fat mayonnaise
1	tablespoon adobo sauce, from canned chipotle in adobo
1½	pounds salmon fillet, skin removed, cut into 1-inch pieces
1	sweet red pepper, cored, seeded and coarsely chopped
2	scallions, trimmed and coarsely chopped
½	cup panko bread crumbs
2	tablespoons lemon juice
¼	teaspoon salt
¼	teaspoon black pepper
16	party-size potato rolls (from a 15-ounce package of 24) Lettuce (optional)

• Combine ½ cup of the reduced-fat mayonnaise and the adobo. Cover and refrigerate until ready to serve.

• In work bowl of a food processor, add salmon, red pepper, scallions, panko, remaining 2 tablespoons mayonnaise, the lemon juice, salt and black pepper. Pulse until just combined. Form into 16 patties, about a scant ¼ cup each. Place on a greased baking sheet.

• Heat a large nonstick skillet over medium-high heat and lightly coat with nonstick cooking spray. Cook patties in batches for 2 to 3 minutes per side, until browned and cooked through.

• Place patties on rolls and spread about 1½ teaspoons chipotle mayonnaise over each. Add lettuce, if desired, and serve.

PER SLIDER 188 **CAL**; 8 g **FAT** (1 g **SAT**); 13 g **PRO**; 16 g **CARB**; 1 g **FIBER**; 280 mg **SODIUM**; 31 mg **CHOL**

Grilled Chicken with Peach Barbecue Sauce

MAKES 8 servings **PREP** 15 minutes **COOK** 30 minutes **GRILL** 30 minutes

1	**cup ketchup**
½	**cup peach preserves**
¼	**cup cider vinegar**
1	**small onion, chopped**
1	**large ripe peach, peeled, pitted and finely chopped**
1	**tablespoon Dijon mustard**
8	**bone-in chicken thighs (about 5 ounces each)**
8	**thin boneless, skinless chicken breasts (about 4 ounces each)**
1	**teaspoon salt**
¼	**teaspoon black pepper**
	Lemon and lime wedges

• In a medium heavy saucepan, combine ketchup, preserves, vinegar, onion, peach and mustard. Simmer on low 30 minutes, stirring occasionally.

• Set up a gas grill or charcoal grill on medium-high heat for indirect grilling. Lightly grease grill rack. Season chicken with salt and pepper. Grill thighs on direct heat, skin side down, 5 minutes. Turn and place over indirect heat; close grill and grill 10 minutes skin side up. Baste every 5 minutes with barbecue sauce and continue to grill, covered, over indirect heat for 15 minutes or until internal temperature reaches 160°.

• Baste chicken breasts with sauce. Grill over direct heat 5 to 7 minutes per side or until internal temperature reaches 160°.

• Meanwhile, place any remaining sauce in a small saucepan and simmer 2 minutes. Serve chicken with remaining barbecue sauce and lemon and lime wedges for squeezing over the top.

PER SERVING 392 **CAL**; 10 g **FAT** (3 g **SAT**); 51 g **PRO**; 24 g **CARB**; 1 g **FIBER**; 826 mg **SODIUM**; 201 mg **CHOL**

GRILLED SUMMER VEGETABLES AND ROMESCO SAUCE

GRILLED CHICKEN WITH PEACH BARBECUE SAUCE

Grilled Summer Vegetables and Romesco Sauce

MAKES 8 servings PREP 30 minutes
GRILL 10 minutes

SAUCE

1	jar (12 ounces) roasted red peppers, drained
¼	cup slivered almonds
3	tablespoons olive oil
2	tablespoons red wine vinegar
2	cloves garlic, chopped
¼	teaspoon salt
¼	teaspoon black pepper

VEGETABLES

2	large zucchini, cut lengthwise into ¼-inch planks
2	large summer squash, cut lengthwise into ¼-inch planks
4	sweet peppers (combination of red and orange) cored, seeded and quartered
1	pound asparagus, woody ends removed
¼	cup olive oil
½	teaspoon salt
½	teaspoon black pepper

• **Sauce.** Place roasted red peppers, almonds, olive oil, vinegar, garlic, salt and pepper in a blender. Blend until smooth. Cover and refrigerate until serving.

• **Vegetables.** Heat a gas grill to medium-high or a charcoal grill to medium-hot. Lightly grease grill rack.

• In a large bowl, toss vegetables with olive oil and season with salt and pepper. Grill vegetables about 4 to 5 minutes per side, turning as needed to avoid burning.

• Serve warm or at room temperature with romesco sauce on the side.

PER SERVING 197 CAL; 15 g FAT (2 g SAT); 4 g PRO; 13 g CARB; 5 g FIBER; 381 mg SODIUM; 0 mg CHOL

STRAWBERRY CORNMEAL SHORTCAKE

Strawberry Cornmeal Shortcake

MAKES 8 servings PREP 25 minutes BAKE at 400° for 15 minutes

BISCUITS

2	cups all-purpose flour
1	cup cornmeal
1½	teaspoons baking soda
¾	teaspoon cream of tartar
½	teaspoon salt
2	cups sour cream
1	egg
¼	cup sugar

TOPPING

8	ounces mascarpone cheese
1	tablespoon sugar
3	tablespoons milk

FILLING

16	ounces strawberries, sliced
1	to 2 tablespoons sugar

• **Biscuits.** Heat oven to 400°. Lightly coat a large baking sheet with nonstick cooking spray.

• In a large bowl, whisk together flour, cornmeal, baking soda, cream of tartar and salt. In a small bowl, combine sour cream, egg and sugar. Make a well in dry ingredients and add sour cream mixture. Blend until dry ingredients are moistened. Knead 6 times in bowl.

• Drop ½-cup mounds of batter onto prepared baking sheet. Bake at 400° for 14 to 15 minutes, or until a wooden pick inserted in center comes out clean. Remove biscuits to a wire rack to cool completely.

• **Topping.** Combine mascarpone cheese, sugar and milk. Stir until smooth.

• **Filling.** Combine strawberries and sugar.

• To serve, split biscuits and fill with sliced strawberries. Top with mascarpone mixture.

PER SERVING 494 CAL; 25 g FAT (15 g SAT); 10 g PRO; 56 g CARB; 4 g FIBER; 430 mg SODIUM; 103 mg CHOL

HEIRLOOM TOMATO
CAPRESE SALAD,
PAGE 207

AUGUST

211   216   225

20-MINUTE MEALS

It's about time!

SHANGHAI SHRIMP
STIR-FRY, PAGE 211

GRILLED PORK WITH
PASTA SALAD,
PAGE 208

HEIRLOOM TOMATO
CAPRESE SALAD

MANGO-RASPBERRY GRILLED CHICKEN SALAD

Heirloom Tomato Caprese Salad

MAKES 6 servings **PREP** 5 minutes
GRILL 15 minutes

5	assorted heirloom tomatoes, such as Green Zebra, beefsteak, Brandywine, yellow or orange, Cherokee Purple and Black Russian
6	chicken or turkey sausage links
2	cups mixed baby greens
1	package (6 ounces) fresh mozzarella cheese
	Fresh basil leaves
2	tablespoons white balsamic vinegar
1	tablespoon extra-virgin olive oil
¼	teaspoon sea salt
	Freshly cracked black pepper
	Crusty Italian bread (optional)

• Heat grill or grill pan to medium-high. Rinse tomatoes and gently pat dry. Cut each tomato into ¼-inch-thick slices, starting from bottom of tomato.

• Meanwhile, grill sausages for 12 to 15 minutes, turning frequently, until cooked through.

• Place greens on a large platter. Cut mozzarella into thin slices. Decoratively fan tomato slices, mozzarella and basil over greens, alternating varieties of tomatoes for contrast.

• Drizzle salad with vinegar and olive oil, and sprinkle with salt and pepper. Serve alongside grilled sausages and, if desired, Italian bread.

PER SERVING 264 **CAL**; 17 g **FAT** (7 g **SAT**); 20 g **PRO**; 9 g **CARB**; 2 g **FIBER**; 668 mg **SODIUM**; 85 mg **CHOL**

Mango-Raspberry Grilled Chicken Salad

MAKES 5 servings **PREP** 8 minutes **GRILL** 12 minutes

DRESSING

2	tablespoons raspberry balsamic vinegar
1	tablespoon lemon juice
1	tablespoon chopped chives
1	teaspoon grainy mustard
¾	teaspoon sugar
½	teaspoon salt
⅛	teaspoon black pepper
⅓	cup extra-virgin olive oil

SALAD

1	pound boneless chicken breasts
1	package (5 ounces) baby spinach
2	cups sliced mango (or 1 whole, pitted, peeled and sliced)
1	cup raspberries
½	small red onion, sliced
¼	cup crumbled goat cheese

• Heat grill or grill pan to medium-high.

• **Dressing.** In bowl, whisk together vinegar, lemon juice, chives, mustard, sugar, salt and pepper. While whisking, add oil in a thin stream.

• **Salad.** Combine chicken and ¼ cup of the dressing in a glass dish or resealable plastic bag.

• Remove chicken from marinade and grill, turning once, for 12 minutes or until internal temperature registers 160° on an instant-read thermometer. Cool slightly.

• Meanwhile, combine spinach, mango, raspberries and onion in a large bowl. Toss with remaining dressing.

• Slice chicken into bite-size pieces and either toss with salad or fan over top of greens. Sprinkle salad with goat cheese and serve.

PER SERVING 337 **CAL**; 18 g **FAT** (4 g **SAT**); 25 g **PRO**; 20 g **CARB**; 4 g **FIBER**; 406 mg **SODIUM**; 58 mg **CHOL**

GRILLED PORK WITH
PASTA SALAD

Grilled Pork with Pasta Salad

MAKES 6 servings **PREP AND LET REST** 12 minutes **COOK AND GRILL** 8 minutes

2	**pork tenderloins (about 2 pounds total)**
½	**cup light Caesar salad dressing**
½	**box (8 ounces; about 2¾ cups) radiatore (or your favorite short-shape pasta)**
1	**can (15.5 ounces) reduced-sodium chickpeas, drained and rinsed**
1	**can (14 ounces) artichoke hearts, drained and quartered**
1	**pint cherry tomatoes, cut in half**
1	**cucumber, cut into half-moons**
¼	**cup pitted olives (optional)**
¼	**cup light mayonnaise**

• Heat grill to medium-high. Bring a large pot of lightly salted water to boiling. Split tenderloins lengthwise almost all the way through and flatten like a book.

• Place in a glass dish and add ¼ cup of the Caesar dressing, turning to coat.

• Cook pasta in boiling water for 7 minutes or per package directions. Drain and rinse. Meanwhile, grill pork, covered, for 4 minutes per side, turning once. Transfer to a cutting board and let rest 5 minutes.

• Combine pasta, chickpeas, artichoke hearts, tomatoes, cucumber and, if desired, olives. Blend remaining ¼ cup dressing and the mayonnaise. Toss with pasta mixture. Slice pork; serve with pasta salad.

PER SERVING 469 **CAL**; 11 g **FAT** (3 g **SAT**); 44 g **PRO**; 54 g **CARB**; 9 g **FIBER**; 773 mg **SODIUM**; 105 mg **CHOL**

South Pacific Grilled Steak

MAKES 4 servings **PREP AND COOK** 6 minutes **GRILL AND LET REST** 11 minutes

1	**cored fresh pineapple (20 ounces) from produce department (reserve any juice in container)**
¼	**cup pineapple or orange juice**
4	**pieces beef filet (5 to 6 ounces each)**
1	**teaspoon salt**
1	**each green, red and orange or yellow sweet pepper, sliced alongside core into 4 flat pieces**
2	**tablespoons packed dark brown sugar**
1	**tablespoon olive oil**
1	**tablespoon chopped fresh ginger**
2	**teaspoons cornstarch**
½	**teaspoon crushed red pepper**
¼	**teaspoon ground black pepper**

• Heat grill to medium-high. Slice pineapple into 8 rings; pour juice from container into a measuring cup. Add enough pineapple juice to equal ⅓ cup. Set aside.

• Season beef on all sides with ½ teaspoon of the salt. Coat pineapple and sweet pepper pieces with nonstick cooking spray and season with ¼ teaspoon of the salt.

• In a small saucepan, whisk together pineapple juice, ¼ cup water, the brown sugar, olive oil, ginger, cornstarch, crushed red pepper, remaining ¼ teaspoon salt and the black pepper. Bring to a boil over high heat; simmer 1 minute.

• Add filets and pineapple slices to grill, then cover. Grill 3 minutes; uncover, turn over and grill another 3 minutes or until desired doneness. Let beef and pineapple rest 5 minutes. Meanwhile, grill peppers, covered, 5 minutes. Uncover, flip over and grill an additional 3 minutes.

• Divide pineapple rings among 4 plates. Top each with 3 pepper pieces (one of each color) and a filet. Drizzle pineapple glaze over beef and serve.

PER SERVING 499 **CAL**; 17 g **FAT** (6 g **SAT**); 51 g **PRO**; 36 g **CARB**; 4 g **FIBER**; 690 mg **SODIUM**; 134 mg **CHOL**

SOUTH PACIFIC
GRILLED STEAK

GRILLED
FISH TACOS

Grilled Fish Tacos

MAKES 5 servings **PREP** 10 minutes
GRILL 10 minutes

- ½ cup light mayonnaise
- 3 tablespoons Hidden Valley spicy chipotle pepper sandwich spread
- ⅓ cup lime juice (from 2 medium limes)
- 2 tablespoons olive oil
- 2 teaspoons honey
- ¾ teaspoon salt
- 1 bag (8 ounces) shredded red cabbage
- 1¼ pounds mahi mahi fillets (thawed if frozen)
- ¼ fresh jicama (see Note)
- 1 package (5 ounces) fresh arugula
- 10 corn tortillas (warmed)

• Heat grill or grill pan to medium-high. In a small bowl, whisk together mayo and 2 tablespoons of the chipotle spread. In a second bowl, whisk lime juice, oil, honey and ¼ teaspoon of the salt.

• Toss cabbage with 3 tablespoons of the lime dressing and ⅛ teaspoon of the salt and set aside.

• Whisk 3 tablespoons of the mayo-chipotle mixture into lime dressing. Pour ¼ cup of the lime mixture into a resealable plastic bag with remaining 1 tablespoon chipotle spread and the fish.

• Brush grill or grill pan with oil. Add fish to grill and cook 4 to 5 minutes. Flip over and grill an additional 4 to 5 minutes, or until cooked through.

• Meanwhile, using a vegetable peeler, peel jicama and shave into ribbons. Toss with arugula, remaining lime mixture and ⅛ teaspoon of the salt.

• Break fish apart with a fork and sprinkle with remaining ¼ teaspoon salt. Spread remaining mayo-chipotle mixture onto tortillas. Top with grilled fish and cabbage. Serve with arugula-jicama salad.

PER SERVING 407 **CAL**; 17 g **FAT** (2 g **SAT**); 25 g **PRO**; 40 g **CARB**; 7 g **FIBER**; 709 mg **SODIUM**; 91 mg **CHOL**

Note: For a healthy snack, cut remaining jicama into matchsticks, then drizzle with lime and paprika.

SHANGHAI SHRIMP STIR-FRY

Shanghai Shrimp Stir-Fry

MAKES 6 servings **PREP** 5 minutes **COOK** 15 minutes

- 1 package (7 ounces) rice stick noodles
- 3 tablespoons canola oil
- 3 tablespoons low-sodium soy sauce
- 3 tablespoons rice vinegar
- ¼ teaspoon plus ⅛ teaspoon salt
- ¾ pound mini sweet peppers, tops trimmed, quartered
- 8 ounces sugar snap peas
- 1 medium onion, thinly sliced
- 1½ pounds raw cleaned shrimp (thawed if frozen)
- ½ cup sweet chili sauce
- 2 tablespoons fresh lemon juice
- 1 to 2 teaspoons Asian chili-garlic sauce

• Bring a large pot of lightly salted water to boiling. Add rice noodles and cook 3 minutes. Drain.

• Heat 1 tablespoon of the oil in a wok or very large skillet over medium-high heat. Add noodles, 1 tablespoon each of the soy sauce and rice vinegar and ¼ teaspoon of the salt. Stir-fry 2 minutes. Transfer to a platter.

• Return wok or skillet to medium-high heat and add remaining 2 tablespoons oil. Add peppers, snap peas and onion. Stir-fry 4 minutes. Add shrimp and cook 5 minutes, stirring, until opaque. Season with remaining ⅛ teaspoon salt.

• Meanwhile, whisk together sweet chili sauce, remaining 2 tablespoons each soy sauce and rice vinegar, the lemon juice and chili-garlic sauce. Stir into wok and cook 1 minute. Pour over noodles on platter and serve.

PER SERVING 397 **CAL**; 8 g **FAT** (1 g **SAT**); 23 g **PRO**; 53 g **CARB**; 5 g **FIBER**; 790 mg **SODIUM**; 168 mg **CHOL**

LEAVE ROOM FOR DESSERT

Here are 10 sweet ways to end the evening.

BANANA SPLIT
CAKE, PAGE 223

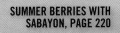

SUMMER BERRIES WITH SABAYON, PAGE 220

FROZEN MOCHA PIE

Frozen Mocha Pie

MAKES 10 servings **PREP** 20 minutes
BAKE at 350° for 15 minutes
MICROWAVE 1 minute
FREEZE 2 hours, then overnight
LET STAND 10 minutes

CRUST

1	package (9 ounces) Nabisco Famous chocolate wafers, finely crushed
1	tablespoon sugar
1	stick (½ cup) unsalted butter, melted

FILLING

1	cup milk chocolate chips
¾	cup light sour cream
2	tablespoons coffee liqueur
2	tablespoons sugar
½	teaspoon vanilla extract
1	tub (8 ounces) reduced-fat whipped topping, thawed
¼	cup unsweetened cocoa powder
¼	cup dark chocolate mini chunks

• **Crust.** Heat oven to 350°. In a large bowl, combine wafer crumbs and sugar; mix in butter until crumbs are moistened. Press crumbs into a 9-inch pie plate. Bake at 350° for 15 minutes; cool.

• **Filling.** Place chocolate chips in a small bowl; microwave on high 1 minute. Stir until smooth. In a medium bowl, combine sour cream, liqueur, sugar and vanilla. Stir in melted chocolate; spread evenly over cookie crust. Freeze 2 hours.

• In a medium bowl, whisk together whipped topping and cocoa powder; fold in mini chunks. Swirl mixture over pie and freeze overnight.

• Let stand 10 minutes before serving.

PER SERVING 415 **CAL**; 24 g **FAT** (14 g **SAT**); 5 g **PRO**; 47 g **CARB**; 2 g **FIBER**; 210 mg **SODIUM**; 41 mg **CHOL**

GRILLED PEACHES WITH RICOTTA, HONEY AND PISTACHIOS

Grilled Peaches with Ricotta, Honey and Pistachios

MAKES 6 servings **PREP** 10 minutes **GRILL** 8 minutes

3	peaches, halved and pitted
1	cup ricotta cheese
¼	cup honey
¼	cup roughly chopped pistachios
6	mint leaves

• Heat grill or grill pan to medium-high. Grill peaches 4 minutes per side, until charred and slightly softened.

• Whip ricotta and 2 tablespoons of the honey with a hand mixer until well combined. Spoon evenly over peaches, then sprinkle with pistachios and drizzle with remaining 2 tablespoons honey. Garnish with mint leaves. Serve warm.

PER SERVING 164 **CAL**; 8 g **FAT** (4 g **SAT**); 6 g **PRO**; 19 g **CARB**; 1 g **FIBER**; 36 mg **SODIUM**; 21 mg **CHOL**

COCONUT CHIP
ICE CREAM

When the weather is warm, chill out with a cool (even cold!) dessert.

Mango-Raspberry Trifle

MAKES 12 servings **PREP** 20 minutes
COOK 6 minutes **COOL** 30 minutes
REFRIGERATE overnight

2	packages (2.75 ounces each) vanilla pudding and pie filling (not instant)
4	cups 2% milk
1	container (6 ounces) low-fat mango Greek yogurt
6	cups angel food cake cubes (from 10 ounce cake)
4	ripe mangoes, peeled and cut into ½-inch dice
2	containers (6 ounces each) raspberries
1	cup heavy cream
1	tablespoon sugar
½	teaspoon vanilla extract
⅓	cup toasted sliced almonds

• Cook pudding with milk according to package directions, 4 to 6 minutes. Cool 30 minutes in refrigerator; stir in yogurt.

• In a 14- to 16-cup footed glass trifle dish, layer 2 cups of the cake cubes, one-third of the pudding mixture, one-third of the mangoes and one-third of the raspberries. Repeat layering twice. Cover and refrigerate overnight.

• Whip cream, sugar and vanilla until medium-soft peaks form. Swirl over top of trifle. Top with almonds.

PER SERVING 325 **CAL**; 12 g **FAT** (6 g **SAT**); 7 g **PRO**; 50 g **CARB**; 4 g **FIBER**; 342 mg **SODIUM**; 35 mg **CHOL**

Coconut Chip Ice Cream

MAKES Twelve ½-cup servings **PREP** 15 minutes **COOK** 8 minutes **BAKE** at 350° for 8 minutes
FREEZE 1 hour

5	egg yolks
½	cup sugar
1	cup coconut milk
1	cup heavy cream
1	cup whole milk
⅛	teaspoon salt
1	cup shredded coconut
1	cup dark chocolate morsels

• Whisk together egg yolks and ¼ cup of the sugar in a large bowl; set aside. In a small pot, combine coconut milk, heavy cream, whole milk, remaining ¼ cup sugar and the salt; bring to a simmer. Remove from heat and slowly pour into yolk-sugar mixture while whisking. Return to pot and stir over medium-low heat until it coats the back of a wooden spoon or reaches 170° to 180°, about 4 to 8 minutes. Strain and cool.

• Heat oven to 350°. Scatter ½ cup of the coconut on a baking sheet. Bake at 350° for 5 minutes; stir and bake another 2 to 3 minutes, until lightly browned. Cool.

• Process cooled mixture in an ice cream maker according to manufacturer's directions. During the last 5 minutes, stir in toasted coconut, remaining ½ cup coconut and the chocolate morsels. Transfer to a lidded container and freeze at least 1 hour.

PER SERVING 255 **CAL**; 20 g **FAT** (13 g **SAT**); 3 g **PRO**; 20 g **CARB**; 2 g **FIBER**; 65 mg **SODIUM**; 115 mg **CHOL**

MANGO-RASPBERRY
TRIFLE

PICNIC-PERFECT BROWNIES

Picnic-Perfect Brownies

MAKES 16 brownies **PREP** 15 minutes
BAKE at 350° for 22 minutes
MICROWAVE 1 minute

BROWNIES

- ½ **cup all-purpose flour**
- ½ **cup unsweetened cocoa powder**
- ¼ **teaspoon salt**
- ¼ **teaspoon baking powder**
- ¾ **cup sugar**
- ¼ **cup vegetable oil**
- 2 **eggs**
- 1 **teaspoon vanilla extract**
- 1 **teaspoon coffee extract**
- ½ **cup coarsely chopped walnuts**
- ½ **cup butterscotch baking chips**

DRIZZLE

- ¼ **cup semisweet chocolate baking chips**
- 2 **teaspoons vegetable oil**
- ¼ **cup butterscotch baking chips**

• **Brownies.** Heat oven to 350°. Coat an 8 x 8-inch baking pan with nonstick cooking spray.

• In a medium bowl, whisk together flour, cocoa, salt and baking powder. Set aside. In a large bowl, combine sugar, oil, eggs and extracts. Stir in flour mixture until just moistened. Fold in walnuts and butterscotch chips. Spoon into prepared baking pan.

• Bake at 350° for 22 minutes or until a toothpick inserted in center comes out clean. Cool completely.

• **Drizzle.** Place chocolate chips and 1 teaspoon of the oil in a small bowl. Microwave on high 1 minute. Stir until melted. Place in a small resealable plastic bag and make a tiny snip in one corner. Pipe over cooled brownies. Repeat with butterscotch chips and remaining 1 teaspoon oil. Cut into 16 brownies.

PER SERVING 185 **CAL**; 11 g **FAT** (4 g **SAT**); 2 g **PRO**; 20 g **CARB**; 1 g **FIBER**; 64 mg **SODIUM**; 26 mg **CHOL**

MERINGUE-TOPPED LEMON-POPPY SEED CUPCAKES

Meringue-Topped Lemon-Poppy Seed Cupcakes

MAKES 15 cupcakes **PREP** 25 minutes **BAKE** at 350° for 21 minutes **BROIL** 45 seconds
REFRIGERATE 1 hour

CUPCAKES

- 1¾ **cups all-purpose flour**
- 1 **tablespoon poppy seeds**
- 1½ **teaspoons baking powder**
- ¼ **teaspoon salt**
- ½ **cup (1 stick) unsalted butter, softened**
- ¾ **cup sugar**
- 2 **eggs**
- ½ **teaspoon vanilla extract**
- ½ **teaspoon lemon extract**
- 2 **tablespoons lemon juice**
- 1 **teaspoon lemon zest**
- ⅔ **cup milk**
- ½ **cup jarred lemon curd**

MERINGUE

- 4 **pasteurized egg whites**
- ¼ **teaspoon cream of tartar**
- 6 **tablespoons sugar**

• **Cupcakes.** Heat oven to 350°. Line fifteen 2½-inch muffin cups with paper baking cups.

• In a large bowl, whisk together flour, poppy seeds, baking powder and salt. Set aside. In a second large bowl, beat butter and sugar on medium-high for 2 minutes, until light and fluffy.

Gradually add in eggs, one at a time, until just combined. Beat in extracts, lemon juice and zest. On low, beat in flour mixture, alternating with milk, until just combined.

• Evenly spoon batter into muffin cups, filling each about three-fourths full. Bake at 350° for 20 to 21 minutes or until a wooden pick inserted in the center comes out clean. Remove to a wire rack and cool completely.

• Fill cupcakes by placing lemon curd in a pastry bag fitted with a medium star piping tip. Press the end of the tip into each cupcake and gently press until top of cupcake starts to rise up a little.

• **Meringue.** Heat broiler. Place egg whites in a clean bowl and beat on medium-high until foamy. Beat in cream of tartar and gradually add in sugar. Beat until stiff peaks form. Frost each cupcake with meringue. Broil 6 inches from heat for about 45 seconds, until tops start to lightly brown.

• Refrigerate for 1 hour before serving.

PER SERVING 196 **CAL**; 8 g **FAT** (5 g **SAT**); 4 g **PRO**; 30 g **CARB**; 0 g **FIBER**; 118 mg **SODIUM**; 45 mg **CHOL**

SUMMER BERRIES WITH SABAYON

Sabayon is a light, foamy egg custard made with sweetened wine that pairs perfectly with fresh fruit.

Melon Bomb Pops

MAKES 12 servings **PREP** 30 minutes
FREEZE 2 hours, then overnight

½	**cup sugar**
2	**tablespoons lemon juice**
2½	**cups diced cantaloupe**
2½	**cups diced seedless watermelon**
2½	**cups honeydew melon**

• In a small saucepan, stir together sugar and ½ cup water. Bring to a simmer and stir until sugar is dissolved. Cool and stir in lemon juice.

• Place cantaloupe in a food processor; add one-third of the simple syrup. Process until smooth. Spoon 1½ tablespoons of the puree into 12 rocket pop molds and freeze for 1 hour or until top starts to set.

• Process watermelon with another third of the simple syrup. Spoon 1½ tablespoons of the puree into each rocket pop mold. Freeze for 1 hour. Repeat with honeydew melon and remaining third of the simple syrup. Insert handles into each mold and freeze overnight.

• To serve, run under warm water for a few seconds and slide each pop out of its mold.

PER SERVING 53 **CAL**; 0 g **FAT** (0 g **SAT**); 1 g **PRO**; 15 g **CARB**; 1 g **FIBER**; 13 mg **SODIUM**; 0 mg **CHOL**

Summer Berries with Sabayon

MAKES 6 servings **PREP** 15 minutes **COOK** 5 minutes

¾	**cup sweet Marsala or moscato wine**
⅓	**cup sugar**
6	**egg yolks**
6	**ounces blackberries**
6	**ounces blueberries**
6	**ounces raspberries**
1	**pint strawberries, hulled and diced**
5	**gingersnap cookies, crushed**

• Fill a small pot with 2 inches of water. Bring to a simmer. In a metal bowl large enough to fit over pot, whisk together wine and sugar. Add in egg yolks, whisking constantly over simmering water until mixture is frothy and thickens, about 5 minutes. (Temperature should reach 165°.) Be careful not to scramble yolks.

• In a large bowl, toss together blackberries, blueberries, raspberries and diced strawberries. Distribute among 6 glasses. Spoon sabayon over berries. Garnish with crushed cookies. Serve warm or chilled.

PER SERVING 211 **CAL**; 5 g **FAT** (2 g **SAT**); 4 g **PRO**; 32 g **CARB**; 5 g **FIBER**; 12 mg **SODIUM**; 205 mg **CHOL**

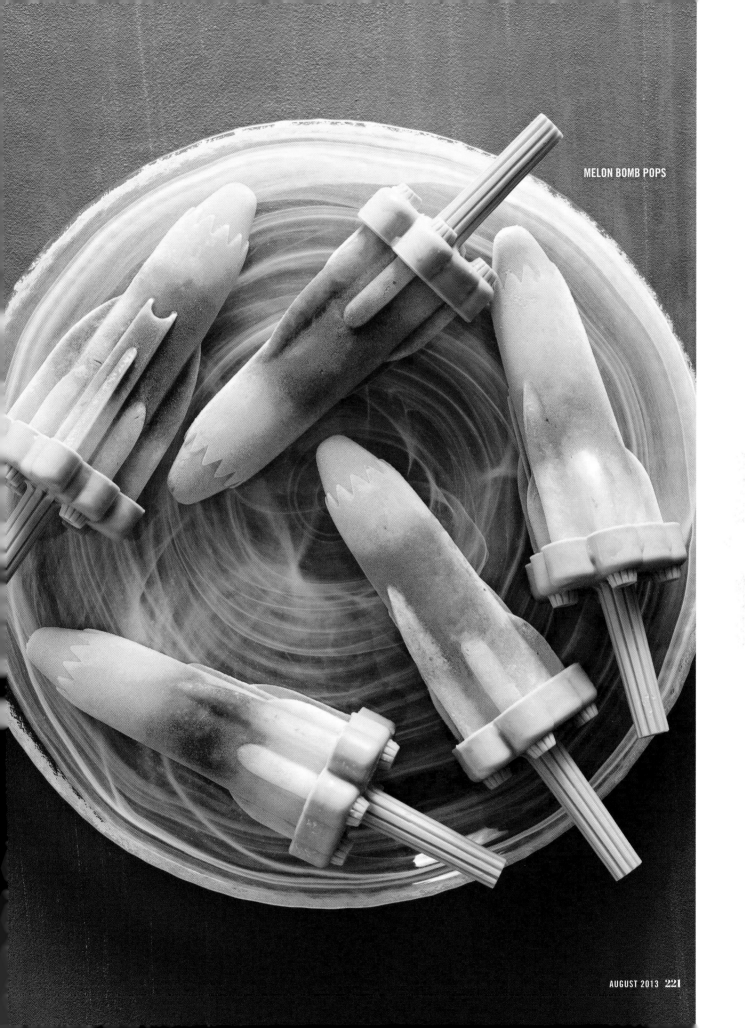

PLUM TART

BANANA SPLIT CAKE

Plum Tart

MAKES 8 servings **PREP** 20 minutes
BAKE at 400° for 40 minutes

- ⅓ **cup raw almonds**
- 1 **cup all-purpose flour**
- ½ **cup packed brown sugar**
- 6 **tablespoons unsalted butter, chilled and cut into cubes**
- 1 **egg yolk**
- ¼ **teaspoon salt**
- 2 **pounds red plums, pitted and thinly sliced**
- ½ **teaspoon lemon zest**
- 2 **tablespoons apricot preserves**

• Heat oven to 400°. Place almonds in a food processor; process until finely ground. Add flour, ¼ cup of the sugar, the butter, egg yolk and salt; pulse until butter forms coarse crumbs. (If it seems too dry, add 1 tablespoon cold water.) Press mixture into a 9-inch tart pan with a removable bottom.

• Toss plums with remaining ¼ cup brown sugar and the lemon zest. Arrange in the tart pan in 3 concentric circles, alternating the direction of the slices with each circle. Bake at 400° for 40 minutes on the middle rack, until crust is lightly browned and plums are tender.

• In a small bowl, combine apricot preserves with 1 tablespoon water; brush on plums. Cool completely on a wire rack.

PER SERVING 288 **CAL**; 12 g **FAT** (6 g **SAT**); 4 g **PRO**; 42 g **CARB**; 3 g **FIBER**; 81 mg **SODIUM**; 48 mg **CHOL**

Banana Split Cake

MAKES 18 servings **PREP** 20 minutes **BAKE** at 350° for 40 minutes **COOL** 15 minutes
LET STAND 10 minutes

- 3½ **cups all-purpose flour**
- 1½ **teaspoons baking soda**
- 1 **teaspoon salt**
- 1½ **cups sugar**
- 1¼ **cups (2½ sticks) unsalted butter, softened**
- 4 **eggs**
- 4 **medium very ripe bananas, mashed**
- 1 **teaspoon vanilla extract**
- ½ **cup buttermilk**
- 12 **ounces semisweet chocolate, finely chopped**
- 1¼ **cups heavy cream**
- ⅔ **cup strawberry preserves**
- ⅔ **cup pineapple preserves**
- ½ **cup chopped walnuts**
- 3 **maraschino cherries**

• Heat oven to 350°. Butter and flour two 8-inch cake pans; line bottom of pans with parchment paper.

• Whisk together flour, baking soda and salt. In another bowl, beat sugar and butter until fluffy, 2 to 3 minutes. Add eggs to butter mixture one at a time, beating after each. Stir in mashed bananas and vanilla. Beat in half of the flour mixture, followed by the buttermilk and then remaining flour mixture. Pour batter evenly into cake pans. Bake at 350° for 35 to 40 minutes, until a toothpick inserted in the middle of the cake comes out clean. Cool in pans for 15 minutes, then turn onto wire racks and cool.

• Place chopped chocolate in the bowl of a stand mixer. Bring cream to a low boil, then pour over chocolate; stir until smooth. Place bowl onto stand mixer fitted with whisk attachment. Beat on medium-high speed until fluffy, 5 to 7 minutes; let stand 10 minutes.

• Trim cakes to flatten tops. Carefully slice each cake in half horizontally, creating 4 layers. Place one layer on stand; spread on strawberry preserves. Top with another layer. Spread ⅔ cup of the ganache on top. Stack on another layer. Spread on pineapple preserves. Top with final layer. Ice cake with remaining ganache. Scatter walnuts over the top and place cherries in the center of the cake. (Cake may be easier to slice if refrigerated for 1 hour before serving.)

PER SERVING 516 **CAL**; 28 g **FAT** (16 g **SAT**); 6 g **PRO**; 65 g **CARB**; 3 g **FIBER**; 266 mg **SODIUM**; 103 mg **CHOL**

FARM TO FORK

Just-harvested fruits and veggies take center stage in these garden-fresh dishes.

HEIRLOOM TOMATO PIE

Heirloom Tomato Pie

MAKES 6 servings **PREP** 15 minutes
LET STAND 10 minutes **BAKE** at 375° for
45 minutes **COOL** 15 minutes

2½	**pounds heirloom tomatoes, sliced ¼ inch thick**
½	**teaspoon salt**
1	**refrigerated piecrust**
¼	**cup plain bread crumbs**
8	**ounces fresh mozzarella, sliced ⅛ inch thick**
½	**cup fresh basil leaves**
¼	**cup shredded Parmesan**
	Freshly cracked pepper
1	**egg, beaten (optional)**

• Heat oven to 375°. Place sliced tomatoes in a single layer on paper towels. Sprinkle one side of tomatoes with ¼ teaspoon of the salt; let stand for 10 minutes. Gently pat salted side of tomatoes with paper towels to absorb some of the moisture. Flip tomatoes and sprinkle with remaining ¼ teaspoon of the salt.

• Meanwhile, fit piecrust into a 9-inch pie plate. Sprinkle bread crumbs evenly on the bottom. Place half the mozzarella over the bread crumbs, along with a third of the tomatoes and a third of the basil. Sprinkle with 2 tablespoons of the Parmesan. Layer with a third of the tomatoes, a third of the basil and remaining mozzarella. Layer with remaining tomatoes, basil and Parmesan. Season with pepper and, if desired, brush edges of crust with beaten egg.

• Bake at 375° for 40 to 45 minutes, until crust is browned. Cool 10 to 15 minutes before slicing.

Note: Pie will have moisture. For a less wet pie, seed the tomatoes.

PER SERVING 347 **CAL**; 20 g **FAT** (11 g **SAT**); 13 g **PRO**; 30 g **CARB**; 3 g **FIBER**; 687 mg **SODIUM**; 36 mg **CHOL**

ZUCCHINI FRITTERS

Zucchini Fritters

MAKES 12 fritters **PREP** 15 minutes **COOK** 18 minutes

1	**container (6 ounces) 2% Greek yogurt**
2	**teaspoons lime juice**
1	**teaspoon lime zest**
1¼	**teaspoons salt**
1½	**pounds zucchini, shredded**
⅔	**cup sliced scallions**
½	**cup cilantro, chopped, plus more for garnish**
1	**egg yolk, beaten**
⅓	**cup all-purpose flour**
½	**teaspoon pepper**
¼	**cup canola oil**

• Heat oven to 200°. In a small bowl, mix yogurt, lime juice, lime zest and ¼ teaspoon of the salt until smooth.

• Squeeze shredded zucchini in a clean kitchen towel until most of the moisture is absorbed. In a medium bowl, combine zucchini, scallions, ½ cup of the cilantro, the egg, flour, remaining 1 teaspoon salt and the pepper.

• Heat 2 tablespoons of the oil over medium-high heat in a large sauté pan. When shimmering, add zucchini mixture in four ¼-cup portions. Flatten fritters with a spatula until they are 3 inches in diameter. (It will require 3 batches.) Cook fritters 3 minutes, until browned, then flip and cook another 3 minutes. Transfer fritters to a baking sheet and place in oven to keep warm. Continue cooking fritters, adding 1 more tablespoon of oil each time. Serve with lime yogurt and garnish with remaining cilantro.

PER FRITTER 79 **CAL**; 5 g **FAT** (1 g **SAT**); 3 g **PRO**; 6 g **CARB**; 1 g **FIBER**; 254 mg **SODIUM**; 18 mg **CHOL**

CUCUMBER, SNOW PEA AND ONION SALAD

BBQ Turkey Burgers

MAKES 4 servings PREP 10 minutes
COOK 10 minutes GRILL 11 minutes

¾	cup ketchup
1	clove garlic, grated
2	tablespoons honey
1	tablespoon cider vinegar
3	teaspoons low-sodium soy sauce
1¼	pounds ground turkey
¼	cup parsley, chopped
	White cheddar cheese (optional)
	Whole wheat buns

• Heat grill or grill pan to medium-high. In a small pot over medium-low heat, combine ketchup, garlic, honey, vinegar and 2 teaspoons of the soy sauce. Bring to a simmer; cook 10 minutes. Set aside to cool.

• In a bowl, combine turkey, ¼ cup of the barbecue sauce, the parsley and remaining 1 teaspoon soy sauce. Form into 4 patties.

• Lightly oil grill or grill pan. Grill burgers 5 minutes; flip and grill another 4 minutes, or until burgers reach 160° on an instant-read thermometer. (If adding cheese, place on burger after flipped.) Grill buns 1 to 2 minutes, until toasted. Serve with remaining barbecue sauce and Apple-Celery Slaw (recipe below), if desired.

PER SERVING 407 CAL; 14 g FAT (4 g SAT); 30 g PRO; 43 g CARB; 3 g FIBER; 993 mg SODIUM; 112 mg CHOL

Cucumber, Snow Pea and Onion Salad

MAKES 6 servings PREP 15 minutes REFRIGERATE 1 hour

2	medium cucumbers, sliced ⅛ inch thick
8	ounces snow peas, thinly sliced into strips (5 cups sliced)
1	cup thinly sliced sweet onion
⅓	cup fresh dill, chopped, plus more for garnish
1	teaspoon salt
½	cup sour cream
2	tablespoons white wine vinegar
1	tablespoon sugar
¼	teaspoon black pepper

• In a large bowl, toss together cucumbers, snow peas, onion, ⅓ cup of the dill and ½ teaspoon of the salt.

• In a separate bowl, mix sour cream, vinegar, sugar, pepper and remaining ½ teaspoon salt until smooth. Pour over vegetables and mix well. Cover and refrigerate 1 hour. Garnish with remaining dill.

PER SERVING 83 CAL; 4 g FAT (2 g SAT); 2 g PRO; 10 g CARB; 2 g FIBER; 399 mg SODIUM; 13 mg CHOL

Apple-Celery Slaw

MAKES 4 servings PREP 15 minutes

¼	cup light mayonnaise
2	teaspoons grainy mustard
2	teaspoons honey
1	teaspoon cider vinegar
2	ribs celery, very thinly sliced
1	Gala apple, cut into matchsticks

• Mix mayonnaise, mustard, honey and vinegar until smooth. Toss with celery and apple.

PER SERVING 80 CAL; 5 g FAT (1 g SAT); 0 g PRO; 9 g CARB; 1 g FIBER; 168 mg SODIUM; 5 mg CHOL

BBQ TURKEY BURGERS
WITH APPLE-CELERY SLAW

SOLE WITH STRAWBERRIES
AND ALMONDS

Sole with Strawberries and Almonds

MAKES 4 servings **PREP** 15 minutes
COOK 16 minutes

1⅓	cups pearl couscous
¼	cup olive oil
¼	cup sliced almonds, toasted
2	tablespoons chopped parsley, plus more for garnish
1¼	teaspoons plus ⅛ teaspoon salt
½	teaspoon black pepper
1	pound strawberries, hulled and diced
2	tablespoons white balsamic vinegar
1	tablespoon unsalted butter
1¼	pounds sole (about 8 small fillets)

• In a medium lidded pot, bring 1⅓ cups water and couscous to a boil. Reduce heat to low and simmer per package directions, covered, until water is absorbed. Stir in 2 tablespoons of the olive oil, 3 tablespoons of the almonds, 2 tablespoons of the parsley, ¾ teaspoon of the salt and ⅛ teaspoon of the pepper. Cover to keep warm.

• Meanwhile, add strawberries and vinegar to a sauté pan over medium heat; cook 8 minutes. Remove from heat. Stir in butter, ⅛ teaspoon of the salt and ⅛ teaspoon of the pepper.

• Pat fillets dry with paper towels; season with remaining ½ teaspoon salt and remaining ¼ teaspoon pepper. In a large nonstick sauté pan, heat 1 tablespoon of the oil on medium-high heat. When shimmering, add 4 fillets to pan. Sauté 2 minutes, then flip and cook 1 to 2 more minutes, until cooked through. Repeat with second batch of fillets, adding remaining 1 tablespoon oil.

• Serve fillets over couscous. Spoon strawberry sauce on top. Garnish with remaining 1 tablespoon almonds and parsley.

PER SERVING 524 **CAL**; 21 g **FAT** (4 g **SAT**); 34 g **PRO**; 48 g **CARB**; 5 g **FIBER**; 921 mg **SODIUM**; 76 mg **CHOL**

BLACKBERRY-RHUBARB COBBLER

Blackberry-Rhubarb Cobbler

MAKES 8 servings **PREP** 15 minutes **BAKE** at 350° for 1 hour **LET STAND** 10 minutes

4	cups blackberries
4	cups sliced rhubarb (1-inch pieces)
2	tablespoons quick-cooking tapioca
1	tablespoon lemon juice
1	tablespoon lemon zest
¾	cup granulated sugar
1	cup old-fashioned oats
¼	cup all-purpose flour
½	cup light brown sugar
5	tablespoons cold butter, cut into small pieces

• Heat oven to 350°. In a bowl, combine blackberries, rhubarb, tapioca, lemon juice, lemon zest and granulated sugar. In a separate bowl, combine oats, flour and brown sugar. Crumble in cold butter; mix with your hands until it resembles coarse crumbs.

• Pour fruit mixture into a 2-quart baking dish. Top with oat mixture. Bake at 350° for 1 hour, or until topping is browned. Let stand 10 minutes before serving.

PER SERVING 292 **CAL**; 8 g **FAT** (5 g **SAT**); 3 g **PRO**; 54 g **CARB**; 6 g **FIBER**; 10 mg **SODIUM**; 19 mg **CHOL**

CHEESY CHICKEN
ENCHILADAS,
PAGE 247

SEPTEMBER

233   236   244

AFTERNOON ENERGY

These kid-friendly mini meals take the edge off until dinner.

Turkey-Cherry Rice Salad

MAKES 8 servings **PREP** 15 minutes

⅓   **cup light mayonnaise**
¼   **cup 0% Greek yogurt**
¼   **teaspoon salt**
¼   **teaspoon pepper**
2   **cups cooked whole grain rice blend**
¾   **pound cooked turkey breast, shredded**
1   **cup sliced celery**
1   **cup sweetened dried cherries**
¼   **cup chopped walnuts**
¼   **cup fresh parsley, chopped**

• In a large bowl, whisk together mayo, yogurt, salt and pepper. Stir in rice, turkey, celery, cherries, walnuts and parsley.

PER SERVING 260 **CAL**; 7 g **FAT** (1 g **SAT**); 21 g **PRO**; 28 g **CARB**; 2 g **FIBER**; 196 mg **SODIUM**; 51 mg **CHOL**

Meatball Sliders

MAKES 12 sliders **PREP** 15 minutes **BROIL** 1 minute

- **1** **package (12 ounces) King's Hawaiian honey wheat rolls, split in half horizontally**
- **1¼** **cups marinara sauce**
- **12** **prepared Italian-style chicken meatballs**
- **3** **slices provolone cheese, sliced into quarters**

• Heat broiler to high. Place rolls on an aluminum-foil-lined baking sheet.

• In a small pot, heat marinara sauce. Stir in meatballs and heat until warmed through.

• Place 1 meatball on each roll and spoon about 2 tablespoons of the sauce over each. Top with a quarter slice of provolone.

• Broil sliders for about 1 minute, until cheese melts and bread is lightly browned.

PER SLIDER 188 **CAL**; 8 g **FAT** (4 g **SAT**); 9 g **PRO**; 21 g **CARB**; 1 g **FIBER**; 434 mg **SODIUM**; 40 mg **CHOL**

CHEESY BROCCOLI AND
TOMATO FLATBREAD

Packed with veggies, whole grains and protein, these super snacks make a great light meal.

Cheesy Broccoli and Tomato Flatbread

MAKES 6 servings **PREP** 10 minutes
COOK 7 minutes **BAKE** at 400° for 12 minutes

2	**tablespoons olive oil**
3	**cups broccoli florets**
1	**cup sliced sweet onion**
3	**cloves garlic, sliced**
¼	**teaspoon salt**
¼	**teaspoon pepper**
1	**flatbread multigrain pizza crust (10.5 ounces)**
1½	**cups grated Fontina cheese**
1	**small tomato, thinly sliced**

• Heat oven to 400°. Heat oil in a skillet over medium heat. Add broccoli and onion; sauté 5 minutes, until onion is soft. Add garlic; sauté 2 minutes. Stir in salt and pepper.

• Place crust on a baking sheet. Scatter ¾ cup of the cheese on top. Distribute tomato slices and broccoli mixture on top, then scatter remaining ¾ cup cheese over it.

• Bake at 400° for 12 minutes. Slice into 6 pieces.

PER SERVING 298 CAL; 15 g FAT (6 g SAT); 12 g PRO; 29 g CARB; 4 g FIBER; 574 mg SODIUM; 31 mg CHOL

BUFFALO CHICKEN SALAD

Buffalo Chicken Salad

MAKES 4 servings **PREP** 15 minutes **COOK** 10 minutes

1½	**pounds boneless, skinless chicken breasts**
2	**large ribs celery, diced, plus more, cut into sticks, for dipping**
¼	**cup buttermilk**
¼	**cup light mayonnaise**
¼	**cup mild Buffalo sauce**
¼	**cup chopped chives**
2	**tablespoons chopped dill**
	Carrot sticks, for dipping

• Bring a large, lidded pot of water to a low simmer. Add chicken breasts; cover and poach 10 minutes or until cooked through. Cool slightly. Dice and place in a large bowl with diced celery.

• In a separate bowl, whisk together buttermilk, light mayo, Buffalo sauce, chives and dill. Pour into bowl with chicken. Mix well. Serve with celery and carrot sticks.

PER SERVING 216 CAL; 7 g FAT (1 g SAT); 34 g PRO; 3 g CARB; 0 g FIBER; 244 mg SODIUM; 88 mg CHOL

SWEET POTATO-
APPLE SOUP

Ham, Swiss and Apple Quesadillas

MAKES 1 serving   **PREP** 5 minutes
GRILL 6 minutes

1	**tablespoon apple preserves, jam or jelly**
1	**8-inch whole wheat tortilla**
¼	**cup shredded Swiss cheese**
1	**ounce (3 tablespoons) diced ham**
4	**thin slices Granny Smith apple**

• Heat a grill or grill pan to medium. Spread apple preserves on half the tortilla. Scatter half the cheese on top, followed by the ham, apple slices and remaining cheese. Fold over tortilla.

• Grill tortilla on medium heat for 2 to 3 minutes per side, until cheese is melted and grill marks are present. Slice into 3 wedges and serve.

PER SERVING 256 **CAL**; 4 g **FAT** (2 g **SAT**); 17 g **PRO**; 41 g **CARB**; 4 g **FIBER**; 631 mg **SODIUM**; 9 mg **CHOL**

Sweet Potato-Apple Soup

MAKES 6 servings   **PREP** 15 minutes   **COOK** 25 minutes

1	**tablespoon olive oil**
1	**cup diced onion**
2	**cloves garlic, chopped**
1½	**pounds sweet potatoes, peeled and cut into 2-inch chunks**
¾	**pound Idaho potatoes, peeled and cut into 2-inch chunks**
2	**Gala apples, peeled, cored and cut into 2-inch chunks**
2	**cups chicken broth**
¼	**cup maple syrup**
½	**teaspoon salt**
¼	**teaspoon pepper**
	Apple chips, for garnish

• Heat oil in a large, lidded pot over medium heat. Add onion; cook 4 minutes. Add garlic; cook 1 minute. Stir in sweet potatoes, Idaho potatoes, apples, chicken broth and 1 cup water. Cover and bring to a simmer. Cook 20 minutes.

• Blend soup in batches until smooth. Return to heat. Stir in maple syrup, salt and pepper. Serve with apple chips.

PER SERVING 221 **CAL**; 3 g **FAT** (0 g **SAT**); 4 g **PRO**; 47 g **CARB**; 5 g **FIBER**; 537 mg **SODIUM**; 0 mg **CHOL**

Pizza Pasta

MAKES 8 servings **PREP** 10 minutes
COOK 12 minutes

1	box (12 ounces) tricolor fusilli
1	pint cherry tomatoes, halved
1	cup baby bocconcini
2	ounces turkey pepperoni, cut into strips
¼	cup olive oil
¼	cup red wine vinegar
½	teaspoon salt
¼	teaspoon pepper

• Bring a large pot of salted water to a boil. Add fusilli; cook 12 minutes. Drain and rinse in cold water until cool. Toss pasta in a bowl with tomatoes, bocconcini and pepperoni.

• In a separate bowl, whisk together oil, vinegar, salt and pepper. Pour over pasta and mix well. Serve at room temperature or chilled.

PER SERVING 294 **CAL**; 11 g **FAT** (1 g **SAT**); 12 g **PRO**; 34 g **CARB**; 2 g **FIBER**; 350 mg **SODIUM**; 27 mg **CHOL**

Veggie Taco Bowls

MAKES 8 servings **PREP** 10 minutes
COOK 7 minutes

- **2** tablespoons vegetable oil
- **½** cup diced red onion
- **2** cups frozen sweet corn
- **2** cloves garlic, chopped
- **1** can (15 ounces) pinto beans, drained and rinsed
- **1** tablespoon lime juice
- **¼** teaspoon salt
- **¼** teaspoon pepper
- **8** Old El Paso Stand 'N Stuff soft flour tortillas
  Shredded iceberg lettuce, prepared guacamole, salsa, shredded cheese blend and sour cream, for topping (optional)

• Heat oil in a skillet over medium heat. Add red onion and corn; cook 5 minutes. Stir in garlic and beans. Cook until beans are warmed through, about 2 minutes. Stir in lime juice, salt and pepper.

• Spoon ½ cup of the corn-bean mixture into each tortilla. Garnish with toppings, if desired.

PER SERVING 197 **CAL**; 7 g **FAT** (2 g **SAT**); 5 g **PRO**; 30 g **CARB**; 4 g **FIBER**; 335 mg **SODIUM**; 0 mg **CHOL**

COLD SESAME-ALMOND NOODLES

Open-Faced Hummus BLTs

MAKES 4 servings **PREP** 10 minutes **BAKE** at
400° for 17 minutes

8	strips turkey bacon
½	cup hummus with Greek yogurt
4	slices multigrain bread, toasted
4	romaine lettuce leaves
1	large tomato, cut into 8 slices

• Heat oven to 400°. Place bacon strips
on a rimmed baking sheet fitted with a
wire rack. Bake at 400° for 17 minutes,
until crisp.

• Spread each toast slice with
2 tablespoons of the hummus;
top with lettuce, 2 tomato slices
and 2 bacon strips.

PER SERVING 220 **CAL**; 11 g **FAT** (2 g **SAT**); 11 g
PRO; 21 g **CARB**; 4 g **FIBER**; 645 mg **SODIUM**;
30 mg **CHOL**

Cold Sesame-Almond Noodles

MAKES 8 servings **PREP** 10 minutes **COOK** 10 minutes

1	box (12 ounces) whole grain linguine
1	small sweet red pepper, thinly sliced
1	cup shredded carrots
1	cup sliced cucumber
¼	cup almond butter
1	tablespoon canola oil
2	tablespoons rice vinegar
1	tablespoon honey
¾	teaspoon salt
½	teaspoon sesame oil
¼	teaspoon pepper
	Sliced almonds (optional)

• Bring a large pot of salted water to a
boil. Cook linguine according to package
directions, about 10 minutes. Drain and
rinse under cold water until cool.
Toss with sweet red pepper, carrots
and cucumber.

• In a separate bowl, whisk together
almond butter and canola oil until
smooth. Whisk in vinegar, honey, salt,
sesame oil and pepper. Pour over
linguine and mix well. Serve at room
temperature or chilled. Garnish with
sliced almonds, if desired.

PER SERVING 223 **CAL**; 7 g **FAT** (1 g **SAT**); 8 g
PRO; 37 g **CARB**; 6 g **FIBER**; 275 mg **SODIUM**;
0 mg **CHOL**

GLOBAL WARMING

Innovative slow cooker dinners feature flavors from around the world.

ITALIAN-STYLE STEAK, MUSHROOMS AND ONIONS

Italian-Style Steak, Mushrooms and Onions

MAKES 4 servings **PREP** 15 minutes
SLOW COOK on HIGH for 6 hours or LOW for 8 hours

- 1½ pounds boneless chuck steak, cut into 4 equal pieces
- 1 teaspoon dried Italian seasoning
- ¼ teaspoon salt
- ¼ teaspoon black pepper
- 2 Cubanelle peppers, seeds removed, sliced
- 1 red sweet pepper, seeds removed, sliced
- 1 sweet onion, sliced
- 1 package (10 ounces) white mushrooms, quartered
- ½ cup beef broth
- 2 tablespoons red wine vinegar
- 1 tablespoon Worcestershire sauce
- 1 tablespoon brown sugar
  Fresh basil leaves
  Purchased tube polenta, sliced into rounds and grilled (optional)

• Coat bowl of slow cooker with nonstick cooking spray.

• Season both sides of steaks with Italian seasoning, salt and pepper. Place in slow cooker. Scatter Cubanelle peppers, red pepper, onion and mushrooms over top. In a small bowl, combine broth, vinegar, Worcestershire sauce and brown sugar. Pour over peppers, onions and mushrooms.

• Cover and cook on HIGH for 6 hours or LOW for 8 hours.

• Serve steaks with peppers, onions, mushrooms and some of the cooking liquid spooned over the top. Garnish with basil and, if desired, serve with grilled polenta rounds.

PER SERVING 280 **CAL**; 7 g **FAT** (2 g **SAT**); 37 g **PRO**; 19 g **CARB**; 4 g **FIBER**; 432 mg **SODIUM**; 97 mg **CHOL**

Variation: Stir Up a Stew Cut the chuck steak into 1½-inch pieces. In place of Cubanelle peppers and red pepper, add 1 pound small red-skinned potatoes, halved. Increase broth to 1 cup. During last 15 minutes of cooking time, add 1 package (10 ounces) frozen peas, thawed.

TUSCAN CHICKEN AND BEANS

Tuscan Chicken and Beans

MAKES 6 servings **PREP** 15 minutes **SLOW COOK** on HIGH for 6 hours or LOW for 8 hours

- 1 large onion, chopped
- 2 cloves garlic, chopped
- 3 pounds skinless, bone-in chicken thighs
- 1½ teaspoons dried Greek seasoning
- ½ teaspoon dried thyme
- ¼ teaspoon black pepper
- 2 tablespoons lemon juice
- 1 can (15 ounces) fire-roasted diced tomatoes
- ½ cup pitted Kalamata olives, halved
- 1 can (15 ounces) Great Northern beans, drained and rinsed
- ¼ cup fresh oregano leaves
- 3 cups cooked orzo
  Lemon slices, for garnish

• Coat bowl of slow cooker with nonstick cooking spray. Place onion and garlic in bottom of slow cooker. Season chicken on both sides with Greek seasoning, thyme and black pepper; arrange in bottom of slow cooker. Drizzle lemon juice over chicken and evenly spoon tomatoes and olives on top.

• Cover and cook on HIGH for 6 hours or LOW for 8 hours. During last 30 minutes of cooking time, stir in beans.

• To serve, stir in fresh oregano and spoon over cooked orzo. Garnish with lemon slices.

PER SERVING 502 **CAL**; 16 g **FAT** (4 g **SAT**); 41 g **PRO**; 46 g **CARB**; 6 g **FIBER**; 520 mg **SODIUM**; 114 mg **CHOL**

Variation: Make Lamb Stew Substitute 2 pounds lamb stew meat, cut into 1½-inch pieces, for chicken. Use traditional diced tomatoes instead of fire-roasted. Replace oregano with mint.

ASIAN FIVE-SPICE
MEATBALLS

Jamaican Country Ribs

MAKES 6 servings   PREP 15 minutes
SLOW COOK on HIGH for 6 hours or LOW
for 8 hours

1	large onion, sliced
4	cloves garlic, sliced
6	bone-in pork country ribs (about 3 pounds)
2	tablespoons jerk seasoning
1	can (20 ounces) pineapple chunks in juice
1	large green pepper, seeded and sliced
1	tablespoon all-purpose flour
1	can (15 ounces) black beans, drained and rinsed
4	cups cooked brown rice
4	scallions, sliced

• Coat bowl of slow cooker with nonstick cooking spray. Place onion and garlic in bottom of slow cooker. Season ribs with 1 tablespoon of the jerk seasoning and place over onion and garlic. Drain pineapple, reserving ¾ cup of the juice, and scatter over ribs. Add green pepper.

• Combine reserved pineapple juice, flour and remaining 1 tablespoon jerk seasoning. Pour over ribs.

• Cover and cook on HIGH for 6 hours or LOW for 8 hours. Stir in black beans during the last 30 minutes of cooking time. Serve with brown rice and garnish with scallions.

PER SERVING 644 CAL; 21 g FAT (7 g SAT); 52 g PRO; 59 g CARB; 8 g FIBER; 581 mg SODIUM; 145 mg CHOL

Variation: Try a Southern Spin
Omit jerk seasoning, pineapple juice and flour. Add 2 cups prepared barbecue sauce. Replace black beans with black-eyed peas. Serve with french fries and coleslaw.

Asian Five-Spice Meatballs

MAKES 6 servings   PREP 20 minutes   SLOW COOK on HIGH for 6 hours or LOW for 8 hours

1½	pounds ground meatloaf mix (beef, pork and veal)
1	cup panko bread crumbs
2	eggs, lightly beaten
3	scallions, sliced, plus more for garnish
2	tablespoons finely chopped ginger root
1	teaspoon onion powder
1	teaspoon Chinese five-spice powder
1	tablespoon reduced-sodium soy sauce
1	cup beef broth
½	cup ketchup
1	can (8 ounces) tomato sauce
3	tablespoons rice vinegar
3	cups cooked white rice

• Coat slow cooker bowl with nonstick cooking spray.

• In a large bowl, combine meatloaf mix, panko, eggs, scallions, ginger, onion powder, five-spice powder and soy sauce. Form into 12 meatballs, about ⅓ cup of mixture for each.

• Combine beef broth, ketchup, tomato sauce and vinegar. Pour into slow cooker; place meatballs in bottom in a single layer. Cover and cook on HIGH for 6 hours or LOW for 8 hours.

• Serve with rice and garnish with sliced scallions.

PER SERVING 450 CAL; 19 g FAT (7 g SAT); 29 g PRO; 40 g CARB; 1 g FIBER; 843 mg SODIUM; 148 mg CHOL

Variation: Turn It into an Asian-Inspired Meatloaf
Reduce panko to ¾ cup; shape meat mixture into a 7 x 4-inch loaf. Set aside 2 tablespoons of the ketchup mixture and pour remainder into slow cooker. Place meatloaf on top and spread with reserved ketchup mixture. Instead of rice, serve with cooked Chinese egg noodles and steamed snow peas.

JAMAICAN
COUNTRY RIBS

A small amount of spicy chorizo infuses this hearty bean stew with savory flavor.

Mexican 16-Bean Tomato and Chorizo Stew

MAKES 10 cups **PREP** 15 minutes **SOAK** overnight **SLOW COOK** on HIGH for 6 hours or LOW for 8 hours

1	**package (16 ounces) Goya 16-bean soup mix**
1	**large onion, chopped**
2	**ribs celery, sliced**
2	**large carrots, peeled and diced**
4	**cloves garlic, chopped**
1	**can (14½ ounces) reduced-sodium chicken broth**
1	**can (14½ ounces) chili-style diced tomatoes**
4	**ounces cured chorizo, chopped**
¾	**teaspoon salt**
½	**cup cilantro, chopped, plus more for serving (optional)**
	Tortilla chips and sour cream (optional)

• Rinse beans and place in a large saucepan. Cover with cold water and soak overnight.

• Coat bowl of slow cooker with nonstick cooking spray. Drain beans and add to slow cooker. Stir in onion, celery, carrots, garlic, broth, tomatoes, chorizo and 2 cups water.

• Cover and cook on HIGH for 6 hours or LOW for 8 hours.

• To serve, stir in salt and cilantro. Accompany with tortilla chips, sour cream and additional cilantro, if desired.

PER CUP 217 **CAL**; 5 g **FAT** (2 g **SAT**); 13 g **PRO**; 30 g **CARB**; 8 g **FIBER**; 667 mg **SODIUM**; 10 mg **CHOL**

Variation: Tweak It for Kids
Substitute tomatoes seasoned with garlic and olive oil for chili-style tomatoes. Add 2 packets Goya Sazón seasoning. Replace chorizo with ¾ pound boneless, skinless chicken breasts, cut into 1½-inch pieces. Serve with warm corn tortillas.

CASSEROLE SEASON

When the weather cools, warm bodies and souls with a bubbling dish of deliciousness.

Two kinds of cheese—lower-fat cream cheese and shredded Mexican cheese blend—give this family favorite a comforting creaminess.

Cheesy Chicken Enchiladas

MAKES 8 servings **PREP** 20 minutes **BAKE** at 375° for 20 minutes, then at 400° for 5 minutes

- **1** **can (19 ounces) mild enchilada sauce**
- **4** **cups shredded chicken (from a large rotisserie chicken) or 1¼ pounds poached chicken breast**
- **1** **bag (8 ounces) shredded Mexican cheese blend**
- **⅔** **cup Neufchâtel (⅓-less-fat cream cheese)**
- **16** **small flour tortillas**
   Sliced fresh jalapeño peppers, fresh cilantro leaves and diced fresh tomato for garnish (optional)

• Heat oven to 375°. Coat one 4-quart or two 2-quart baking dishes with nonstick cooking spray. If using 1 dish, spread ⅓ cup of the enchilada sauce in bottom. If using 2 dishes, spread 3 tablespoons of the enchilada sauce in bottom of each dish.

• In a bowl, combine chicken, 1 cup of the shredded cheese and ¾ cup of the enchilada sauce.

• Spread 2 teaspoons Neufchâtel on a tortilla. Spoon 2 to 3 tablespoons chicken mixture in a strip in center of tortilla. Roll up tightly to enclose filling; transfer to prepared dish(es). Repeat with remaining tortillas, cream cheese and chicken mixture to yield 16 enchiladas.

• Pour remaining sauce over enchiladas, dividing evenly between dishes (if using two). Top with remaining cheese. Bake at 375° for 20 minutes. Increase temperature to 400° and bake an additional 5 minutes, until cheese begins to brown slightly. Garnish with jalapeño slices, cilantro and tomato, if desired.

PER SERVING 415 **CAL**; 20 g **FAT** (10 g **SAT**); 25 g **PRO**; 30 g **CARB**; 0 g **FIBER**; 930 mg **SODIUM**; 77 mg **CHOL**

CANDY APPLES,
PAGES 262–263

OCTOBER

257   267   271

GOOD TO GO!

Take-it-with-you ideas for tailgates, potlucks or anywhere there's a hungry crowd.

ITALIAN HOAGIE ON A STICK, PAGE 253

SLOW COOKER BEER-
BRAISED SMOKED
SAUSAGES AND ONIONS,
PAGE 254

Pork Burgers Stuffed with Manchego

MAKES 8 servings **PREP** 20 minutes **GRILL** 10 minutes

- **2** pounds ground pork
- **¼** cup light mayonnaise, plus more for serving (optional)
- **1** teaspoon dried oregano
- **½** teaspoon salt
- **½** teaspoon coarsely ground pepper
- **½** teaspoon dried thyme
- **½** teaspoon onion powder
- **½** teaspoon hot paprika
- **4** ounces Manchego cheese
- **8** egg challah rolls, split
- **8** tablespoons dried onion topping

Sliced hot cherry peppers (optional)

- In large bowl, combine pork, mayonnaise, oregano, salt, pepper, thyme, onion powder and paprika. Form into 8 burgers.

- Cut Manchego into pieces about 1 inch square and ¼ inch thick. Make an indentation in each burger and insert a piece of cheese into it. Close meat around cheese and flatten burger.

- Heat a gas grill to medium-high or the coals in a charcoal grill to medium-hot. Lightly grease grates. Grill burgers about 5 minutes per side, until internal temperature reaches 160°.

- Place burgers on rolls and top each with 1 tablespoon of the onion topping. Add slices of hot cherry peppers and additional mayonnaise, if desired.

PER SERVING 621 **CAL**; 36 g **FAT** (13 g **SAT**); 30 g **PRO**; 41 g **CARB**; 2 g **FIBER**; 888 mg **SODIUM**; 135 mg **CHOL**

PORK BURGERS STUFFED WITH MANCHEGO

Double the fun with totable food you can take to a game, tailgate, fall picnic or potluck.

Italian Hoagie on a Stick

MAKES 12 servings **PREP** 20 minutes

12	10-inch wooden skewers
4	ounces provolone, cut into 1-inch cubes
4	ounces cheddar, cut into 1-inch cubes
4	ounces sliced Genoa salami, rolled
4	ounces sliced mortadella, rolled
4	ounces sliced capicola, rolled
12	large pimiento-stuffed olives
18	grape tomatoes
6	small sweet gherkins
6	artichoke hearts in oil, drained and quartered
½	cup light mayonnaise
3	tablespoons grainy mustard
2	tablespoons honey

• Thread skewers, alternating cheese cubes and rolled meat with olives, tomatoes, gherkins and artichokes in the order you prefer.

• Combine mayonnaise, mustard and honey. Serve as a dipping sauce.

PER SERVING 211 **CAL**; 15 g **FAT** (6 g **SAT**); 10 g **PRO**; 9 g **CARB**; 1 g **FIBER**; 861 mg **SODIUM**; 39 mg **CHOL**

GAME DAY DEVILED EGGS

Game Day Deviled Eggs

MAKES 24 egg halves **PREP** 25 minutes **REFRIGERATE** 1 hour

12	hard-cooked eggs, peeled
½	cup light mayonnaise
1	tablespoon Dijon mustard
¼	teaspoon black pepper
3	tablespoons finely diced ham
2	tablespoons finely shredded cheddar
	Chives for garnish (optional)

• Cut eggs in half lengthwise and spoon yolks into a bowl. Reserve whites. Mash yolks with a fork. Stir in mayonnaise, mustard and black pepper.

• Fold in ham and cheddar.

• Fill whites with yolk mixture. If desired, cut chives into small pieces and arrange on top of eggs so that they resemble a football. Refrigerate at least 1 hour before serving.

PER EGG HALF 62 **CAL**; 5 g **FAT** (1 g **SAT**); 4 g **PRO**; 1 g **CARB**; 0 g **FIBER**; 136 mg **SODIUM**; 110 mg **CHOL**

Slow Cooker Chipotle Beef and Black Bean Chili

MAKES 8 servings **PREP** 15 minutes
SLOW COOK on HIGH for 6 hours or LOW for 8 hours

1	large onion, chopped
4	cloves garlic, chopped
1	large red pepper, seeded and diced
1	large green pepper, seeded and diced
1½	pounds ground beef chuck
2	cans (14.5 ounces each) stewed tomatoes
3	tablespoons chili powder
2	tablespoons tomato paste
2	teaspoons ground cumin
2	teaspoons dried oregano
1	teaspoon salt
2	chipotle peppers in adobo, seeded and chopped
2	cans (15 ounces each) black beans, drained and rinsed
	Tortilla chips and sour cream (optional)

● Coat the bowl of a slow cooker with nonstick cooking spray. Place onion, garlic, peppers and ground beef in bottom of slow cooker.

● In a medium bowl, combine tomatoes, chili powder, tomato paste, cumin, oregano, salt and chipotle peppers. Pour over ground beef.

● Cover and cook on HIGH for 6 hours or LOW for 8 hours. Stir in beans during last 30 minutes of cooking time.

● Serve with crushed tortilla chips and sour cream, if desired.

PER SERVING 324 **CAL**; 14 g **FAT** (5 g **SAT**); 23 g **PRO**; 25 g **CARB**; 9 g **FIBER**; 793 mg **SODIUM**; 58 mg **CHOL**

Slow Cooker Beer-Braised Smoked Sausages and Onions

MAKES 12 servings **PREP** 15 minutes **COOK** 10 minutes **SLOW COOK** on HIGH for 4 hours

12	smoked sausages with cheese
3	tablespoons butter, melted
1	tablespoon brown sugar
1	tablespoon grainy mustard
3	large onions, sliced into ¼-inch rings
1	teaspoon caraway seeds
½	teaspoon salt
¼	teaspoon black pepper
1	can (12 ounces) beer
12	hoagie rolls, split
	Mustard and shredded cheddar (optional)

● Heat a large nonstick skillet over medium-high heat. Add sausages and brown on all sides, about 10 minutes.

● Meanwhile, coat the bowl of a slow cooker with nonstick cooking spray. Place butter, brown sugar and mustard in slow cooker; stir in onions, caraway seeds, salt and pepper. Place sausages over onions and pour beer over the top.

● Cover and cook on HIGH for 4 hours. Serve sausages on rolls with onions. Top with mustard and cheddar, if desired.

PER SERVING 446 **CAL**; 24 g **FAT** (10 g **SAT**); 16 g **PRO**; 43 g **CARB**; 3 g **FIBER**; 1,031 mg **SODIUM**; 43 mg **CHOL**

SLOW COOKER CHIPOTLE BEEF
AND BLACK BEAN CHILI

Turkey and Roast Beef Muffuletta

MAKES 10 servings **PREP** 15 minutes **LET STAND** 1 hour

- **1** jar (4.75 ounces) pimiento-stuffed olives, drained and chopped
- **1** large tomato, seeded and chopped
- **¼** cup olive oil
- **1** rib celery, diced
- **2** cloves garlic, chopped
- **2** tablespoons red wine vinegar
- **½** teaspoon dried oregano
- **½** teaspoon salt
- **⅛** teaspoon black pepper
- **1** large round crusty Italian bread (about 1¼ pounds)
- **¼** pound sliced deli roast beef
- **¼** pound sliced Swiss cheese
- **1** jar (12 ounces) roasted red peppers, drained
- **¼** pound sliced deli turkey
- **¼** pound sliced American cheese

• In a small bowl, combine olives, tomato, olive oil, celery, garlic, red wine vinegar, oregano, salt and black pepper.

• Cut Italian bread in half crosswise. Spread bottom of cut side with half of olive mixture. Layer on roast beef, Swiss cheese, red peppers, turkey and American cheese. Spread remaining olive mixture over cheese and top with other half of bread.

• Wrap tightly in plastic wrap and weigh down with a heavy pot filled with canned goods for at least an hour. Slice into 10 wedges to serve.

PER SERVING 364 **CAL**; 18 g **FAT** (6 g **SAT**); 17 g **PRO**; 33 g **CARB**; 2 g **FIBER**; 1,006 mg **SODIUM**; 34 mg **CHOL**

MULLED CIDER

ONE-POT SHRIMP GUMBO

Mulled Cider

MAKES 8 servings PREP 5 minutes
STEEP 2 hours

- 2 quarts apple cider
- 1 orange, cut into ¼-inch slices
- 1 tablespoon brown sugar
- 4 cloves
- 2 star anise pods
- 2 cinnamon sticks

• In a large saucepan, combine apple cider, orange slices, brown sugar, cloves, star anise pods and cinnamon sticks. Bring to a simmer. Remove from heat and allow to steep at least 2 hours.

• Strain out spices before serving.

PER SERVING 131 CAL; 0 g FAT (0 g SAT); 0 g PRO; 33 g CARB; 0 g FIBER; 25 mg SODIUM; 0 mg CHOL

One-Pot Shrimp Gumbo

MAKES 12 servings PREP 15 minutes COOK 38 minutes

- ¼ cup vegetable oil
- ¼ cup all-purpose flour
- 1 large onion, sliced
- 1 green pepper, seeded and diced
- 3 ribs celery, sliced
- 3 cloves garlic, chopped
- 2 cans (14.5 ounces each) stewed tomatoes
- 1 package (16 ounces) frozen chopped okra, thawed
- 8 ounces kielbasa (from a 13-ounce package), cut into ½-inch dice
- 2 large vegetable bouillon cubes (from a 2.1-ounce package)
- 1¼ cups white rice
- ¼ teaspoon cayenne
- 1 pound shrimp, peeled and deveined, sliced in half lengthwise

• Heat oil in a large pot over medium heat. Add flour and cook 4 to 5 minutes, stirring constantly, until lightly browned.

• Add onion, green pepper, celery and garlic; cook 10 minutes, stirring occasionally. Add tomatoes, okra, kielbasa, bouillon, rice, cayenne and 10 cups water. Cover and bring to a boil over high heat. Reduce heat to medium and simmer 20 minutes with cover ajar. Stir occasionally.

• Stir in shrimp and cook 2 to 3 minutes, until cooked through.

PER SERVING 182 CAL; 11 g FAT (3 g SAT); 11 g PRO; 12 g CARB; 3 g FIBER; 750 mg SODIUM; 69 mg CHOL

RASPBERRY-CHIP
CRUMB CAKE

Raspberry-Chip Crumb Cake

MAKES 9 servings **PREP** 20 minutes
BAKE at 350° for 40 minutes

CAKE

1¼	**cups all-purpose flour**
¾	**cup sugar**
2	**teaspoons baking powder**
¼	**teaspoon salt**
1	**egg**
½	**cup whole milk**
2	**tablespoons vegetable oil**
½	**teaspoon vanilla extract**
½	**cup dark mini chocolate baking chunks**
1	**container raspberries (6 ounces), about 1½ cups**

TOPPING

½	**cup all-purpose flour**
¾	**cup sugar**
4	**tablespoons unsalted butter, chilled and cut into pieces**
⅓	**cup chopped walnuts**

• **Cake.** Heat oven to 350°. Coat an 8 x 8 x 2-inch baking pan with nonstick cooking spray.

• In a large mixing bowl, whisk together flour, sugar, baking powder and salt. In a small bowl, whisk together egg, milk, oil and vanilla.

• Make a well in center of flour mixture. Add egg mixture to well and beat with a wooden spoon 1 minute, until evenly moistened; stir in chocolate chunks. Spoon into prepared pan and top with raspberries.

• **Topping.** In a small bowl, combine flour and sugar. Cut in butter with pastry blender until crumbly. Stir in walnuts. Sprinkle topping over raspberries.

• Bake at 350° for 35 to 40 minutes or until wooden pick inserted in center comes out clean. Cool in pan on a wire rack. Cut into 9 squares. This cake is best eaten on the day it's made.

PER SERVING 357 **CAL**; 16 g **FAT** (7 g **SAT**); 5 g **PRO**; 54 g **CARB**; 3 g **FIBER**; 168 mg **SODIUM**; 38 mg **CHOL**

LOADED BROWNIES

Loaded Brownies

MAKES 36 brownies **PREP** 20 minutes **BAKE** at 325° for 35 minutes

1¼	**cups all-purpose flour**
¾	**cup unsweetened cocoa powder**
½	**teaspoon salt**
¼	**teaspoon baking powder**
1	**cup (2 sticks) unsalted butter, softened**
1	**package (3 ounces) cream cheese, softened**
1½	**cups sugar**
3	**eggs**
1	**teaspoon vanilla extract**
½	**cup macadamia nuts, chopped**
½	**cup milk chocolate chips**
½	**cup semisweet chocolate chips**
½	**cup cherry-juice-infused sweetened dried cranberries**

• Heat oven to 325°. Coat 13 x 9 x 2-inch baking pan with nonstick cooking spray.

• In a bowl, whisk together flour, cocoa powder, salt and baking powder. Set aside.

• In a large bowl, beat together butter, cream cheese and sugar on medium-high for 2 minutes, until smooth. Beat in eggs and vanilla 1 minute, until combined.

• On low, gradually beat flour mixture into butter mixture; beat 2 minutes. Stir in nuts, chocolate chips and dried cranberries. Spoon batter into prepared pan, spreading evenly.

• Bake at 325° for 35 minutes or until brownies begin to pull away from pan. Cool in pan on a wire rack.

• To serve, cut into 36 pieces.

PER BROWNIE 146 **CAL**; 10 g **FAT** (5 g **SAT**); 2 g **PRO**; 15 g **CARB**; 1 g **FIBER**; 51 mg **SODIUM**; 34 mg **CHOL**

A FRIGHTFULLY SWEET CELEBRATION

No tricks here! Just an easy menu of sliders, mac and cheese, candy apples and more.

INDIVIDUAL MAC
AND CHEESE,
PAGE 267

CANDY APPLES,
PAGES 262–263

PUMPKIN PIE NOG,
PAGE 264

Drizzled Chocolate Apples

MAKES 4 servings **PREP** 30 minutes **MICROWAVE** about 9 minutes

- **4**   **small to medium Gala apples**
- **4**   **6-inch wooden dowels**
- **1**   **bag (12 ounces) semisweet chocolate morsels**
- **3**   **teaspoons canola oil**
- **4**   **ounces orange candy melts (from a 12-ounce bag)**
- **4**   **ounces yellow candy melts (from a 12-ounce bag)**

• Remove stems from apples. Insert a dowel into each apple at the stem end.

• In a microwave-safe bowl, combine semisweet chocolate and 1 teaspoon of the oil. Microwave at 50% power for 1 minute; stir. Continue microwaving at 50% power in 30-second intervals until melted. Dip apples in chocolate until evenly coated. Allow excess chocolate to drip back into bowl. Place apples on a parchment-paper-lined baking sheet to partially dry.

• In a separate microwave-safe bowl, combine orange candy melts and 1 teaspoon of the oil. Melt according to package directions, then transfer to a piping bag or a small resealable bag with one small corner snipped off. Repeat with yellow candy melts and remaining 1 teaspoon oil. Drizzle both colors over apples. Return apples to parchment-paper-lined baking sheet to dry.

PER SERVING 492 **CAL**; 29 g **FAT** (18 g **SAT**); 3 g **PRO**; 63 g **CARB**; 4 g **FIBER**; 50 mg **SODIUM**; 0 mg **CHOL**

Chocolate Apples with Sprinkles

MAKES 4 servings PREP 30 minutes
MICROWAVE about 3 minutes

4	small to medium Gala apples
4	6-inch wooden dowels
1	bag (12 ounces) semisweet chocolate morsels
1	teaspoon canola oil
⅓	cup orange nonpareils or sprinkles

• Remove stems from apples. Insert a dowel into each apple at the stem end.

• In a microwave-safe bowl, combine semisweet chocolate and oil. Microwave at 50% power for 1 minute; stir. Continue microwaving at 50% power in 30-second intervals until melted.

• Dollop several spoonfuls of the chocolate on top of an apple around the dowel. Holding dowel, gently tap apple on a flat surface, creating drips. Sprinkle nonpareils over chocolate. Place apple on a parchment-paper-lined baking sheet to dry. Repeat with each apple.

PER SERVING 409 CAL; 22 g FAT (13 g SAT); 4 g PRO; 58 g CARB; 4 g FIBER; 19 mg SODIUM; 7 mg CHOL

White Chocolate-Oreo Apples

MAKES 4 servings PREP 30 minutes

4	small to medium Gala apples
4	6-inch wooden dowels
1	bag (12 ounces) white candy melts
2	teaspoons canola oil
	Oreo cookies (about 6), chopped

• Remove stems from apples. Insert a dowel into each apple at the stem end.

• In a microwave-safe bowl, combine candy melts and oil; melt according to package directions. Dip apples in candy until evenly coated, making sure some red peeks out. Allow excess candy to drip back into bowl. Sprinkle chopped Oreos around the top of each candy-coated apple.

• Place apples on a parchment-paper-lined baking sheet to dry.

PER SERVING 473 CAL; 24 g FAT (17 g SAT); 2 g PRO; 63 g CARB; 2 g FIBER; 178 mg SODIUM; 0 mg CHOL

White Chocolate-Pistachio Apples

MAKES 4 servings PREP 30 minutes

4	small to medium Granny Smith apples
4	6-inch wooden dowels
1	bag (12 ounces) white candy melts
2	teaspoons canola oil
	Shelled pistachios, chopped

• Remove stems from apples. Insert a dowel into each apple at the stem end.

• In a microwave-safe bowl, combine candy melts and oil; melt according to package directions. Dip apples in candy until evenly coated, making sure some green peeks out. Allow excess candy to drip back into bowl. Sprinkle chopped pistachios around top of each candy-coated apple.

• Place apples on a parchment-paper-lined baking sheet to dry.

PER SERVING 449 CAL; 26 g FAT (17 g SAT); 5 g PRO; 50 g CARB; 3 g FIBER; 90 mg SODIUM; 0 mg CHOL

Salted Caramel Apples

MAKES 4 servings PREP 30 minutes
REFRIGERATE 1 hour

4	small to medium Granny Smith apples
4	6-inch wooden dowels
1	bag (11 ounces) caramel bits
	Sea salt flakes (such as Maldon)

• Remove stems from apples. Insert a dowel into each apple at the stem end.

• In a microwave-safe bowl, melt caramel bits according to package directions. Dip apples in caramel until evenly coated, making sure some green peeks out. Allow excess caramel to drip back into bowl. Sprinkle with sea salt.

• Place apples on a parchment-paper-lined baking sheet coated with nonstick cooking spray. Refrigerate 1 hour. Remove from refrigerator at least 15 minutes before serving. (If refrigerated for too long, salt will dissolve.)

PER SERVING 227 CAL; 4 g FAT (1 g SAT); 3 g PRO; 49 g CARB; 2 g FIBER; 413 mg SODIUM; 3 mg CHOL

Double Chocolate Apples

MAKES 4 servings PREP 30 minutes
MICROWAVE about 6 minutes

4	small to medium Granny Smith or Gala apples
4	6-inch wooden dowels
1	bag (12 ounces) semisweet chocolate morsels
2	teaspoons canola oil
6	ounces white candy melts (from a 12-ounce bag)
2	tubes M&M's Minis (use only the orange, yellow and red)

• Remove stems from apples. Insert a dowel into each apple at the stem end.

• In a microwave-safe bowl, combine semisweet chocolate and 1 teaspoon of the oil. Microwave at 50% power for 1 minute; stir. Continue microwaving at 50% power in 30-second intervals until melted. Dip apples in chocolate until evenly coated. Allow excess chocolate to drip back into bowl. Place apples on a parchment-paper-lined baking sheet to dry.

• In a separate microwave-safe bowl, combine candy melts and remaining 1 teaspoon oil; melt according to package directions. Dollop several spoonfuls of the candy on top of an apple around the dowel. Holding dowel, gently tap apple on a flat surface, creating drips. Sprinkle M&M's on white chocolate. Return apple to parchment-paper-lined baking sheet to dry. Repeat with each apple.

PER SERVING 503 CAL; 29 g FAT (19 g SAT); 4 g PRO; 66 g CARB; 5 g FIBER; 53 mg SODIUM; 1 mg CHOL

The taste of fall is encompassed in a single bite of crisp, sweet-tart apple covered in chewy caramel, chocolate or creamy white candy melt.

Pumpkin Pie Nog

MAKES 16 servings **COOK** 15 minutes

- **2** cups cooked fresh sugar pumpkin puree, or 1 can (15 ounces) pumpkin
- **1** bottle (46 ounces) peach-mango smoothie drink or peach nectar (5½ cups)
- **2** teaspoons pumpkin pie spice
- **1** quart vanilla or pumpkin ice cream

• If using cooked fresh pumpkin puree, add to a blender with 1 cup of the smoothie drink; cover and blend until smooth.

• In a 5- to 6-quart saucepan combine remaining smoothie drink, the blended pumpkin mixture or canned pumpkin, and pumpkin pie spice; heat about 10 minutes until warm.

• Add about three-quarters of the ice cream by spoonfuls. Heat and stir 3 to 5 minutes more, until just melted. Pour into a punch bowl. Top with scoops of remaining ice cream. Serve immediately (nog will be slightly warm).

PER SERVING 142 **CAL**; 8 g **FAT** (5 g **SAT**); 2 g **PRO**; 17 g **CARB**; 0 g **FIBER**; 39 mg **SODIUM**; 43 mg **CHOL**

Mini-Burger Party Platter

MAKES 8 sliders **PREP** 25 minutes
BROIL 11 minutes

- **¼** cup finely chopped green onions or onion
- **2** tablespoons fine dry bread crumbs
- **1** teaspoon Worcestershire sauce or steak sauce
- **¾** teaspoon Montreal steak seasoning or Cajun seasoning
- **1** pound lean ground beef
- **2** slices Swiss or cheddar cheese (1 ounce each), cut into fourths
- **8** dinner rolls or cocktail-size hamburger buns, split
  Shredded red leaf lettuce
- **1** plum tomato, thinly sliced
  Citrus Ketchup and/or Balsamic Mayo (recipes follow)
  Hot waffle fries

• In a large bowl, combine onions, bread crumbs, 2 tablespoons water, Worcestershire sauce and steak seasoning. Add beef and mix well.

• Shape meat mixture on waxed paper into a 10 x 5-inch rectangle. Cut into 8 square patties. Place patties on the unheated rack of a broiler pan. Broil 4 to 5 inches from heat, turning once, for 8 to 10 minutes or until internal temperature registers 160° on an instant-read thermometer. Top with cheese slices and broil 30 seconds or until melted.

• On a serving platter, top each dinner roll or hamburger bun bottom with lettuce, a mini burger, tomato slice, Citrus Ketchup or Balsamic Mayo and roll or bun top. If desired, decorate burgers with party toothpicks. Add hot waffle fries to platter.

PER SERVING 402 **CAL**; 24 g **FAT** (6 g **SAT**); 16 g **PRO**; 35 g **CARB**; 3 g **FIBER**; 689 mg **SODIUM**; 48 mg **CHOL**

Citrus Ketchup

MAKES ½ cup **PREP** 5 minutes

- **½** cup ketchup
- **¼** teaspoon finely shredded lemon peel
- **1** teaspoon lemon juice
- **¼** teaspoon finely shredded orange peel
- **1** teaspoon orange juice

• In a small bowl, combine ketchup, lemon peel, lemon juice, orange peel and orange juice. Cover and chill until ready to use.

Balsamic Mayo

MAKES ½ cup **PREP** 5 minutes

- **½** cup mayonnaise
- **2** tablespoons balsamic vinegar
- **⅛** teaspoon freshly ground black pepper

• In a small bowl, combine mayonnaise, balsamic vinegar and freshly ground black pepper. Cover and chill until ready to use.

PUMPKIN PIE NOG

MINI-BURGER
PARTY PLATTER

INDIVIDUAL MAC
AND CHEESE

Individual Mac and Cheese

MAKES 8 servings **PREP** 45 minutes
COOK 15 minutes **BAKE** at 350° for 20 minutes

- **4**   **tablespoons unsalted butter**
- **1**   **small onion, chopped**
- **1**   **rib celery, chopped**
- **1½**   **teaspoons chopped fresh thyme**
- **2**   **tablespoons all-purpose flour**
- **1½**   **cups hot whole milk**
- **¼**   **pound cheddar cheese, coarsely grated**
- **¼**   **pound Fontina cheese, coarsely grated**
- **½**   **teaspoon finely grated fresh nutmeg**
- **¾**   **pound tubular pasta, such as tubetti or tubettini**
-     **Salt and pepper to taste**
- **1½**   **cups fresh bread crumbs (from about 3 slices firm white sandwich bread)**

• Melt 2 tablespoons of the butter in a large skillet over medium heat. Add onion, celery and thyme; cook, stirring, until vegetables are softened, about 4 minutes. Add flour and cook, stirring constantly, until flour is golden, about 4 minutes. Add milk in a slow stream, whisking constantly. Cook until thickened and reduced to 1½ cups, about 4 minutes. Remove pan from heat; whisk in cheeses and nutmeg.

• Meanwhile, bring a large pot of salted water to a boil. Stir in pasta; cook until al dente, about 7 minutes. Drain pasta and return to pot. Gently stir together pasta, cheese mixture and salt and pepper to taste. Spoon into eight 5- to 8-ounce ovenproof dishes.

• Heat oven to 350°. Melt remaining 2 tablespoons butter in a nonstick skillet over medium heat. Add bread crumbs and cook, stirring, until golden, about 3 minutes. Transfer to a bowl. Sprinkle tops of macaroni and cheese with crumbs. Bake on a cookie sheet at 350° on the middle rack until hot and crumbs are golden brown, about 20 minutes.

PER SERVING 390 **CAL**; 18 g **FAT** (11 g **SAT**); 15 g **PRO**; 42 g **CARB**; 2 g **FIBER**; 432 mg **SODIUM**; 53 mg **CHOL**

VEGGIE BRUSCHETTA

Veggie Bruschetta

MAKES 36 pieces **PREP** 25 minutes **ROAST** at 425° for 40 minutes **BAKE** at 375° for 6 minutes

- **1½**   **pounds plum tomatoes, seeded and cut into 1-inch pieces**
- **2**   **small sweet red and/or yellow peppers, seeded and cut into 1-inch pieces**
- **½**   **or 1 whole medium red onion, cut into ½-inch wedges**
- **3**   **cloves garlic, peeled**
- **2**   **tablespoons olive oil**
- **½**   **teaspoon kosher salt or sea salt**
- **½**   **teaspoon freshly ground black pepper**
- **2**   **tablespoons balsamic vinegar**
- **2**   **teaspoons snipped fresh thyme**
- **¼**   **cup snipped fresh basil**
- **1**   **whole grain baguette (1 pound)**
- **2**   **ounces Parmesan cheese, thinly shaved**

• Heat oven to 425°. In a large bowl, combine tomatoes, sweet peppers, onion wedges and garlic. Add oil, salt and black pepper; toss to coat. Transfer mixture to a foil-lined shallow roasting pan.

• Roast at 425° for 35 to 40 minutes or until vegetables are tender and slightly charred on the edges, stirring twice. Cool slightly on a wire rack. Lower oven temperature to 375°.

• Transfer tomato mixture to a food processor. Cover and pulse with several on-off turns until mixture is chopped but still slightly chunky. Stir in balsamic vinegar and thyme.

• Slice baguette crosswise into ¼-inch-thick slices (about 36 slices). Lightly coat bread slices with nonstick cooking spray. Place on a baking sheet. Bake at 375° for 4 to 6 minutes or until golden and crisp, turning once. Cool bread on a wire rack.

• Stir basil into tomato mixture. Top each bread slice with 1 tablespoon of the mixture and some of the Parmesan.

PER SERVING 52 **CAL**; 2 g **FAT** (0 g **SAT**); 3 g **PRO**; 7 g **CARB**; 1 g **FIBER**; 114 mg **SODIUM**; 1 mg **CHOL**

POWER BREAKFASTS

Healthy make-ahead options keep morning madness to a minimum.

PUMPKIN WAFFLES WITH
CINNAMON MAPLE SYRUP

APPLE-CINNAMON
PARFAITS

Pumpkin Waffles with Cinnamon Maple Syrup

MAKES 12 waffles **PREP** 15 minutes **COOK** per manufacturer's directions **LET STAND** 15 minutes

1	cup pure maple syrup
1	cinnamon stick
1½	cups all-purpose flour
1	cup white whole wheat flour
1	teaspoon baking soda
½	teaspoon salt
2	cups buttermilk
1	cup canned packed pumpkin
4	eggs, beaten
⅓	cup packed brown sugar
¼	cup unsalted butter, melted

• Heat waffle iron according to manufacturer's directions. In a small lidded pot over medium heat, combine maple syrup and cinnamon stick. Cook, uncovered, until it steams (do not boil). Turn off heat, cover and let stand 15 minutes. If not immediately serving, transfer to an airtight container with cinnamon stick. Cool; refrigerate until ready to use.

• Whisk together both flours, baking soda and salt. In a separate bowl, blend buttermilk, pumpkin, eggs, brown sugar and butter. Stir dry mixture into wet mixture until smooth.

• Coat waffle iron with nonstick cooking spray. Cook waffles according to manufacturer's directions.

• If not immediately serving, cool and freeze in resealable bags in a single layer or stack with parchment paper in between waffles. To serve: Toast frozen waffles and reheat syrup.

PER WAFFLE 270 **CAL**; 6 g **FAT** (3 g **SAT**); 7 g **PRO**; 47 g **CARB**; 3 g **FIBER**; 274 mg **SODIUM**; 82 mg **CHOL**

Apple-Cinnamon Parfaits

MAKES 6 servings **PREP** 5 minutes **COOK** 10 minutes

2	tablespoons unsalted butter
3	Granny Smith apples, peeled, cored and cut into ½-inch chunks
2	tablespoons packed light brown sugar
1	teaspoon ground cinnamon
4	containers (6 ounces each) Chobani 0% apple-cinnamon yogurt
1	cup cinnamon-raisin granola

• In a skillet, melt butter over medium heat. Stir in diced apples, light brown sugar and cinnamon. Cook 8 to 10 minutes, until slightly tender, stirring periodically. Cool cooked apples and store in an airtight container until ready to use.

• To assemble parfaits, layer a scant ¼ cup yogurt in the bottom of a cup or glass. Sprinkle 2 tablespoons of the granola on top, followed by 3 tablespoons of the cooked apples. Repeat layering. Serve.

Note: Assemble parfaits just before serving or granola may lose its crunch.

PER SERVING 239 **CAL**; 6 g **FAT** (2 g **SAT**); 11 g **PRO**; 36 g **CARB**; 2 g **FIBER**; 59 mg **SODIUM**; 10 mg **CHOL**

CARROT-COCONUT
BREAD

Whether it's a slice of veggie-rich whole wheat sweet bread or a protein-packed quiche, a homemade breakfast starts the day off right.

Carrot-Coconut Bread

MAKES 10 servings **PREP** 15 minutes
BAKE at 350° for 1 hour

½	**cup coconut oil, at room temperature**
⅔	**cup packed light brown sugar**
2	**eggs**
1½	**cups grated carrots**
1	**cup white whole wheat flour**
1	**cup all-purpose flour**
1	**teaspoon baking powder**
¼	**teaspoon salt**
1	**cup sweetened flaked coconut**
⅓	**cup chopped unsalted macadamia nuts (optional)**

• Heat oven to 350°. Lightly coat an 8½ x 4½-inch loaf pan with nonstick cooking spray.

• In a large bowl, beat oil, sugar and eggs 3 minutes, until well combined and fluffy. Beat in carrots until just combined. In a separate bowl, whisk together white whole wheat flour, all-purpose flour, baking powder and salt. Beat dry mixture into wet mixture until just combined. Stir in coconut and, if desired, macadamia nuts.

• Transfer the mixture to pan, smoothing out the top. Bake at 350° for 55 minutes to 1 hour. Cool 15 minutes in pan, then turn onto a rack and cool completely. Wrap in plastic wrap, then aluminum foil.

PER SERVING 297 **CAL**; 14 g **FAT** (12 g **SAT**); 5 g **PRO**; 39 g **CARB**; 3 g **FIBER**; 151 mg **SODIUM**; 42 mg **CHOL**

MINI BACON-BROCCOLI QUICHES

Mini Bacon-Broccoli Quiches

MAKES 12 quiches **PREP** 15 minutes **COOK** 10 minutes **BAKE** at 375° for 25 minutes
MICROWAVE 45 seconds

3	**cups broccoli florets**
4	**ounces (6 strips) turkey bacon**
9	**eggs**
3	**egg whites**
½	**cup 2% milk**
½	**cup grated cheddar**
½	**teaspoon salt**
¼	**teaspoon pepper**

• Heat oven to 375°. Bring a large pot of lightly salted water to a boil. Add broccoli. Cook 3 minutes; drain. Roughly chop and cool slightly. Set aside.

• Meanwhile, heat a skillet over medium heat. Cook bacon until crispy, 8 to 10 minutes. Dice and set aside to cool.

• Whisk the eggs, egg whites and milk together. Stir in cheese, salt, pepper, broccoli and bacon.

• Coat a 12-cup nonstick muffin tin with nonstick cooking spray. Ladle mixture among cups. Bake at 375° for 20 to 25 minutes, until cooked through.

• Cool slightly. Remove quiches with a small offset spatula. Cool completely and refrigerate.

• To serve: Wrap a mini quiche in a paper towel and microwave for 30 to 45 seconds, until warm.

PER QUICHE 111 **CAL**; 7 g **FAT** (3 g **SAT**); 9 g **PRO**; 2 g **CARB**; 1 g **FIBER**; 316 mg **SODIUM**; 173 mg **CHOL**

BANANA NUT OATMEAL

Silver Dollar Pancake Breakfast Sandwiches

MAKES 6 sandwiches **PREP** 15 minutes
COOK 8 minutes **MICROWAVE** 90 seconds

¾	cup white whole wheat flour
½	teaspoon baking powder
¼	teaspoon baking soda
½	teaspoon salt
3	whole eggs plus 2 egg whites
¾	cup buttermilk
1	tablespoon sugar
1	tablespoon unsalted butter, melted
	Special equipment: Silver dollar pancake pan
⅛	teaspoon pepper
1	box (8 ounces) maple-flavor veggie sausage patties, unwrapped

• In a large bowl, whisk together flour, baking powder, baking soda and ¼ teaspoon of the salt. In another bowl, beat 1 of the whole eggs, then whisk in buttermilk, sugar and melted butter. Stir dry mixture into wet mixture until just combined. In a third bowl, whisk together remaining 2 whole eggs, the egg whites, remaining ¼ teaspoon salt and the pepper.

• Heat a silver dollar pancake pan over medium heat. Coat with nonstick cooking spray. Spoon 2 tablespoons of the batter into each cavity; spread batter with an offset spatula if necessary. Cook pancakes until bubbles appear, about 2 minutes. Flip and cook 1 minute, until browned. Remove pancakes; spray pan again and cook 5 more pancakes (2 cavities will be empty). Remove pancakes and spray again. Pour beaten egg mixture evenly into 6 of the cavities. Cook 1 to 1½ minutes; flip and cook another 30 seconds.

• To assemble: Stack an egg patty on top of a pancake; add an unwrapped frozen sausage patty and top with another pancake. Freeze in individual resealable bags until using.

• To serve: Wrap frozen sandwich in a paper towel and reheat on a microwave-safe plate for 45 seconds. Flip sandwich and heat another 30 to 45 seconds, until heated through.

PER SERVING 215 **CAL**; 8 g **FAT** (3 g **SAT**); 15 g **PRO**; 19 g **CARB**; 3 g **FIBER**; 614 mg **SODIUM**; 112 mg **CHOL**

Banana-Nut Oatmeal

MAKES 8 servings **PREP** 10 minutes **COOK** 10 minutes **REFRIGERATE** overnight
MICROWAVE 2 minutes

2	cups steel-cut oats
½	teaspoon salt
3	large very ripe bananas, mashed
¼	cup packed light brown sugar, plus more for serving (optional)
1	tablespoon fresh lemon juice
8	12-ounce canning jars with metal rings and lids
½	cup buttermilk or milk
½	cup chopped walnuts
	Sliced bananas, for garnish (optional)

• In a medium pot, combine oats, 5 cups water and salt; bring to a boil. Reduce to a simmer and cover. Cook 10 minutes. (Oatmeal will be very watery.) Remove from heat; stir in bananas, sugar and lemon juice. Distribute oatmeal evenly among glass jars; screw on lids. Cool on countertop and refrigerate overnight.

• To serve: Remove metal rings and lids. For each jar, stir in 1 tablespoon buttermilk, 1 tablespoon chopped walnuts and, if desired, additional brown sugar. Reheat in microwave for 1½ to 2 minutes, until hot; let stand 1 minute. Carefully remove, stir and garnish with sliced bananas, if desired.

PER SERVING 266 **CAL**; 8 g **FAT** (1 g **SAT**); 8 g **PRO**; 47 g **CARB**; 6 g **FIBER**; 165 mg **SODIUM**; 1 mg **CHOL**

SILVER DOLLAR PANCAKE
BREAKFAST SANDWICHES

HEALTHY FAMILY DINNERS

Simple prep on Sunday jump-starts delicious meals all week long.

SUNDAY PREP

- ❑ **Prepare a batch of meatballs** (see below)
- ❑ **Assemble and bake gratin** (see page 275)
- ❑ **Cook brown rice** (see below)
- ❑ **Cook quinoa** (see below)
- ❑ **Stuff chicken; prep veggies for roasting** (see page 276)
- ❑ **Finely dice 2 large onions** (for soup, portobellos and fried rice)
- ❑ **Dice 1 each sweet yellow, red and orange peppers** (for gratin, burritos and soup)
- ❑ **Chop 3 cloves garlic** (for soup and fried rice)

Meatballs

MAKES 90 meatballs **PREP** 25 minutes
COOK 15 minutes

1	package (20.8 ounces) ground turkey
1	pound ground chicken
1	large egg
⅓	cup seasoned bread crumbs
½	teaspoon dried Italian seasoning
½	teaspoon salt
½	teaspoon ground black pepper
3	tablespoons olive oil

• Combine turkey, chicken, egg, bread crumbs, Italian seasoning, salt and pepper in a bowl. Gently work together with your hands until mixed.

• Have a bowl of water handy. With wet hands, form 90 meatballs (rewetting hands as needed), using about 1 scant tablespoon for each.

• Heat 1 tablespoon of the oil in a large skillet over medium-high heat. Brown one-third of the meatballs on all sides, shaking pan to maintain shape, for 5 minutes. Transfer to a platter; repeat twice more with remaining oil and meatballs.

• Refrigerate the meatballs in a resealable container. Save half for Italian Wedding Soup (page 276). Use the remaining half for Rigatoni and Meatball Gratin (page 275).

Quinoa

MAKES 4½ cups **PREP** 5 minutes
COOK 20 minutes

1¼	cups dry quinoa
¼	teaspoon salt
½	teaspoon oil

• Bring 2 cups water to a boil in a medium lidded saucepan. Add quinoa, salt and oil. Cover and reduce heat to medium-low. Simmer 15 to 20 minutes, until water is absorbed.

• Store cooked quinoa in a resealable container for Black Bean and Quinoa Burritos (page 275). Refrigerate until needed.

Brown Rice

MAKES 5½ cups **PREP** 5 minutes
COOK 45 minutes **LET STAND** 5 minutes

1⅓	cups brown rice
½	teaspoon salt

• Combine 2¾ cups water, brown rice and salt in a medium lidded saucepan. Bring to a boil and stir once. Cover, reduce heat to medium-low and simmer 40 minutes until almost all the water is absorbed. Let stand, covered, 5 minutes.

• Store cooked rice in a resealable container for Stuffed Chicken Breasts (page 276) and Shrimp Fried Rice (page 277). Refrigerate until needed.

SUNDAY

Rigatoni and Meatball Gratin

MAKES 8 servings PREP 15 minutes
COOK 14 minutes BAKE at 350° for 45 minutes

1	pound rigatoni
1¼	cups diced sweet peppers
45	meatballs (see page 274)
1	jar (28 ounces) marinara sauce
1	cup shredded cheddar-Jack cheese
1	package (15 ounces) fat-free or part-skim ricotta cheese

• Bring a large pot of lightly salted water to a boil. Heat oven to 350°.

• Add rigatoni to boiling water and cook al dente, as per package directions, about 14 minutes. Add peppers during last 2 minutes. Drain and return to pot.

• Stir in meatballs, marinara sauce and shredded cheese. Transfer to a greased 2½-quart baking dish. Top with spoonfuls of ricotta.

• Carefully cover with foil and bake at 350° for 25 minutes. Uncover and continue to bake for an additional 20 minutes or until bubbly. Stir gently before serving.

PER SERVING 506 CAL; 18 g FAT (6 g SAT); 31 g PRO; 54 g CARB; 4 g FIBER; 713 mg SODIUM; 95 mg CHOL

RIGATONI AND MEATBALL GRATIN

BLACK BEAN AND QUINOA BURRITOS

MONDAY

Black Bean and Quinoa Burritos

MAKES 6 servings PREP 15 minutes COOK 6 minutes MICROWAVE 30 seconds
BAKE at 350° for 25 minutes

1	tablespoon vegetable oil
1¼	cups diced sweet peppers
2	scallions, sliced
1	tablespoon chili powder
1	can (15.5 ounces) low-sodium black beans, drained and rinsed
1	tablespoon lime juice
2	cups cooked quinoa (see page 274)
⅔	cup jarred medium salsa, plus more for serving (optional)
6	burrito-size tortillas
1	cup shredded cheddar-Jack cheese blend
	Sour cream for serving (optional)

• Heat oven to 350°. Heat oil in a large nonstick skillet over medium heat. Add peppers, scallions and chili powder; cook 5 minutes. Stir in beans and lime juice; cook 1 more minute. Remove from heat.

• Meanwhile, in a medium bowl, combine quinoa and salsa. Microwave tortillas for 30 seconds to soften.

• Spread a tortilla on a work surface. Top with ⅓ cup of the pepper mixture, a heaping 2 tablespoons cheese and ⅓ cup quinoa. Fold up, envelope-style, to enclose filling. Place seam side down on a foil-lined baking sheet. Repeat with remaining tortillas, pepper mixture, cheese and quinoa.

• Bake at 350° for 20 to 25 minutes until hot (filling should register 150°). Serve with sour cream and additional salsa, if desired.

PER SERVING 419 CAL; 15 g FAT (8 g SAT); 12 g PRO; 64 g CARB; 7 g FIBER; 795 mg SODIUM; 37 mg CHOL

STUFFED CHICKEN BREASTS WITH ROASTED VEGETABLES AND HERBED BROWN RICE

TUESDAY

Stuffed Chicken Breasts with Roasted Vegetables and Herbed Brown Rice

MAKES 6 servings PREP 20 minutes COOK 12 minutes ROAST at 425° for 30 minutes
MICROWAVE 2 minutes

3	ounces feta cheese, crumbled (¾ cup)
¼	cup soft sun-dried tomatoes, chopped
1	tablespoon unsalted butter, softened
2	teaspoons fresh oregano, minced
½	teaspoon salt
½	teaspoon black pepper
12	thin-sliced chicken breast halves (about 2 pounds)
12	thin slices Genoa salami
1	pound carrots, peeled and cut into sticks
½	pound green beans, trimmed
7	teaspoons olive oil
2	cups cooked brown rice (see page 274)
1	tablespoon fresh parsley, chopped

• In a bowl, with a fork, mash together feta cheese, sun-dried tomatoes, butter, 1 teaspoon of the oregano, ¼ teaspoon of the salt, ¼ teaspoon of the pepper and 2 tablespoons warm water.

• Place 6 pieces of the chicken on a cutting board. Press about 2 tablespoons of the cheese mixture down the center of each piece of chicken. Sandwich with remaining pieces of chicken, making sure to cover all the filling. Wrap each piece of stuffed chicken with 2 slices of the salami, pressing to adhere. Wrap each piece in plastic and refrigerate until cooking.

• Place carrot sticks, green beans, 3 teaspoons of the oil, remaining ¼ teaspoon each of the salt and pepper in a resealable plastic bag. Toss to coat; refrigerate until roasting.

• Heat oven to 425°. Heat 2 teaspoons of the remaining olive oil in a large stainless-steel skillet over medium-high heat. Remove plastic from chicken and brown 3 pieces for 3 minutes. Flip and brown an additional 3 minutes. Transfer to a large baking dish. Repeat with remaining oil and chicken.

• Meanwhile, spread carrots and green beans on a large baking sheet. Roast at 425° for 10 minutes; stir. Add browned chicken to oven and roast veggies and chicken for an additional 15 to 20 minutes, until veggies are tender and internal temperature of chicken registers 165°.

• Warm rice in microwave 2 minutes. Stir in remaining 1 teaspoon oregano and the parsley. Serve with chicken and vegetables.

PER SERVING 404 CAL; 17 g FAT (6 g SAT); 37 g PRO; 23 g CARB; 4 g FIBER; 726 mg SODIUM; 110 mg CHOL

WEDNESDAY

Italian Wedding Soup

MAKES 6 servings PREP 10 minutes
COOK 18 minutes

2	tablespoons olive oil
1¼	cups diced sweet peppers
⅔	cup diced onion
3	carrots, peeled and diced
1½	teaspoons minced garlic
1	large bouillon cube
½	teaspoon Italian seasoning
½	teaspoon salt
1¼	cups pearl couscous
45	meatballs (see page 274)
1	can (14.5 ounces) diced tomatoes
1	bag (6 ounces) baby spinach
	Grated Parmesan (optional)

• Heat oil in a large pot over medium heat. Add peppers, onion and carrots and sauté for 5 minutes. Stir in garlic; cook 1 minute.

• Add 8 cups water, the bouillon cube, Italian seasoning and salt to pot. Increase heat to high and bring to a boil. Stir in couscous, reduce heat to medium-high and simmer mixture for 10 minutes.

• Stir in meatballs, diced tomatoes with their liquid and spinach. Cook 2 minutes, until spinach is wilted and meatballs are heated. Serve with Parmesan, if desired.

PER SERVING 385 CAL; 17 g FAT (4 g SAT); 21 g PRO; 37 g CARB; 6 g FIBER; 733 mg SODIUM; 102 mg CHOL

ITALIAN WEDDING SOUP

SAUSAGE-AND-QUINOA-TOPPED PORTOBELLOS

THURSDAY

Sausage-and-Quinoa-Topped Portobellos

MAKES 6 servings   **PREP** 5 minutes
COOK 7 minutes   **BAKE** at 400° for 20 minutes

1	pound mild pork sausage links, casings removed
⅔	cup diced onion
2½	cups cooked quinoa (see page 274)
¼	cup fresh parsley leaves, chopped
1	tablespoon balsamic vinegar
1	large egg, lightly beaten
6	tablespoons shredded Asiago cheese
3	tablespoons plain dry bread crumbs
12	portobello mushroom caps
9	cups mixed green salad (optional)

• Heat oven to 400°. Heat a large nonstick skillet over medium-high heat. Crumble in sausage and add onion. Cook 5 minutes, breaking sausage apart with a wooden spoon.

• Stir in quinoa and cook 2 minutes. Remove from heat. Stir in parsley and balsamic vinegar and let cool slightly. Fold in egg and 3 tablespoons of the shredded Asiago. In a small bowl, combine remaining 3 tablespoons shredded Asiago and the bread crumbs.

• Coat rounded side of mushroom caps with nonstick cooking spray. Place rounded side down on 2 large baking sheets. Divide filling among mushroom caps, about ⅓ cup per portobello. Sprinkle each with ½ tablespoon of the bread crumb mixture.

• Bake at 400° for 18 to 20 minutes, until tops are browned and filling registers 160° on an instant-read thermometer. Serve 2 mushroom caps per person with, if desired, 1½ cups green salad on the side.

PER SERVING 322 **CAL**; 15 g **FAT** (5 g **SAT**); 18 g **PRO**; 28 g **CARB**; 4 g **FIBER**; 632 mg **SODIUM**; 63 mg **CHOL**

SHRIMP FRIED RICE

FRIDAY

Shrimp Fried Rice

MAKES 6 servings   **PREP** 15 minutes   **COOK** 14 minutes   **LET STAND** 5 minutes

2	tablespoons vegetable oil
⅔	cup diced onion
2	teaspoons chopped garlic
3½	cups cooked brown rice (see page 274)
1	can (8 ounces) sliced water chestnuts, drained
3	large eggs, beaten
1½	pounds frozen raw cleaned shrimp, thawed
1	box (10 ounces) frozen peas, thawed
3	tablespoons low-sodium soy sauce
2	tablespoons rice vinegar
2	teaspoons Sriracha hot sauce

• Heat oil in a large, lidded nonstick skillet over medium heat. Sauté onion for 4 minutes. Add garlic and cook 1 minute.

• Stir in brown rice and water chestnuts. Increase heat to medium-high; cook 1 minute.

• Push rice mixture to one side of pan and add eggs. Cook, scrambling, 1 minute. Stir into rice mixture and add shrimp, peas and soy sauce. Cover and cook 6 to 7 minutes, until shrimp are opaque. Remove from heat and let stand 5 minutes. Stir in vinegar and Sriracha before serving.

PER SERVING 355 **CAL**; 10 g **FAT** (2 g **SAT**); 31 g **PRO**; 34 g **CARB**; 2 g **FIBER**; 664 mg **SODIUM**; 278 mg **CHOL**

MAPLE-BACON
BRUSSELS SPROUTS,
PAGE 299

NOVEMBER

283   303   305

SWEET ON DESSERT

Fresh twists on classic fall flavors.

PUMPKIN CAKE ROLL,
PAGE 286

PEAR UPSIDE-DOWN
CAKE, PAGE 284

The crumble topping on this autumnal pie is essentially granola—oats, almonds and cinnamon—cut together with bits of butter that give it crispness when it bakes. Raisins—a customary ingredient in granola—are included in the filling instead of the topping to keep them from burning.

Apple Granola Pie

MAKES 8 servings PREP 25 minutes BAKE at 400° for 25 minutes, then at 325° for 25 minutes COOL 30 minutes

| 1 | refrigerated rolled piecrust (from a 14.1-ounce package) |

FILLING

4	Granny Smith apples (about 2 pounds), peeled, cored and thinly sliced
½	cup golden raisins
⅓	cup plus 2 tablespoons granulated sugar
2	tablespoons lemon juice
½	teaspoon ground cinnamon
2	tablespoons cornstarch

TOPPING

¾	cup all-purpose flour
½	cup old-fashioned oats (not quick-cooking)
¼	cup packed light brown sugar
¼	teaspoon ground cinnamon
	Pinch of salt
7	tablespoons cold unsalted butter, cut into small pieces
¼	cup sliced almonds

• Heat oven to 400°. Unroll crust and fit into a standard 9-inch pie plate. Flute edge as desired and refrigerate while preparing filling and topping.

• **Filling.** In a large bowl, combine apples, golden raisins, ⅓ cup of the granulated sugar, the lemon juice and ground cinnamon. Toss to coat and let stand for 10 minutes.

• **Topping.** In a medium bowl, whisk together flour, oats, brown sugar, cinnamon and salt. Cut butter into mixture with a pastry blender or rub between your fingers until crumbly. Stir in sliced almonds.

• In a small bowl, combine remaining 2 tablespoons granulated sugar and the cornstarch. Sprinkle over apple mixture and toss to combine. Pour mixture into crust, mounding slightly in center. Cover with topping and transfer to oven.

• Bake at 400° for 25 minutes. Cover pie with foil, reduce oven temperature to 325° and continue baking for 20 to 25 minutes, until apples can be easily pierced with a small knife. Cool at least 30 minutes before slicing.

PER SERVING 447 CAL; 19 g FAT (9 g SAT); 4 g PRO; 69 g CARB; 4 g FIBER; 143 mg SODIUM; 31 mg CHOL

PEAR UPSIDE-DOWN
CAKE

Pear Upside-Down Cake

MAKES 16 servings **PREP** 30 minutes **BAKE** at 350° for 60 minutes **COOL** 5 minutes

2	tablespoons cold unsalted butter
½	cup packed dark brown sugar
2	Bartlett pears (about 1 pound), peeled, cored and thinly sliced
2	cups all-purpose flour
1	tablespoon ground ginger
2	teaspoons baking powder
½	teaspoon salt
½	teaspoon ground cardamom
½	cup (1 stick) unsalted butter, softened
1	cup granulated sugar
2	large eggs
1	teaspoon vanilla extract
⅔	cup milk
	Vanilla or brown sugar ice cream (optional)

• Heat oven to 350°.

• Add cold butter to a 10-inch springform pan. Heat in oven until melted, about 3 minutes. Swirl pan to coat bottom with melted butter. Sprinkle evenly with brown sugar.

• Fan slices of pears over sugar, with pointed ends toward center of pan, overlapping slightly. Set aside.

• In a small bowl, whisk together flour, ginger, baking powder, salt and cardamom. With a stand mixer, beat softened butter in a large bowl until smooth. Add granulated sugar and beat 2 minutes, until creamy. Beat in eggs, one at a time, beating well after each addition. Beat in vanilla.

• On low speed, beat in flour mixture, alternating with milk, beginning and ending with flour mixture. Spoon batter over pears and spread to pan edge with a spatula. Wrap bottom of pan with foil and bake at 350° for 55 to 60 minutes. Test center of cake with a toothpick; if pick tests clean, remove to a wire rack. Cool 5 minutes.

• Invert cake onto plate; remove side of pan. Carefully lift off pan bottom and cool cake to room temperature. Serve slightly warm with ice cream, if desired.

PER SERVING 302 **CAL**; 11 g **FAT** (7 g **SAT**); 4 g PRO; 48 g **CARB**; 2 g **FIBER**; 186 mg **SODIUM**; 62 mg **CHOL**

Maple Pudding with Quick Praline

MAKES 6 servings **PREP** 10 minutes
COOK 11 minutes **REFRIGERATE** 4 hours

3	cups whole milk
3	large egg yolks
3	tablespoons plus 1 teaspoon cornstarch
⅔	cup maple syrup
½	teaspoon maple flavoring
¼	teaspoon salt
	Quick Praline (recipe follows)

• In a medium bowl, whisk together 1 cup of the milk, the egg yolks and cornstarch.

• In a medium saucepan, combine remaining 2 cups milk, the maple syrup, maple flavoring and salt. Cook over medium heat until just steaming, about 6 minutes.

• Whisk about 1½ cups of the hot milk mixture into the egg yolk mixture. Whisk egg-milk mixture back into saucepan. Cook, stirring constantly with a wooden spoon, to a bare simmer, until thick and large bubbles break the surface, about 5 minutes. Strain into 6 dessert cups or glasses. Place plastic wrap directly on surface of puddings and refrigerate at least 4 hours. Just before serving, remove plastic wrap and sprinkle each pudding with a little Quick Praline. Reserve any extra praline for snacking.

PER SERVING 320 **CAL**; 13 g **FAT** (4 g **SAT**); 6 g PRO; 47 g **CARB**; 1 g **FIBER**; 190 mg **SODIUM**; 115 mg **CHOL**

Quick Praline

MAKES 8 servings **PREP** 5 minutes
TOAST at 350° for 10 minutes **COOK** 5 minutes
COOL 30 minutes

• Spread ⅔ **cup pecans** on a baking sheet. Toast at 350° for 10 minutes. Line a large baking sheet with nonstick foil.

• In a small saucepan, combine ½ **cup sugar, 2 tablespoons water** and a pinch of **salt**. Cook over medium-high heat until bubbly, then cook at a low boil without stirring until light amber, about 5 minutes. Stir in pecans until coated and quickly spread onto foil-lined sheet. Cool 30 minutes, then chop into pieces.

MAPLE PUDDING WITH
QUICK PRALINE

When it comes to dessert this time of year, it seems to be all about pies, tarts, crisps and crumbles. For a change of pace, try this creamy and cool cake roll spiced with the warm and familiar flavors of cinnamon, ginger, nutmeg and allspice.

Pumpkin Cake Roll

MAKES 12 servings **PREP** 20 minutes **COOK** 5 minutes **BAKE** at 375° for 12 minutes **COOL** 1 hour **REFRIGERATE** 20 minutes

CAKE

1	cup all-purpose flour
1½	teaspoons baking powder
1	teaspoon pumpkin pie spice, plus more for serving (optional)
¼	teaspoon salt
4	eggs, at room temperature
¾	cup granulated sugar
¾	cup canned pumpkin puree
½	cup confectioners' sugar

FILLING AND FROSTING

¾	cup canned pumpkin puree
1	large egg yolk
6	tablespoons granulated sugar
1½	cups heavy cream

• **Cake.** Heat oven to 375°. Coat a 15 x 10 x 1-inch pan with nonstick cooking spray. Line pan with wax paper; coat paper with spray.

• In a medium bowl, whisk flour, baking powder, pumpkin pie spice and salt.

• In a large bowl or in a stand mixer, whip eggs at medium speed until slightly thickened, about 2 minutes. On high speed, beat in granulated sugar 1 tablespoon at a time until thick and lemon-colored, about 5 to 7 minutes. On low, beat in pumpkin puree. Fold in flour mixture in 2 batches. Spread evenly in prepared pan.

• Bake at 375° for 10 to 12 minutes, until cake springs back slightly when pressed. Meanwhile, sift ¼ cup of the confectioners' sugar over a clean kitchen towel. When cake is done, loosen edges and immediately invert onto prepared towel. Remove pan and wax paper. Sift remaining ¼ cup confectioners' sugar over cake. From a short end, roll up cake with towel, jelly roll fashion. Cool completely on a wire rack for at least an hour.

• **Filling.** In a small saucepan, whisk pumpkin puree, egg yolk and 3 tablespoons of the granulated sugar. Cook for 5 minutes over medium heat, stirring frequently (mixture should reach 160°). Transfer to a medium bowl. Refrigerate for 20 minutes.

• Once cake is cool, gently unroll. Whip ¼ cup of the heavy cream with 1 tablespoon of the remaining granulated sugar to stiff peaks. Fold into filling and spread over cake. Re-roll without towel.

• **Frosting.** Whip remaining 1¼ cups cream with remaining 2 tablespoons sugar to stiff peaks. Spread over cake roll. Dust with a little pumpkin pie spice, if desired. Refrigerate until serving.

PER SERVING 271 **CAL**; 13 g **FAT** (8 g **SAT**); 5 g **PRO**; 35 g **CARB**; 2 g **FIBER**; 135 mg **SODIUM**; 128 mg **CHOL**

BEYOND THE BIRD

Starters and sides that take the celebration up a notch.

GREEN BEANS WITH
CRISPY GARLIC, PAGE 299

SWEET POTATO
GRATIN, PAGE 296

BUTTERNUT
SQUASH-GOAT
CHEESE BITES

Butternut Squash-Goat Cheese Bites

MAKES 30 bites **PREP** 20 minutes
BAKE at 350° for 10 minutes **FRY** 30 seconds

- **1** cup frozen cooked winter squash puree, thawed (such as Birds Eye, from a 12-ounce package)
- **2** tablespoons heavy cream
- **4** ounces soft goat cheese, at room temperature
- **1** egg yolk
- **¾** teaspoon salt
- **⅛** teaspoon ground white pepper
- **2** boxes (1.9 ounces each) Athens Mini Fillo Shells
- **⅓** cup canola oil
- **30** sage leaves

• Heat oven to 350°. In a small pot, whisk together butternut squash and heavy cream over medium-low heat. When hot, whisk in goat cheese until melted. Remove from heat and stir in egg yolk, ½ teaspoon of the salt and the pepper. Cool slightly.

• Place pastry shells on a baking sheet. Transfer squash mixture into a resealable plastic bag; snip corner. Pipe into pastry shells. Bake at 350° for 8 to 10 minutes, until set.

• In a small skillet, heat canola oil until shimmering. Fry sage leaves (in 2 batches) for 30 seconds, until crisp. Remove to a paper towel and sprinkle with remaining ¼ teaspoon salt. Garnish bites with fried sage leaves.

PER BITE 37 **CAL**; 2 g **FAT** (1 g **SAT**); 1 g **PRO**; 3 g **CARB**; 0 g **FIBER**; 81 mg **SODIUM**; 10 mg **CHOL**

CHILE-CHEDDAR MASHED POTATOES

Chile-Cheddar Mashed Potatoes

MAKES 8 servings **PREP** 15 minutes **COOK** 10 minutes

- **2½** pounds baking potatoes, peeled and cut into 1-inch chunks
- **2** large cloves garlic, peeled and halved
- **1** cup 2% milk, heated
- **3** tablespoons unsalted butter
- **4** ounces sharp white cheddar cheese, shredded
- **1** can (4 ounces) diced mild green chiles
- **1** teaspoon salt

• Place diced potatoes and garlic in a lidded pot. Fill with cold water until potatoes are covered by 1 inch. Cover pot and bring to a boil. Reduce heat to a simmer and cook 10 minutes, until fork-tender.

• Drain potatoes and immediately return to pot. Stir in milk and butter; mash until smooth. Stir in cheese, chiles and salt.

PER SERVING 216 **CAL**; 9 g **FAT** (6 g **SAT**); 7 g **PRO**; 27 g **CARB**; 2 g **FIBER**; 451 mg **SODIUM**; 29 mg **CHOL**

CREAMED KALE

Get some greens on the Thanksgiving table: Classic creamed spinach gets an update with nutrient-packed kale.

Creamed Kale

MAKES 8 servings PREP 20 minutes COOK 12 minutes

- 2 **pounds kale, tough stems discarded, roughly chopped**
- 3 **tablespoons unsalted butter**
- ½ **cup finely diced shallots**
- 2 **cloves garlic, chopped**
- 3 **tablespoons all-purpose flour**
- 2 **cups whole milk**
- ¾ **teaspoon salt**
- ⅛ **teaspoon nutmeg**
- ⅛ **teaspoon black pepper**

• Bring a large pot of lightly salted water to a boil. Add chopped kale. Return to a boil and cook 2 minutes. Drain and press out most of the liquid.

• Meanwhile, melt butter in a large skillet over medium heat. Add shallots and sauté 3 minutes, until softened. Add garlic; cook 1 minute. Stir in flour; cook 1 minute. Whisk in milk. Bring to a low simmer and cook 3 to 5 minutes, until thickened. Stir in salt, nutmeg and pepper. Fold in kale until well coated with sauce.

PER SERVING 122 CAL; 7 g FAT (4 g SAT); 4 g PRO; 13 g CARB; 1 g FIBER; 267 mg SODIUM; 17 mg CHOL

Roasted Carrots with Chestnuts and Golden Raisins

MAKES 8 servings PREP 10 minutes
ROAST at 400° for 30 minutes

- 2 **pounds carrots (about ½ to ¾ inch thick), peeled and tops trimmed**
- 2 **tablespoons olive oil**
- ½ **teaspoon salt**
- ¼ **teaspoon pepper**
- 1 **cup peeled and roasted chestnuts, roughly chopped**
- ½ **cup golden raisins**
- 1 **tablespoon honey**

• Heat oven to 400°. On a rimmed baking sheet, toss carrots with olive oil, ¼ teaspoon of the salt and the pepper. Roast at 400° for 15 minutes. Stir in chestnuts, raisins and honey. Roast another 10 to 15 minutes, until fork-tender. Gently toss carrots with remaining ¼ teaspoon salt.

PER SERVING 156 CAL; 4 g FAT (0 g SAT); 2 g PRO; 30 g CARB; 4 g FIBER; 235 mg SODIUM; 0 mg CHOL

ROASTED CARROTS
WITH CHESTNUTS AND
GOLDEN RAISINS

Chorizo-Cornbread Stuffing

MAKES 10 servings **PREP** 15 minutes
COOK 10 minutes **BAKE** at 350° for 30 minutes

6	ounces dried chorizo, diced into ¼-inch pieces
1	tablespoon unsalted butter
3	cloves garlic, chopped
1½	cups frozen corn
1	tablespoon chopped fresh oregano
¾	teaspoon salt
¼	teaspoon plus ⅛ teaspoon black pepper
2	eggs, beaten
1½	cups chicken broth
1	cup sliced scallions
7	cups day-old cornbread, cut into ¾-inch cubes

• Heat oven to 350°. Heat a large skillet over medium heat. Add chorizo; sauté 5 minutes, stirring occasionally. Add butter; melt. Stir in garlic; cook 2 minutes. Raise heat to medium-high and stir in corn; sauté 3 minutes. Mix in oregano and ¼ teaspoon each of the salt and pepper. Set aside.

• In a large bowl, beat eggs, chicken broth, remaining ½ teaspoon salt and remaining ⅛ teaspoon pepper. Stir in scallions and chorizo-corn mixture. Gently fold in cornbread until just combined.

• Coat an 8 x 8-inch baking dish with nonstick cooking spray. Transfer mixture to dish and bake, uncovered, at 350° for 30 minutes, until top is toasted.

PER SERVING 258 **CAL**; 13 g **FAT** (5 g **SAT**); 10 g **PRO**; 26 g **CARB**; 2 g **FIBER**; 929 mg **SODIUM**; 78 mg **CHOL**

CRANBERRY-HIBISCUS SPRITZER

Cranberry-Hibiscus Spritzer

MAKES 8 servings **PREP** 5 minutes **STEEP** 4 minutes

¼	cup plus 2 tablespoons sugar
2	hibiscus tea bags
1	cup chilled unsweetened cranberry juice (such as R.W. Knudsen Just Cranberry)
1	bottle (750 ml) dry sparkling wine, chilled
2	cups ice
1	cup frozen cranberries (for garnish and to keep punch cold)

• In a small, lidded pot, bring 2½ cups water and sugar to a boil. Turn off heat. Add tea bags; cover and steep 4 minutes. Cool.

• In a medium punch bowl, combine cooled tea, cranberry juice, sparkling wine and ice. Stir. Pour in frozen cranberries. Serve cold.

PER SERVING 107 **CAL**; 0 g **FAT**; 0 g **PRO**; 11 g **CARB**; 0 g **FIBER**; 1 mg **SODIUM**; 0 mg **CHOL**

SWEET POTATO GRATIN

Can't decide between sweet potatoes and white potatoes? This rich, two-toned gratin featuring both is elegant and absolutely delicious.

Crab Toasts

MAKES 16 toasts PREP 15 minutes
BAKE at 400° for 12 minutes COOK 5 minutes

1	French baguette (about 12 ounces), cut on the bias into sixteen ½-inch-thick slices
2	tablespoons olive oil
2	tablespoons unsalted butter
1	cup cleaned and sliced leeks
¼	teaspoon crushed red pepper flakes
¼	cup light mayonnaise
¼	cup fresh chopped parsley, plus more for garnish
1	tablespoon fresh lemon juice, plus 1 teaspoon zest
1	teaspoon Dijon mustard
⅛	teaspoon salt
1	pound lump crabmeat, drained

• Heat oven to 400°. Brush baguette slices on both sides with olive oil. Place on a baking sheet. Bake at 400° for 7 minutes; flip and bake another 5 minutes.

• Melt butter in a skillet. Add leeks and red pepper flakes; sauté on medium heat for 5 minutes, until soft. Cool.

• In a bowl, mix sautéed leeks with mayonnaise, parsley, lemon juice and zest, mustard and salt. Gently fold in crabmeat. Evenly spoon mixture onto toasts. Garnish with parsley. Chill in refrigerator until serving.

PER TOAST 134 CAL; 5 g FAT (2 g SAT); 8 g PRO; 13 g CARB; 1 g FIBER; 290 mg SODIUM; 30 mg CHOL

Sweet Potato Gratin

MAKES 12 servings PREP 30 minutes BAKE at 400° for 55 minutes COOL 15 minutes

3	cloves garlic, chopped
1	tablespoon chopped fresh rosemary
1	tablespoon chopped fresh thyme
2	pounds sweet potatoes, peeled and sliced ⅛ inch thick
1	pound baking potatoes, peeled and sliced ⅛ inch thick
1¼	teaspoons salt
¼	teaspoon plus ⅛ teaspoon black pepper
5	ounces Gruyère cheese, grated
1	cup heavy cream, heated

• Heat oven to 400°. In a small bowl, mix together chopped garlic, rosemary and thyme. In a 2-quart baking dish, layer one-third of the sweet potato and baking potato slices, slightly overlapping some of the edges. Sprinkle with ¼ teaspoon of the salt, ⅛ teaspoon of the pepper, half the garlic-herb mixture and one-third of the shredded cheese. Repeat layering a second and third time. Mix remaining ½ teaspoon salt with heavy cream; pour over potatoes.

• Place baking dish on a rimmed baking sheet. Cover with aluminum foil. Bake at 400° for 30 minutes. Uncover and bake another 25 minutes, until bubbling and top is golden-brown. Cool 15 minutes before serving.

PER SERVING 178 CAL; 11 g FAT (7 g SAT); 5 g PRO; 15 g CARB; 2 g FIBER; 310 mg SODIUM; 40 mg CHOL

CRAB TOASTS

MAPLE-BACON
BRUSSELS SPROUTS

Try something different this year. Instead of the ubiquitous green bean casserole (which can be a bit heavy), serve this crisp and light green-bean dish flavored with ginger, sesame and slices of caramelized garlic.

GREEN BEANS WITH CRISPY GARLIC

Maple-Bacon Brussels Sprouts

MAKES 8 servings **PREP** 15 minutes
COOK 23 minutes

8	**ounces maple bacon, diced**
2	**pounds Brussels sprouts, trimmed and halved**
½	**cup heavy cream**
¼	**cup pure maple syrup**
¾	**teaspoon salt**
¼	**teaspoon black pepper**

• Heat a large skillet over medium heat. Cook bacon until crispy, about 8 minutes. Remove with a slotted spoon to a paper-towel-lined plate.

• In the same pan, pour off all but 3 tablespoons of the bacon fat (if not enough fat, add canola oil to compensate). Add Brussels sprouts and cook 10 minutes, stirring occasionally. Pour in heavy cream; reduce by half, about 3 minutes. Stir in cooked bacon, maple syrup, salt and pepper. Cook 2 more minutes, until Brussels sprouts are tender and sauce has thickened.

PER SERVING 215 **CAL**; 15 g **FAT** (7 g **SAT**); 7 g **PRO**; 16 g **CARB**; 4 g **FIBER**; 473 mg **SODIUM**; 35 mg **CHOL**

Green Beans with Crispy Garlic

MAKES 8 servings **PREP** 15 minutes **COOK** 8 minutes, 30 seconds

¼	**cup canola oil**
8	**large cloves garlic, thinly sliced**
1½	**pounds green beans, trimmed and cut on the bias**
1	**teaspoon salt**
3	**tablespoons rice vinegar**
1	**tablespoon grated ginger**
2	**tablespoons sesame seeds**
1	**teaspoon sesame oil**

• In a small skillet, heat canola oil until shimmering. Fry garlic cloves for 15 to 30 seconds, until golden. (Be careful not to burn.) Remove garlic with a slotted spoon to a paper-towel-lined plate. Carefully pour 2 tablespoons of the oil into a large skillet and place on medium heat.

• Add beans, ⅔ cup water and ½ teaspoon of the salt. Increase heat to medium-high. Bring to a boil and cook 5 to 7 minutes, until liquid evaporates and beans are tender-crisp. Add rice vinegar and ginger; cook 1 minute. Stir in sesame seeds, sesame oil and remaining ½ teaspoon salt. Transfer to a serving platter and garnish with crispy garlic.

PER SERVING 67 **CAL**; 4 g **FAT** (1 g **SAT**); 2 g **PRO**; 8 g **CARB**; 3 g **FIBER**; 293 mg **SODIUM**; 0 mg **CHOL**

FUN FALL DESSERTS

For the holidays or just because—here are some new ways to enjoy autumnal treats.

CARAMEL APPLE
CAKE IN A JAR

CHOCOLATE
TIRAMISU IN A JAR

CARROT CAKE
IN A JAR

MACARONS

FROSTED
PUMPKINS

WHOOPIE PIES

Caramel Apple Cake in a Jar

MAKES 12 desserts **PREP** 25 minutes
BAKE at 325° for 28 minutes **COOK** 8 minutes

CAKE

1	box (18.25 ounces) yellow cake mix
⅓	cup vegetable oil
3	eggs
1	Gala apple, peeled, cored and coarsely grated
1	teaspoon ground cinnamon

FILLING

2	tablespoons unsalted butter
	Pinch of salt
3	Gala apples, peeled, cored and diced into ¼-inch pieces
⅛	teaspoon ground cinnamon
1¼	cups heavy cream
1	tablespoon sugar
12	9-ounce canning jars
1½	cups jarred caramel, plus more for drizzling

• **Cake.** Heat oven to 325°. Coat 12 cups of a jumbo muffin tin with nonstick cooking spray. (**Note:** Cake can alternately be baked in a 15 x 10 x 1-inch jelly roll pan; follow baking and layering instructions for Chocolate Tiramisu in a Jar at right.)

• Prepare cake mix as per package directions with oil, eggs and 1 cup water. Fold in grated apple and cinnamon. Divide evenly among prepared muffin cups. Bake at 325° for 25 to 28 minutes, until crowned slightly and dry to the touch.

• Cool in pans for 10 minutes, then run a thin knife or spatula around edge and remove cakes directly to a wire rack; cool completely.

• **Filling.** Melt butter in a large nonstick skillet over medium heat. Add salt, diced apples and cinnamon. Cook 7 to 8 minutes, until slightly tender. Set aside.

• Whip heavy cream and sugar to medium-stiff peaks.

• Once cakes have cooled, slice each in half horizontally. Fit 1 cake round into a jar, pressing with fingers until flush with bottom of jar. Top with 1 tablespoon of the caramel, 1 tablespoon of the apple mixture and 2 tablespoons of the whipped cream. Repeat layers of cake, 1 tablespoon of the caramel and 1 tablespoon of the apple mixture. Repeat process in remaining jars. Refrigerate, then top with a dollop of whipped cream and drizzle with a little of the remaining caramel just before serving.

PER JAR (1 TO 2 SERVINGS) 477 **CAL**; 24 g **FAT** (9 g **SAT**); 5 g **PRO**; 65 g **CARB**; 2 g **FIBER**; 430 mg **SODIUM**; 93 mg **CHOL**

Chocolate Tiramisu in a Jar

MAKES 8 desserts **PREP** 25 minutes
BAKE at 350° for 22 minutes

CAKE

1	box (18.25 ounces) French vanilla cake mix
1⅓	cups brewed coffee, cooled slightly
⅓	cup vegetable oil
3	eggs
3	tablespoons unsweetened cocoa powder
⅛	teaspoon ground cinnamon

FILLING

1	package (8 ounces) Neufchâtel cheese, softened
1¼	cups heavy cream
1	container (6 ounces) low-fat French vanilla yogurt
5	tablespoons sugar
8	9-ounce canning jars
1	cup brewed coffee
2	ounces semisweet chocolate

• **Cake.** Heat oven to 350°. Coat a 15 x 10 x 1-inch jelly roll pan with nonstick cooking spray. Line pan with wax paper; coat paper with spray. (**Note:** Cake can alternately be baked in a jumbo muffin tin; follow baking and layering instructions for Caramel Apple Cake in a Jar at left.)

• Prepare cake mix according to package directions, substituting coffee for water and using oil, eggs, cocoa powder and cinnamon. Spread into prepared pan. Bake at 350° for 22 minutes or until dry to the touch. Cool in pan on a wire rack for 10 minutes, then invert onto rack and remove wax paper. Cool completely.

• **Filling.** In a medium bowl, beat together Neufchâtel, ½ cup of the heavy cream, the yogurt and ¼ cup of the sugar on medium speed until blended and fluffy. Beat remaining ¾ cup heavy cream with remaining 1 tablespoon sugar.

• Use a 2¾-inch cookie cutter to cut 8 cake rounds. Cut 8 more rounds with a 2½-inch cookie cutter. Trim cakes level.

• Use the back of a spoon to spread 2 tablespoons of the whipped cream in bottom of a jar. Grate ½ tablespoon semisweet chocolate over whipped cream (a Microplane grater works well for this). Top with 1 of the 2½-inch cake layers, compressing with fingers to fit. Spoon 1 tablespoon of the brewed coffee over cake layer and allow to soak into cake. Top cake with another 2 tablespoons of the Neufchâtel mixture and ½ tablespoon grated chocolate. Place a 2¾-inch cake layer over chocolate and spoon 1 tablespoon of the brewed coffee over cake. Let soak. Top with another 2 tablespoons of the Neufchâtel mixture and ½ tablespoon grated chocolate. Dollop with whipped cream and more grated chocolate. Repeat process in remaining jars, using all cake layers and filling. Refrigerate until serving.

PER JAR (1 TO 2 SERVINGS) 498 **CAL**; 33 g **FAT** (16 g **SAT**); 7 g **PRO**; 45 g **CARB**; 1 g **FIBER**; 378 mg **SODIUM**; 113 mg **CHOL**

Carrot Cake in a Jar

MAKES 8 desserts **PREP** 25 minutes
BAKE at 350° for 18 minutes

CAKE

1	box (18.25 ounces) spice cake mix
⅓	cup vegetable oil
3	eggs
1	cup grated fresh carrot

FILLING

1	package (8 ounces) Neufchâtel cheese, softened
1	cup heavy cream
¼	cup plus 1 teaspoon sugar
1	teaspoon vanilla extract
8	9-ounce canning jars
¾	cup glazed walnuts, coarsely chopped

• **Cake.** Heat oven to 350°. Coat two 13 x 9 x 2-inch baking pans with nonstick cooking spray. Line pan bottoms with wax paper; coat paper with spray.

• Prepare cake mix according to package directions with oil, eggs and 1⅓ cups water. Fold in grated carrot. Divide evenly between prepared pans and spread level. Bake at 350° for 18 minutes or until dry to the touch and cakes have pulled slightly away from edges of pans. Cool in pans for 10 minutes, then invert onto wire racks and remove wax paper.

• **Filling.** In a medium bowl, beat Neufchâtel, ¾ cup of the cream and ¼ cup of the sugar until smooth and fluffy. Beat in vanilla extract.

• In a separate bowl, beat remaining ¼ cup cream and remaining 1 teaspoon sugar to medium-stiff peaks.

• Cut 16 rounds of cake with a 2½-inch cookie cutter. Cut 8 rounds with a 2¾-inch cutter (keep cuts close together in order to fit). Place one 2½-inch round into bottom of a jar, compressing with fingers to fit. Spread with 2 tablespoons of the cream cheese filling and 2 teaspoons of the coarsely chopped nuts. Repeat layering with a second 2½-inch cake layer, 2 tablespoons of the cream cheese and 2 teaspoons of the nuts. Top with one 2¾-inch cake layer. Repeat process in other jars with remaining cake rounds and most of the remaining cream cheese filling and nuts. Fold remaining cream cheese filling (about ⅓ cup) into whipped cream. Top each jar with 2 tablespoons of the whipped cream mixture and sprinkle with a few nuts to garnish.

PER JAR (1 TO 2 SERVINGS) 644 **CAL**; 38 g **FAT** (14 g **SAT**); 9 g **PRO**; 68 g **CARB**; 1 g **FIBER**; 650 mg **SODIUM**; 140 mg **CHOL**

Macarons

MAKES 36 servings **PREP** 8 minutes **LET STAND** 20 minutes **BAKE** at 350° for 30 minutes

COOKIES

1½	cups sifted confectioners' sugar
¾	cup sifted almond flour (such as Bob's Red Mill)
3	egg whites
	Pinch of salt
3	tablespoons granulated sugar
3	drops orange gel food coloring

GANACHE

4	ounces bittersweet chocolate, chopped
½	cup heavy cream

FILLING

1	stick (½ cup) unsalted butter, softened
2	cups confectioners' sugar
	Pinch of salt
2	to 3 tablespoons heavy cream
	Orange gel food coloring

• **Cookies.** Combine confectioners' sugar and almond flour in a food processor. Pulse until blended and finely ground. Line 2 large baking sheets with parchment paper. Heat oven to 350°.

• Whip egg whites and salt in a stand mixer on medium-high speed until frothy. Gradually beat in granulated sugar, 1 tablespoon at a time, until stiff peaks form, about 2 minutes.

• Fold one-third of the confectioners' sugar mixture into beaten whites. Fold in remaining confectioners' sugar mixture and the food coloring. Transfer to a large piping bag (use half the batter so bag is not overfilled) and snip off a ½-inch opening.

• Pipe batter in 1¼-inch circles onto parchment paper. Let stand at room temperature for 15 to 20 minutes.

• Bake cookies, one sheet at a time, at 350° for 15 minutes. Cool completely on paper on wire racks.

• **Ganache.** Place chopped chocolate in a small bowl. In a small saucepan, heat cream just until steaming. Pour over chocolate and stir until smooth. Refrigerate until good spreading consistency.

• **Filling.** Beat butter until smooth. Add confectioners' sugar and salt; beat on low speed until blended. Add heavy cream and beat until good spreading consistency. Divide in half; tint half orange with gel food coloring.

• Carefully remove cookies from parchment. Spread ganache or white or orange filling onto flat side of a cookie. Sandwich with a second cookie. Repeat with all cookies.

PER SERVING 117 **CAL**; 7 g **FAT** (3 g **SAT**); 1 g **PRO**; 15 g **CARB**; 0 g **FIBER**; 8 mg **SODIUM**; 13 mg **CHOL**

Whoopie Pies

MAKES 12 servings **PREP** 20 minutes
BAKE at 350° for 13 minutes

COOKIES

1½	cups all-purpose flour
½	cup unsweetened cocoa powder
½	teaspoon baking soda
¼	teaspoon salt
½	cup (1 stick) unsalted butter, softened
¾	cup packed light brown sugar
1	large egg
1	teaspoon vanilla extract
1	cup buttermilk or sour milk

FILLING

¼	cup (½ stick) unsalted butter, softened
4	ounces (½ package) cream cheese, softened

1   jar (7 ounces) marshmallow crème
        Orange gel food coloring

• **Cookies.** Heat oven to 350°. Have 2 whoopie pie pans ready. In a medium bowl, whisk flour, cocoa powder, baking soda and salt.

• In a large bowl, beat butter with an electric mixer for 30 seconds, until creamy. Beat in brown sugar for 1 minute, until fluffy, and beat in egg for 1 minute. Beat in vanilla. On low speed, beat in flour mixture, alternating with buttermilk, beginning and ending with flour. Divide evenly between pans, spreading batter slightly until level.

• Bake at 350° for 11 to 13 minutes or until dry to the touch. Remove from pans to a wire rack to cool.

• **Filling.** In a medium bowl, beat butter and cream cheese until smooth. Fold in marshmallow crème and tint with food coloring to desired color. Spread 1 to 2 tablespoons of the filling onto flat side of a cookie. Sandwich with a second cookie. Repeat; refrigerate pies in an airtight container up to 4 days. Let stand at room temperature before serving.

PER SERVING 338 **CAL**; 16 g **FAT** (10 g **SAT**); 4 g **PRO**; 46 g **CARB**; 1 g **FIBER**; 178 mg **SODIUM**; 59 mg **CHOL**

Frosted Pumpkins

MAKES 12 servings   PREP 25 minutes
BAKE at 350° for 36 minutes

CAKE
1   package (16 ounces) pound cake mix
¼   cup (½ stick) unsalted butter, softened
2   large eggs
⅔   cup milk or water
2   teaspoons pumpkin pie spice

FROSTING
¾   cup (1½ sticks) unsalted butter, softened
4   cups confectioners' sugar
6   tablespoons milk

1   teaspoon vanilla extract
        Orange gel or paste food coloring
        Assorted brown paper cupcake liners
        Pretzel rods

• **Cake.** Heat oven to 350°. Generously coat 1 mini Bundt pan (or 2 pans if you have them) with nonstick cooking spray.

• Prepare cake mix as per package directions, with butter, eggs, milk and pumpkin pie spice. Spoon batter into Bundt cups, filling each halfway. Bake at 350° for 15 to 18 minutes or until dry to the touch. Cool cakes in pan on a wire rack for 5 minutes, then turn out directly onto rack.

• Clean pan, coat again with spray and make a second batch of cakes. Let cakes cool completely.

• **Frosting.** Beat butter in a large bowl until creamy. Gradually add confectioners' sugar and milk. Beat on low speed until good spreading consistency, adding more milk as needed. Beat in vanilla and divide frosting into thirds. Tint varying shades of orange with food coloring.

• Trim cakes level and sandwich 2 of them with a little frosting. Spread frosting on sandwiched cakes, starting at the bottom and spreading toward top in lines to resemble the ridges on a pumpkin. Place pumpkin in a paper liner. Top with a pretzel piece trimmed to look like a stem. Repeat with all cakes, frosting and pretzels, varying the frosting color for variety.

PER SERVING 489 **CAL**; 22 g **FAT** 12 g **SAT**); 3 g **PRO**; 70 g **CARB**; 1 g **FIBER**; 234 mg **SODIUM**; 77 mg **CHOL**

NEW IN THE SLOW COOKER

Lasagna, lentil soup and more delicious fall recipes.

SAUSAGE AND
VEGGIE LASAGNA

Sausage and Veggie Lasagna

MAKES 8 servings **PREP** 25 minutes
COOK 6 minutes **SLOW COOK** on LOW for
4 hours **COOL** 30 minutes

1	pound chicken sausage, casings removed
1	package (8 ounces) sliced mushrooms
2	large carrots, peeled and grated
1	zucchini (8 ounces), trimmed and grated
1	jar (24 ounces) marinara sauce
1	container (15 ounces) part-skim ricotta cheese
1	bag (7 ounces) 2% shredded Italian cheese blend
⅓	cup fresh basil, chopped
12	traditional lasagna noodles (not no-boil)

• Line a 5-quart slow cooker with a slow cooker liner. Coat liner with nonstick cooking spray. Crumble sausage into a nonstick skillet and cook over medium to medium-high heat for 6 minutes, breaking apart with a wooden spoon.

• Meanwhile, in a large bowl, combine mushrooms, carrots, zucchini and 1 cup of the marinara sauce. Stir remaining sauce into the sausage.

• In a medium bowl, stir together ricotta, 1 cup of the shredded cheese and the basil.

• Begin layering: Break 3 noodles into thirds and spread on bottom of slow cooker. Top with half the vegetable mixture, spreading level, and 3 more noodles, broken into thirds. Spread noodles with sausage sauce and top with 3 more noodles, broken into thirds. Spread noodles with ricotta mixture and remaining 3 noodles (in thirds). Top noodles with remaining vegetable mixture and remaining shredded cheese. Cover and slow cook on LOW for 4 hours.

• Remove crock insert from slow cooker and cool for 30 minutes. Uncover and use liner bag to lift lasagna from crock. Remove slow cooker liner and cut lasagna into pieces.

PER SERVING 487 **CAL**; 20 g **FAT** (9 g **SAT**); 33 g **PRO**; 45 g **CARB**; 4 g **FIBER**; 1,083 mg **SODIUM**; 91 mg **CHOL**

BEEF BURGUNDY

Beef Burgundy

MAKES 6 servings **PREP** 15 minutes **COOK** 7 minutes **SLOW COOK** on HIGH for 5 hours or LOW for 6½ hours

2	pounds beef chuck for stew, cut into 1½- to 2-inch chunks
5	tablespoons all-purpose flour
½	teaspoon salt
½	teaspoon black pepper
1	tablespoon unsalted butter
1	tablespoon canola oil
1	can (14.5 ounces) low-sodium beef broth
4	large carrots, peeled and cut on the diagonal into 1½-inch pieces
1	package (10 ounces) brown mushrooms, cleaned (halved or quartered if large)
2	cloves garlic, sliced
1	cup red wine
1	bag (14.4 ounces) frozen pearl onions, thawed
	Mashed potatoes or hot buttered noodles (optional)

• Combine beef in a large resealable plastic bag with 2 tablespoons of the flour, ¼ teaspoon of the salt and the pepper. Shake to coat. Melt butter and oil in a large stainless-steel skillet over medium-high heat. Add beef and brown for 5 minutes, stirring to sear all sides (cook in 2 batches, if needed). Spoon into slow cooker. Reduce heat under pan to medium and add 1 cup of the broth. Cook for 2 minutes, stirring up any brown bits on bottom of pan. Pour into slow cooker along with carrots, mushrooms, garlic, red wine and remaining beef broth. Scatter onions over top of vegetables.

• Cover and slow cook on HIGH for 5 hours or LOW for 6½ hours. With a slotted spoon, remove beef and vegetables to a large serving bowl.

• Whisk together remaining 3 tablespoons flour with 3 tablespoons water in a small bowl. Strain hot liquid from slow cooker into a medium saucepan. Whisk in flour mixture and bring to a boil over medium-high heat. Boil 3 minutes, until thickened, then stir into stew with remaining ¼ teaspoon salt. Serve stew over mashed potatoes or noodles, if desired.

PER SERVING 500 **CAL**; 12 g **FAT** (4 g **SAT**); 39 g **PRO**; 51 g **CARB**; 6 g **FIBER**; 797 mg **SODIUM**; 69 mg **CHOL**

Red Lentil Soup

MAKES 8 servings **PREP** 15 minutes **SLOW COOK** on HIGH for 4 hours or LOW for 6 hours

¾ **cup blanched almonds, plus more for garnish (optional)**

2 **large carrots, peeled and sliced into 2-inch pieces**

1 **medium onion, peeled and quartered**

2 **ribs celery, finely diced**

1 **bag (16 ounces) red lentils**

2 **large vegetable bouillon cubes, crumbled**

1 **tablespoon curry powder**

½ **teaspoon salt**

2 **cloves garlic, halved**

¾ **cup heavy cream**

Chopped cilantro for garnish (optional)

• Combine blanched almonds, carrots, onion and celery in slow cooker. Pick through lentils and rinse. Add lentils to slow cooker along with bouillon, curry powder, salt, garlic and 7 cups water.

• Cover and slow cook on HIGH for 4 hours or LOW for 6 hours. Uncover and puree with an immersion blender until smooth (alternately, transfer soup in batches to a blender and puree until smooth). Stir in heavy cream and heat through. Garnish with cilantro and additional blanched almonds, if desired.

PER SERVING 370 **CAL**; 16 g **FAT** (6 g **SAT**); 18 g **PRO**; 40 g **CARB**; 6 g **FIBER**; 675 mg **SODIUM**; 31 mg **CHOL**

Roasted Turkey Breast

MAKES 6 servings **PREP** 5 minutes **SLOW COOK** on LOW for 5 hours **LET REST** 10 minutes

1	bone-in turkey breast (5 to 5½ pounds), thawed if frozen
1	medium onion, sliced
1	cup chicken broth
2	teaspoons dried Italian seasoning
½	teaspoon salt
½	teaspoon ground black pepper

• Place turkey breast on a cutting board and pat dry with paper towels. Spread onion slices on bottom of slow cooker and pour in chicken broth. Rub Italian seasoning, salt and pepper on and under skin of turkey breast.

• Place turkey breast in slow cooker on top of onion and broth. Cover and slow cook on LOW for 5 hours or until an instant-read thermometer inserted in breast registers 165°.

• Remove turkey to a clean cutting board. Cover and let rest 10 minutes. Remove and discard skin; slice breast meat from bones. Cut meat crosswise into slices.

PER SERVING 334 **CAL**; 2 g **FAT** (1 g **SAT**); 71 g **PRO**; 3 g **CARB**; 1 g **FIBER**; 473 mg **SODIUM**; 196 mg **CHOL**

ROASTED TURKEY BREAST

ASIAN PORK WRAPS

Asian Pork Wraps

MAKES 8 servings **PREP** 15 minutes **COOK** 12 minutes **SLOW COOK** on HIGH for 4½ hours or LOW for 6 hours **MICROWAVE** 30 seconds

PORK WRAPS

1	teaspoon onion powder
1	teaspoon ground ginger
1	teaspoon sugar
½	teaspoon ground cumin
½	teaspoon ground allspice
¼	teaspoon cayenne pepper
¼	teaspoon salt
2½	pounds boneless pork loin roast
1	teaspoon toasted sesame oil
1	tablespoon canola oil
¾	cup hoisin sauce, plus more for serving (optional)
8	large flour tortillas

SLAW

2	tablespoons rice vinegar
1	teaspoon sugar
½	teaspoon salt
½	teaspoon black pepper
3	tablespoons canola oil
1	teaspoon toasted sesame oil
1	bag (14 ounces) coleslaw mix

• **Pork.** In a small bowl, combine onion powder, ginger, sugar, cumin, allspice, cayenne pepper and salt. Rub the pork with sesame oil, then rub spice mixture into the pork.

• Heat canola oil in a large stainless-steel skillet over medium-high heat. Brown pork on all sides, about 3 minutes per side. Transfer to slow cooker. Whisk ¼ cup of the hoisin sauce with 1 cup water. Pour around pork in slow cooker. Cover and slow cook on HIGH for 4½ hours or LOW for 6 hours.

• Remove pork to a large bowl. Shred with 2 forks into large pieces and toss with remaining ½ cup hoisin sauce.

• **Slaw.** In a large bowl, combine rice vinegar, sugar, salt and pepper. Whisk in canola oil and sesame oil. Toss with coleslaw mix.

• To serve, microwave tortillas for 30 seconds or until heated through. Spread each tortilla with additional hoisin sauce, if desired. Top with slaw and shredded pork. Fold up and serve.

PER SERVING 443 **CAL**; 20 g **FAT** (4 g **SAT**); 31 g **PRO**; 39 g **CARB**; 4 g **FIBER**; 737 mg **SODIUM**; 70 mg **CHOL**

OREO SNOWMEN,
PAGE 318

DECEMBER

316   321   328

HOMEMADE FOR THE HOLIDAYS

Edible goodies that are perfect for giving.

PEPPERMINT BARK,
PAGE 317

Chocolate-Dipped Marshmallows

MAKES 24 marshmallows **PREP** 30 minutes **MICROWAVE** 75 seconds **REFRIGERATE** 1 hour

2 cups milk chocolate chips
24 large marshmallows (from a 10-ounce bag)
Red and green nonpareils and assorted holiday-themed candies

• Place chocolate chips in a medium bowl and microwave on HIGH for 45 seconds. Stir and microwave for 30 seconds more. Stir until smooth. Spoon into a 1-cup glass measuring cup.

• Line a rimmed baking sheet with wax paper. Using 2 wood toothpicks, dip the marshmallows in the chocolate and shake off excess. Place on prepared baking sheet.

• Sprinkle tops with desired decorations. Refrigerate for at least 1 hour.

PER MARSHMALLOW 93 **CAL**; 4 g **FAT** (2 g **SAT**); 1 g **PRO**; 13 g **CARB**; 0 g **FIBER**; 17 mg **SODIUM**; 3 mg **CHOL**

When you make a homemade gift, you give the gift itself and the time you took to make it—which is an especially cherished commodity.

Cookie Mix

MAKES one 2-quart jar; 3½ dozen baked cookies
PREP 13 minutes

1	2-quart jar
2¾	cups all-purpose flour
1¼	teaspoons baking powder
½	teaspoon baking soda
¼	teaspoon salt
½	cup dark cocoa powder
1	cup packed light brown sugar
1	cup granulated sugar
1	cup milk chocolate chips
1	cup white chocolate chips
1	cup red and green M&M's Minis

• In a bowl, combine 1¾ cups of the flour, the baking powder, baking soda and salt. In another bowl, blend cocoa and remaining 1 cup flour.

• Spoon half the flour-cocoa mixture into jar. Press down to flatten, using a small spice jar. Spoon half the plain flour mixture over cocoa layer; compact. Repeat. Top with brown sugar and granulated sugar, compressing each. Add chips and M&M's to jar.

• Attach baking instructions: Blend 2 sticks cooled, melted unsalted butter with 3 eggs, ⅓ cup milk and 2 teaspoons vanilla extract. Stir in cookie mix until blended. Drop by heaping tablespoons onto cookie sheets. Bake at 350° for 13 minutes or until firm. Cool on pan for 1 minute, then remove to a rack.

PER COOKIE 146 **CAL**; 4 g **FAT** (3 g **SAT**); 2 g **PRO**; 26 g **CARB**; 1 g **FIBER**; 37 mg **SODIUM**; 4 mg **CHOL**

GUMDROP WREATH

Gumdrop Wreath

MAKES one 8-inch wreath   **PREP** 1 hour   **LET DRY** 2 days

1	recipe Royal Frosting (recipe follows)
	Green food coloring
1	8-inch straw, plastic or foam wreath form
6	bags (13 ounces each) red and green gumdrops, separated

• Tint Royal Frosting bright green with food coloring. Spoon frosting into 2 or 3 resealable bags. Seal bags and set aside.

• Wrap wreath form with several sheets of aluminum foil. Tape the ends to secure.

• Place a sheet of wax paper on a work surface. Place wreath form on wax paper.

• Snip a corner from one of the frosting bags. Pipe some frosting over wreath. Spread to make a thick coating on about one-third of the wreath. Starting at the base, arrange green gumdrops close together in rows. Repeat rows to cover wreath. Make sure to work in small areas so frosting doesn't dry out. Add a few clusters of 3 red gumdrops here and there. Allow to dry at least 48 hours before hanging.

Royal Frosting: Combine 1 box (16 ounces) confectioners' sugar with 3 tablespoons powdered egg whites and 6 tablespoons water in a large bowl. Beat until thick.

CARAMEL CORN

These candy shop-quality treats in their pretty packages will elicit oohs and ahhs upon opening.

Ancho Chile Truffles

MAKES 72 truffles **PREP** 1 hour
REFRIGERATE 4 hours

¾	**cup heavy cream**
1	**pound semisweet chocolate, finely chopped**
¼	**cup unsalted butter, cut into pieces**
¼	**cup coffee liqueur**
½	**teaspoon ground cinnamon**
½	**teaspoon ancho chile powder**
⅛	**teaspoon cayenne pepper**
½	**cup flaked coconut, processed with 1 tablespoon confectioners' sugar**
½	**cup dark cocoa powder, mixed with ½ teaspoon ancho chile powder**
¼	**cup red nonpareils**

• Line a rimmed baking sheet with nonstick foil.

• Heat cream in a small saucepan until simmering. Place chocolate and butter in a large bowl; add cream and stir until smooth. Add liqueur, cinnamon, chile powder and cayenne; stir until combined. Refrigerate for 2 hours, until firm enough to roll into balls.

• With wet hands, shape 2 teaspoons of the chocolate mixture into a ball. Roll in coconut, cocoa powder or nonpareils. Place on baking sheet. Repeat with remaining mixture. Refrigerate for 2 hours.

PER TRUFFLE 53 **CAL**; 4 g **FAT** (2 g **SAT**); 0 g **PRO**; 5 g **CARB**; 1 g **FIBER**; 3 mg **SODIUM**; 5 mg **CHOL**

Caramel Corn

MAKES 12 servings **PREP** 10 minutes **COOK** 20 minutes

1	**box (16 ounces) light brown sugar**
1	**cup light corn syrup**
¼	**cup unsalted butter**
1	**tablespoon white vinegar**
1	**teaspoon kosher salt**
1	**bag microwave popcorn (about 10 cups popped)**

• Coat a 15 x 11 x 1-inch jelly roll pan with nonstick cooking spray.

• In a medium heavy-bottomed stainless-steel saucepan, combine brown sugar, corn syrup, butter, vinegar and salt. Cook over medium-high heat, without stirring, until mixture reaches 300° on a candy thermometer, about 20 minutes.

• Meanwhile, microwave popcorn following package directions and spread out on prepared jelly roll pan. Carefully pour hot sugar mixture over popcorn and quickly toss with 2 forks until popcorn is coated. Cool.

• Break into bite-size pieces and store in airtight containers at room temperature.

PER SERVING (¾ cup) 279 **CAL**; 4 g **FAT** (2 g **SAT**); 1 g **PRO**; 63 g **CARB**; 1 g **FIBER**; 227 mg **SODIUM**; 10 mg **CHOL**

Rice Krispies Trees

MAKES 18 trees **PREP** 30 minutes **MICROWAVE** 1 minute **LET COOL** 5 minutes

- **1** **bag (10 ounces) mini marshmallows**
- **3** **tablespoons unsalted butter**
  Green and yellow food coloring
- **6** **cups crisp rice cereal**
- **3** **tablespoons red sprinkles**
- **18** **dark chocolate peanut butter-cup miniatures, unwrapped**
- **18** **yellow M&M's Minis**

• Combine marshmallows and butter in a large glass bowl and microwave until melted, about 1 minute. Stir until smooth. Tint mixture to a bright green with green and yellow food coloring.

• Add cereal and stir until well coated. Let cool about 5 minutes. With greased hands, shape about 1/3 cup of the mixture into a small cone, pressing firmly. Decorate cone with red sprinkles. Repeat with remaining cereal and sprinkles. Top each cone with a yellow candy and place on top of a peanut butter cup.

PER TREE 170 **CAL**; 5 g **FAT** (3 g **SAT**); 2 g **PRO**; 28 g **CARB**; 0 g **FIBER**; 129 mg **SODIUM**; 7 mg **CHOL**

Peppermint Bark

MAKES 36 pieces **PREP** 10 minutes
REFRIGERATE 2 hours

- **1½ pounds bittersweet chocolate, chopped**
- **1 teaspoon mint extract**
- **8 candy canes, broken up into small pieces**

• Line a 15 x 11 x 1-inch jelly roll pan with nonstick aluminum foil.

• Melt chocolate in a large bowl set over a saucepan of gently simmering water. Stir chocolate until smooth. Remove bowl and allow to cool 3 minutes.

• Stir in mint extract and spread chocolate evenly onto prepared pan. Scatter candy cane pieces over top. Refrigerate for 2 hours.

• Invert pan onto a cutting board and peel off foil. Break bark into thirty-six 2-inch pieces.

• Store in an airtight container at room temperature for up to 2 weeks.

PER 2-INCH PIECE 122 **CAL**; 9 g **FAT** (5 g **SAT**); 2 g **PRO**; 14 g **CARB**; 1 g **FIBER**; 1 mg **SODIUM**; 4 mg **CHOL**

PEPPERMINT BARK

SALTED CARAMEL SAUCE

Salted Caramel Sauce

MAKES 2 cups (16 servings) **PREP** 5 minutes **COOK** 16 minutes

- **1½ cups sugar**
- **1 teaspoon sea salt**
- **1 cup heavy cream**
- **1 teaspoon vanilla extract**

• Place sugar in a medium heavy-bottomed saucepan and stir in ½ cup water.

• Place over medium-high heat and cook, without stirring, for 15 to 16 minutes, until dark amber in color. Remove from heat and stir in salt. Gradually stir in cream and add vanilla.

• Cool and spoon into jars. Tightly seal and store in refrigerator for up to 2 weeks.

PER SERVING (2 tablespoons) 97 **CAL**; 6 g **FAT** (3 g **SAT**); 0 g **PRO**; 14 g **CARB**; 0 g **FIBER**; 151 mg **SODIUM**; 20 mg **CHOL**

These whimsical treats are based on familiar purchased cookies that are transformed into characters with personality plus!

Nutter Butter Reindeer

MAKES 24 reindeer pops PREP 30 minutes
MICROWAVE 90 seconds
REFRIGERATE 25 minutes

1	bag (12 ounces) Wilton light cocoa candy melts
1	tablespoon solid vegetable shortening
24	Nutter Butter sandwich cookies
24	pop sticks
24	red peanut butter M&M's
24	thin pretzel twists, cut into small pieces
48	white M&M's
48	brown M&M's Minis

• Combine candy melts and shortening in a 2-cup glass measuring cup. Microwave, stirring often, until smooth, about 60 to 90 seconds.

• Line 2 cookie sheets with wax paper. Separate cookies. Dip one end of a pop stick into melted chocolate and place at one end of an opened cookie. Top with another cookie half and arrange on sheet. Repeat with remaining cookies and refrigerate until set, about 5 minutes.

• Reheat melted chocolate if necessary. Dip a chilled cookie into chocolate to coat. Allow excess to drain off, tapping lightly. Return cookie to sheet. Add pretzel pieces as antlers and red candy as nose, gently pressing into the wet chocolate to adhere. Press white candies into chocolate for eyes. Repeat steps with remaining cookies. Refrigerate until set, about 10 minutes.

• Pipe dots of chocolate on white candies and place brown candies on them. Refrigerate until set, about 10 minutes.

PER POP 190 CAL; 10 g FAT (3 g SAT); 3 g PRO; 24 g CARB; 1 g FIBER; 95 mg SODIUM; 6 mg CHOL

OREO SNOWMEN

Oreo Snowmen

MAKES 24 snowman pops PREP 30 minutes LET DRY 30 minutes

24	white-chocolate-coated Oreo cookies
24	lollipop sticks
½	cup canned dark chocolate frosting
¼	cup canned vanilla frosting
24	Mike and Ike small orange candies

• Insert a lollipop stick into one end of each cookie. (You may first need to use a toothpick or small skewer to make a hole.)

• Spoon frostings into separate resealable bags and snip a small corner from each with scissors.

• Using dark chocolate frosting, pipe eyes and mouth onto cookies. Pipe a dot of vanilla frosting in center of each cookie and place an orange candy on it. Allow cookies to dry for about 30 minutes.

PER POP 149 CAL; 7 g FAT (2 g SAT); 1 g PRO; 21 g CARB; 0 g FIBER; 83 mg SODIUM; 0 mg CHOL

SHARE THE LOVE

Sweet ideas for a cookie swap.

CHERRY AND
APRICOT LINZERS

Cherry and Apricot Linzers

MAKES 18 linzers (from 36 cookies)
PREP 25 minutes **REFRIGERATE** 2 hours
BAKE at 375° for 12 minutes

1½	cups all-purpose flour
⅔	cup almond flour (such as Bob's Red Mill)
¼	teaspoon salt
⅔	cup unsalted butter, softened
⅓	cup granulated sugar
⅔	cup confectioners' sugar, plus more for dusting
1	egg
½	teaspoon almond extract
6	tablespoons cherry or apricot preserves

• In a bowl, whisk together all-purpose flour, almond flour and salt. In another bowl, beat butter and sugars for 2 minutes, until fluffy. Beat in egg and almond extract until just combined. Pour in flour mixture; beat until just combined. Work dough briefly with hands and form 2 disks. Wrap in plastic and refrigerate for 2 hours.

• Heat oven to 375°. Remove a dough disk from refrigerator. Generously flour work surface. Roll to ⅛-inch thickness. Cut out shapes (such as snowmen or Christmas trees) with a 3-inch cookie cutter; place on baking sheets 2 inches apart. On half the cookies, use a smaller cookie cutter to remove a different shape (such as a heart for snowmen or a star for trees). Re-roll dough as needed. Repeat with second dough disk.

• Bake at 375° for 10 to 12 minutes, until golden. Cool completely on a wire rack.

• Separate cookies with cutouts from those without. Spread a scant teaspoon of preserves on non-cutout cookies. Dust cutout cookies with confectioners' sugar and place on top of non-cutouts.

PER LINZER 151 **CAL**; 7 g **FAT** (2 g **SAT**); 3 g **PRO**; 21 g **CARB**; 1 g **FIBER**; 49 mg **SODIUM**; 18 mg **CHOL**

CHOCOLATE
PRETZEL COOKIES

Bourbon Balls

MAKES 36 cookies **PREP** 20 minutes
REFRIGERATE 30 minutes

- **1½ cups finely ground vanilla wafer cookie crumbs (about 40 cookies, ground in a food processor)**
- **1 cup finely ground walnuts (ground in a food processor)**
- **½ cup confectioners' sugar**
- **2 tablespoons unsweetened cocoa powder**
- **¼ cup bourbon**
- **1 tablespoon light corn syrup**
  Decorators' sugar, unsweetened cocoa or confectioners' sugar for rolling (optional)

• In a large bowl, combine cookie crumbs, walnuts, confectioners' sugar and cocoa. Stir in bourbon and corn syrup until well combined. Roll mixture into 1-inch balls; place on a parchment-lined baking sheet and refrigerate 30 minutes. Roll in decorators' sugar, unsweetened cocoa or confectioners' sugar, if desired.

PER COOKIE 57 **CAL**; 3 g **FAT** (0 g **SAT**); 1 g **PRO**; 6 g **CARB**; 1 g **FIBER**; 14 mg **SODIUM**; 1 mg **CHOL**

BOURBON
BALLS

Chocolate Pretzel Cookies

MAKES 30 cookies **PREP** 15 minutes **BAKE** at 350° for 11 minutes

- **1 cup all-purpose flour**
- **¼ cup unsweetened cocoa powder**
- **½ teaspoon baking powder**
- **½ teaspoon baking soda**
- **¼ teaspoon salt**
- **½ cup (1 stick) unsalted butter, softened**
- **⅓ cup granulated sugar**
- **⅓ cup packed light brown sugar**
- **1 egg**
- **½ teaspoon vanilla extract**
- **1 cup semisweet chocolate chips**
- **1 cup roughly chopped mini pretzels, plus 30 whole pretzels for garnish**

• Heat oven to 350°. In a bowl, whisk together flour, cocoa, baking powder, baking soda and salt. In another bowl, beat butter, granulated sugar and brown sugar for 2 minutes, until fluffy. Beat in egg and vanilla extract until just combined. Pour in flour mixture and beat on low until just combined. Carefully fold in chocolate chips and chopped pretzels.

• Drop tablespoonfuls of batter on baking sheets, spacing them about 2 inches apart. Press down lightly to flatten. Gently press a whole pretzel on top of each cookie.

• Bake at 350° for 11 minutes. Transfer to a wire rack to cool completely.

PER COOKIE 101 **CAL**; 5 g **FAT** (3 g **SAT**); 1 g **PRO**; 14 g **CARB**; 1 g **FIBER**; 96 mg **SODIUM**; 15 mg **CHOL**

Chai Gingerbread

MAKES 36 cookies **PREP** 35 minutes **REFRIGERATE** 2 hours, 15 minutes **BAKE** at 350° for 14 minutes

3	cups all-purpose flour
1	teaspoon baking soda
2	teaspoons ginger
2	teaspoons ground cinnamon
1	teaspoon ground cardamom
½	teaspoon ground cloves
½	teaspoon finely ground black pepper
½	teaspoon salt
½	cup (1 stick) unsalted butter, softened
¾	cup packed dark brown sugar
1	egg
½	cup molasses

• In a large bowl, whisk together flour, baking soda, ginger, cinnamon, cardamom, cloves, pepper and salt. In a separate bowl, beat butter and brown sugar 2 minutes, until fluffy. Beat in egg and molasses until just combined. Add flour mixture and beat until just combined. Divide dough in half and shape into disks; wrap tightly in plastic. Refrigerate 2 hours.

• Heat oven to 350°. Remove one dough disk from refrigerator. Generously flour work surface. Roll out dough to ¼-inch thickness. Cut into gingerbread men and women with 3-inch cookie cutters. Place on baking sheets 2 inches apart. Use pastry brush to remove flour from cookies, if desired. Refrigerate 15 minutes. Repeat with second dough disk.

• Bake at 350° in batches until golden brown, about 14 minutes. Cool on wire racks, then decorate, if desired.

PER COOKIE 93 **CAL**; 3 g **FAT** (2 g **SAT**); 1 g **PRO**; 16 g **CARB**; 0 g **FIBER**; 73 mg **SODIUM**; 13 mg **CHOL**

BUCKEYES

ALMOND LACE COOKIES

German Chocolate Bars

MAKES 36 bar cookies **PREP** 10 minutes
BAKE at 350° for 25 minutes **REFRIGERATE** 2 hours

1½	**boxes (9 ounces each) Nabisco Famous chocolate wafers**
½	**cup (1 stick) unsalted butter, melted**
1	**can (14 ounces) sweetened condensed milk**
1	**bag (12 ounces) semisweet chocolate chips**
1¼	**cups sweetened flaked coconut**
1	**cup coarsely chopped pecans**

• Heat oven to 350°. Line a 13 x 9-inch baking pan with nonstick aluminum foil.

• Pulse wafers in a food processor until very fine crumbs. Transfer to a bowl and stir in melted butter until well combined. Press mixture firmly and evenly (the flat side of a measuring cup works well) into foil-lined pan. Pour condensed milk evenly over crust. Sprinkle with chocolate chips, followed by coconut and finally pecans.

• Bake at 350° for 25 minutes. Cool completely. Refrigerate 2 hours. Remove from pan by lifting foil and place on a cutting board. Cut into 36 pieces.

PER COOKIE 182 **CAL**; 11 g **FAT** (5 g **SAT**); 2 g **PRO**; 21 g **CARB**; 1 g **FIBER**; 96 mg **SODIUM**; 12 mg **CHOL**

Almond Lace Cookies

MAKES 42 cookies **PREP** 15 minutes
BAKE at 375° for 8 minutes **COOL** 5 minutes

½	**cup (1 stick) unsalted butter**
½	**cup light brown sugar**
2	**tablespoons light corn syrup**
¾	**cup all-purpose flour**
⅔	**cup sliced almonds**
⅛	**teaspoon salt**

• Heat oven to 375°. In a small pot, combine butter, brown sugar and corn syrup over medium heat. Stir until butter is melted and mixture is smooth. Remove from heat. Stir in flour, almonds and salt until just combined.

• Spoon teaspoonfuls of batter onto parchment-paper-lined cookie sheets, spacing 4 inches apart. Bake at 375° for 7 to 8 minutes, until bubbling and golden-brown. Let sit on baking sheets until firm, about 5 minutes. Carefully transfer to a wire rack to cool completely. (Bake in 2 batches, 2 sheets at a time.) Gently reheat batter, if necessary, for second batch.

PER COOKIE 49 **CAL**; 3 g **FAT** (1 g **SAT**); 1 g **PRO**; 5 g **CARB**; 0 g **FIBER**; 9 mg **SODIUM**; 6 mg **CHOL**

Buckeyes

MAKES 36 cookies **PREP** 30 minutes
FREEZE 30 minutes

1	**cup creamy peanut butter, at room temperature**
⅓	**cup unsalted butter, softened**
2½	**cups confectioners' sugar**
½	**teaspoon vanilla extract**
4	**ounces bittersweet chocolate chips**

• In a large bowl, beat peanut butter, softened butter, confectioners' sugar and vanilla extract until smooth. Roll into 1-inch balls and place on parchment-paper-lined baking sheets. Place in freezer for 30 minutes, until firm.

• Melt chocolate chips per package directions. Using a toothpick, dip peanut butter balls halfway into chocolate, allowing excess to drip off. Return to parchment-lined baking sheets. With a moistened finger, smooth out toothpick holes. Refrigerate to harden chocolate; keep refrigerated until serving.

PER COOKIE 101 **CAL**; 6 g **FAT** (2 g **SAT**); 2 g **PRO**; 11 g **CARB**; 1 g **FIBER**; 33 mg **SODIUM**; 4 mg **CHOL**

GERMAN CHOCOLATE BARS

MAPLE-RAISIN OATMEAL COOKIES

WHITE CHOCOLATE CRANBERRY CLUSTERS

Maple-Raisin Oatmeal Cookies

MAKES 36 cookies **PREP** 15 minutes **BAKE** at 350° for 14 minutes

- ¾ **cup all-purpose flour**
- ½ **teaspoon baking soda**
- ¼ **teaspoon salt**
- ½ **cup (1 stick) unsalted butter, softened**
- ½ **cup packed light brown sugar**
- ¼ **cup plus 3 tablespoons pure maple syrup**
- 1 **egg**
- 1½ **cups quick-cooking oats**
- ½ **cup raisins**
- 1 **cup confectioners' sugar**

• Heat oven to 350°. In a bowl, whisk together flour, baking soda and salt. In another bowl, beat butter, sugar and ¼ cup of the maple syrup for 3 minutes.

Beat in egg until just combined. Pour in flour and beat on low until just combined. Stir in oats and raisins.

• Drop scant tablespoon-size rounds of batter onto baking sheets, spacing about 2 inches apart. Bake at 350° for 12 to 14 minutes, until golden. Remove to a wire rack to cool completely.

• In a bowl, beat confectioners' sugar, remaining 3 tablespoons maple syrup and 1 tablespoon water on low until well combined. Drizzle with a spoon over cooled cookies.

PER COOKIE 88 **CAL**; 3 g **FAT** (2 g **SAT**); 1 g **PRO**; 15 g **CARB**; 0 g **FIBER**; 38 mg **SODIUM**; 13 mg **CHOL**

White Chocolate Cranberry Clusters

MAKES 36 cookies **PREP** 15 minutes

- 2 **cups Kellogg's Original All-Bran cereal**
- 1½ **cups sweetened dried cranberries**
- 12 **ounces white chocolate melting disks (such as Ghirardelli)**
- 1 **cup white chocolate chips**

• Combine cereal and cranberries in a large bowl. In a separate bowl, melt white chocolate disks per package directions. Pour over cereal mixture and stir together until well combined. Stir in white chocolate chips.

• Working quickly, form into very well-packed tablespoon-size balls (a cookie scoop works best) and place on parchment-paper-lined cookie sheets. Refrigerate until set.

PER COOKIE 102 **CAL**; 5 g **FAT** (3 g **SAT**); 1 g **PRO**; 15 g **CARB**; 1 g **FIBER**; 21 mg **SODIUM**; 2 mg **CHOL**

Chocolate-Dipped Pistachio Crescents

MAKES 36 cookies **PREP** 20 minutes
BAKE at 350° for 16 minutes

2	**cups all-purpose flour**
1	**cup unsalted, shelled pistachios, finely ground in a food processor**
¼	**teaspoon salt**
¾	**cup (1½ sticks) unsalted butter, softened**
¾	**cup packed light brown sugar**
1	**egg**
8	**ounces (about 1½ cups) semisweet chocolate chips**
1	**cup unsalted, shelled pistachios, roughly chopped**

• Heat oven to 350°. In a bowl, stir together flour, finely ground pistachios and salt. In another bowl, beat butter and sugar for 2 minutes, until fluffy. Beat in egg. Pour in dry mixture and beat until just combined.

• Shape level tablespoonfuls of dough into 2½-inch logs and bend into crescents. Place on a baking sheet 2 inches apart. Bake at 350° for 14 to 16 minutes, until lightly browned. Remove to a wire rack to cool completely.

• Melt chocolate per package directions. Dip crescents halfway into chocolate, allowing excess to drip off. Sprinkle with chopped pistachios. Place on parchment paper to dry.

PER COOKIE 139 CAL; 8 g FAT (4 g SAT); 3 g PRO; 15 g CARB; 1 g FIBER; 21 mg SODIUM; 16 mg CHOL

ORANGE AND FIG BARS

CHOCOLATE-DIPPED PISTACHIO CRESCENTS

Orange and Fig Bars

MAKES 36 bar cookies **PREP** 15 minutes **COOK** 15 minutes **COOL** 5 minutes **BAKE** at 350° for 25 minutes

2	**cups all-purpose flour**
½	**teaspoon baking powder**
½	**teaspoon ground cinnamon**
¼	**teaspoon salt**
½	**cup (1 stick) unsalted butter, softened**
½	**cup plus 2 tablespoons sugar**
1	**teaspoon vanilla extract**
4	**cups dried figs, roughly chopped**
½	**cup orange juice and 2 teaspoons orange zest (from 1 large orange)**
2	**tablespoons honey**

• Heat oven to 350°. Line a 13 x 9-inch baking pan with aluminum foil.

• In a bowl, whisk together flour, baking powder, cinnamon and salt. In another bowl, beat butter and ½ cup of the sugar for 2 minutes, until fluffy. Beat in vanilla extract. Pour in flour and beat on low until well combined. Press firmly and evenly (the flat side of a measuring cup works well) into foil-lined pan.

• In a medium lidded pot, combine figs, orange juice and zest, honey and remaining 2 tablespoons sugar. Bring to a simmer, cover, reduce heat to medium-low and cook 15 minutes, until softened. Transfer to a food processor and run until smooth. Cool 5 minutes. Using a spatula dipped in warm water, carefully spread fig mixture over cookie layer (re-dip spatula as necessary to prevent sticking).

• Bake at 350° for 25 minutes. Cool completely. Remove from pan by lifting foil and place on a cutting board. Cut into 36 pieces.

PER COOKIE 122 CAL; 3 g FAT (2 g SAT); 2 g PRO; 24 g CARB; 2 g FIBER; 41 mg SODIUM; 7 mg CHOL

HEALTHY FAMILY DINNERS

One day of prep yields a week's worth of meals for the busiest time of the year.

WHIPPED POTATOES

CHICKEN MEATLOAF

Serve half with meatloaf and roasted butternut squash. Form remaining half into 6 potato pancakes for Thursday (page 329) and refrigerate.

PER SERVING 110 **CAL**; 4 g **FAT** (2 g **SAT**); 3 g **PRO**; 15 g **CARB**; 2 g **FIBER**; 202 mg **SODIUM**; 10 mg **CHOL**

Chicken Meatloaf

MAKES 6 servings plus leftovers **PREP** 30 minutes
BAKE at 375° for 55 minutes

¾	**cup unseasoned bread crumbs**
¾	**cup fat-free milk**
3	**pounds ground chicken**
10	**ounces baby bella mushrooms, shredded**
2	**large onions, chopped**
4	**eggs, lightly beaten**
½	**cup parsley, chopped**
1	**package (1.25 ounces) Mrs. Dash meatloaf seasoning**
1	**tablespoon fresh lemon zest**
1½	**teaspoons salt**
1	**can (14.5 ounces) Italian seasoned stewed tomatoes (optional)**

• Heat oven to 375°. Coat a large shallow roasting pan with cooking spray.

• In a large bowl, combine bread crumbs and milk. Add ground chicken, mushrooms, onions, eggs, parsley, meatloaf seasoning, lemon zest and salt. Mix thoroughly; form into 2 meatloaves.

• Place meatloaves in prepared pan and bake at 375° for 55 minutes or until internal temperature reaches 180°. Serve 1 meatloaf with whipped potatoes, roasted butternut squash and, if desired, seasoned stewed tomatoes. Cool remaining meatloaf, wrap in plastic and refrigerate for gyros on Wednesday (page 328).

PER SERVING 222 **CAL**; 11 g **FAT** (3 g **SAT**); 22 g **PRO**; 9 g **CARB**; 1 g **FIBER**; 341 mg **SODIUM**; 146 mg **CHOL**

SUNDAY PREP

❏ **Make 2 meatloaves.** Refrigerate one for Wednesday.
❏ **Prepare potatoes.** Use half to make 6 potato pancakes for Thursday.
❏ **Roast 2 butternut squash.** Refrigerate half for risotto on Monday.
❏ **Chop 3 onions** (for meatloaves and risotto).
❏ **Shred Fontina cheese** (for risotto).
❏ **Slice ½ onion** (for stir-fry).
❏ **Cut broccoli into florets** (for stir-fry).
❏ **Slice 1 red pepper and 1 green bell pepper** (for fra diavolo).

SUNDAY

Whipped Potatoes

MAKES 6 servings plus leftovers
PREP 15 minutes **COOK** 15 minutes

3	**pounds all-purpose potatoes**
½	**cup fat-free milk**
¼	**cup (½ stick) unsalted butter**
1	**teaspoon salt**
¼	**teaspoon black pepper**
¼	**teaspoon ground nutmeg**
3	**tablespoons chopped parsley**

• Peel potatoes and cut into 1-inch pieces. Place in a large saucepan and cover with salted water. Bring to a boil over high heat; reduce heat and simmer for 15 minutes, until tender. Drain.

• Add milk, butter, salt, pepper and nutmeg. On medium speed, whip potatoes until smooth. Stir in parsley.

Roasted Butternut Squash

MAKES 6 servings plus leftovers
PREP 20 minutes BAKE at 375° for 45 minutes

2	large butternut squash (about 2½ pounds each), peeled, seeded and cut into 1-inch pieces
2	tablespoons olive oil
1	teaspoon salt
½	teaspoon black pepper
2	tablespoons chopped fresh sage

• Heat oven to 375°. Toss squash with olive oil and season with salt and pepper. Spread out on 2 baking sheets. Bake at 375° for 45 minutes or until tender. Turn once.

• Sprinkle half the squash with sage. Serve with meatloaf and whipped potatoes. Cool and refrigerate remaining squash for risotto on Monday (below right).

PER SERVING 71 CAL; 2 g FAT (0 g SAT); 1 g PRO; 13 g CARB; 2 g FIBER; 198 mg SODIUM; 0 mg CHOL

BUTTERNUT SQUASH RISOTTO

ROASTED BUTTERNUT SQUASH

MONDAY

Butternut Squash Risotto

MAKES 6 servings PREP 15 minutes COOK 27 minutes

4	cups low-sodium vegetable broth (such as Pacific)
2	tablespoons olive oil
1	large onion, chopped
2	cloves garlic, chopped
1½	cups arborio rice
⅓	cup dry white wine
3	cups Roasted Butternut Squash (see recipe, left)
1½	cups (6 ounces) shredded Fontina cheese
½	teaspoon salt
¼	teaspoon black pepper
2	tablespoons fresh chopped sage

• In a medium saucepan, bring broth and 1 cup water to a simmer. Keep at a low simmer.

• Heat oil in large heavy-bottomed saucepan over medium heat. Add onion and garlic; cook 5 minutes, stirring occasionally. Add rice; cook 1 minute, stirring to coat. Add wine; cook 1 minute or until wine is absorbed.

• Add ½ cup of the simmering broth mixture; cook over medium-low heat, stirring, until all broth is absorbed. Add remaining broth mixture, ½ cup at a time, cooking in the same manner for 20 to 25 minutes until all liquid is absorbed and rice is tender.

• Stir in butternut squash and heat through. Remove from heat and stir in cheese, salt, pepper and sage. Serve immediately.

Note: For a heartier dish, stir in shredded cooked chicken or cooked Italian seasoned chicken sausage, sliced into coins.

PER SERVING 434 CAL; 16 g FAT (6 g SAT); 12 g PRO; 58 g CARB; 5 g FIBER; 715 mg SODIUM; 6 mg CHOL

FLANK STEAK, BROCCOLI AND GREEN BEAN STIR-FRY

Chicken Gyros

MAKES 6 servings **PREP** 15 minutes
MICROWAVE 2 minutes

1	container (7 ounces) 2% fat Greek yogurt
⅓	cup reduced-fat crumbled feta cheese
1	tablespoon lemon juice
1	Chicken Meatloaf, sliced (page 326)
6	whole wheat pita breads, warmed
1	bag (6 ounces) baby spinach
2	cups shredded iceberg lettuce
1	cucumber, peeled and thinly sliced
2	Roma tomatoes, thinly sliced
1	small red onion, thinly sliced

• In a small bowl, combine yogurt, feta and lemon juice. Set aside.

• Gently reheat meatloaf slices in microwave on HIGH for 1 to 2 minutes.

• Assemble gyros: Place pitas on individual serving plates. Top with spinach, meatloaf slices, lettuce, cucumber, tomatoes, onion and yogurt mixture.

PER SERVING 459 **CAL**; 15 g **FAT** (5 g **SAT**); 35 g **PRO**; 53 g **CARB**; 8 g **FIBER**; 800 mg **SODIUM**; 150 mg **CHOL**

CHICKEN GYROS

TUESDAY

Flank Steak, Broccoli and Green Bean Stir-Fry

MAKES 6 servings **PREP** 15 minutes **COOK** 12 minutes

1	cup beef broth
¼	cup reduced-sodium soy sauce
2	tablespoons rice vinegar
1	tablespoon cornstarch
½	teaspoon Chinese five-spice powder
½	teaspoon red pepper flakes
2	tablespoons vegetable oil
1¼	pounds lean beef flank steak, cut into ¼-inch slices against the grain
¼	teaspoon salt
½	large onion, sliced
1	head broccoli, cut into florets (about 6 cups)
½	pound thin green beans, trimmed
1	cup shredded carrot
½	cup sliced almonds
3	cups cooked brown rice

• In a small bowl, whisk together broth, soy sauce, vinegar, cornstarch, five-spice powder and red pepper flakes. Set aside.

• Heat 1 tablespoon of the oil in a large nonstick skillet or wok. Season flank steak with salt and stir-fry for 3 minutes. Remove to a plate. Add remaining 1 tablespoon oil; add onion, broccoli, green beans and carrot. Stir-fry 8 minutes or until crisp-tender. Add ¼ cup water during last 2 minutes of cooking time and cover.

• Add broth and soy sauce mixture; bring to a boil and cook 1 minute, until thickened. Stir in beef and any accumulated juices and heat through.

• Sprinkle with almonds and serve immediately over cooked brown rice.

PER SERVING 388 **CAL**; 15 g **FAT** (3 g **SAT**); 29 g **PRO**; 35 g **CARB**; 6 g **FIBER**; 556 mg **SODIUM**; 31 mg **CHOL**

APRICOT-GLAZED PORK CHOPS AND
POTATO PANCAKES

THURSDAY

Apricot-Glazed Pork Chops and Potato Pancakes

MAKES 6 servings PREP 15 minutes
REFRIGERATE 1 hour COOK 10 minutes
BROIL 7 minutes

6	potato pancakes (page 326)
¼	cup all-purpose flour
½	cup apricot jam
2	teaspoons Dijon mustard
6	center-cut boneless pork chops (about 5 ounces each)
¾	teaspoon salt
¼	teaspoon black pepper
⅓	cup sliced almonds
2	tablespoons vegetable oil
	Broccoli or broccoli rabe (optional)

• Heat broiler. Coat broiler pan with nonstick cooking spray.

• Dredge potato pancakes in flour and place on a plate. Refrigerate for at least 1 hour.

• Combine jam and mustard. Set aside. Season pork chops with salt and pepper. Place on prepared pan and broil 4 inches from heat for 3 minutes per side or until temperature reaches 145°. Evenly spoon jam mixture over each chop and scatter almonds over top. Broil for 45 to 60 seconds, until nuts are lightly browned.

• Meanwhile, heat a large nonstick skillet over medium-high heat. Add oil and swirl. Place potato pancakes in skillet and cook for 5 minutes. Turn with a spatula and cook for an additional 5 minutes.

• Serve pork and potato pancakes with sautéed broccoli or broccoli rabe, if desired.

PER SERVING 410 CAL; 19 g FAT (6 g SAT); 26 g PRO; 34 g CARB; 3 g FIBER; 582 mg SODIUM; 71 mg CHOL

Sautéed Broccoli: Heat 1 tablespoon olive oil in a large nonstick skillet over medium heat; add 3 sliced garlic cloves and cook 1 minute. Add 1 large bunch rinsed broccoli cut into florets and season with ¼ teaspoon salt. Cook for 5 minutes, stirring occasionally.

SCALLOPS
FRA DIAVOLO

FRIDAY

Scallops Fra Diavolo

MAKES 6 servings PREP 15 minutes COOK 10 minutes

1	tablespoon olive oil
1	sweet red pepper, seeded and sliced
1	green bell pepper, seeded and sliced
1	pound frozen bay scallops, thawed (see Note)
¼	teaspoon salt
⅛	teaspoon black pepper
1	jar (24 ounces) fra diavolo sauce (such as Patsy's)
1	can (6.5 ounces) minced clams, drained
1	pound dry pappardelle or fettuccine
½	cup basil leaves

• In a large skillet, heat oil over medium-high heat. Add peppers and cook 5 minutes, stirring occasionally, until crisp-tender. Remove to a plate.

• Season scallops with salt and pepper. Cook 2 minutes, turning once. Return peppers to skillet; stir in sauce and clams. Bring to a boil; reduce heat to medium and simmer 1 minute or until scallops are cooked through.

• Meanwhile, cook pappardelle following package directions, about 10 minutes. Reserve 1 cup cooking water. Drain.

• Add pappardelle to skillet and stir until evenly coated with sauce. Add reserved cooking water as needed to thin sauce. To serve, spoon onto a large serving platter and garnish with basil.

PER SERVING 489 CAL; 10 g FAT (2 g SAT); 32 g PRO; 68 g CARB; 7 g FIBER; 739 mg SODIUM; 132 mg CHOL

Note: To freeze fresh scallops, place on plastic wrap in a single layer and tightly wrap. Wrap in foil and freeze. When ready to cook, first thaw in refrigerator overnight.

INDEX

C

IN-A-PINCH SUBSTITUTIONS

It can happen to the best of us: Halfway through a recipe, you find you're completely out of a key ingredient. Here's what to do:

Recipe Calls For:	You May Substitute:
1 square unsweetened chocolate	3 tbsp. unsweetened cocoa powder + 1 tbsp. butter/margarine
1 cup cake flour	1 cup less 2 tbsp. all-purpose flour
2 tbsp. flour (for thickening)	1 tbsp. cornstarch
1 tsp. baking powder	¼ tsp. baking soda + ½ tsp. cream of tartar + ¼ tsp. cornstarch
1 cup corn syrup	1 cup sugar + ¼ cup additional liquid used in recipe
1 cup milk	½ cup evaporated milk + ½ cup water
1 cup buttermilk or sour milk	1 tbsp. vinegar or lemon juice + enough milk to make 1 cup
1 cup sour cream (for baking)	1 cup plain yogurt
1 cup firmly packed brown sugar	1 cup sugar + 2 tbsp. molasses
1 tsp. lemon juice	¼ tsp. vinegar (not balsamic)
¼ cup chopped onion	1 tbsp. instant minced
1 clove garlic	¼ tsp. garlic powder
2 cups tomato sauce	¾ cup tomato paste + 1 cup water
1 tbsp. prepared mustard	1 tsp. dry mustard + 1 tbsp. water

HOW TO KNOW WHAT YOU NEED

Making a shopping list based on a recipe can be tricky if you don't know how many tomatoes yields 3 cups chopped. Our handy translations:

When the Recipe Calls For:	You Need:
4 cups shredded cabbage	1 small cabbage
1 cup grated raw carrot	1 large carrot
2½ cups sliced carrots	1 pound raw carrots
4 cups cooked cut fresh green beans	1 pound beans
1 cup chopped onion	1 large onion
4 cups sliced raw potatoes	4 medium-size potatoes
1 cup chopped sweet pepper	1 large pepper
1 cup chopped tomato	1 large tomato
2 cups canned tomatoes	16-oz. can
4 cups sliced apples	4 medium-size apples
1 cup mashed banana	3 medium-size bananas
1 tsp. grated lemon rind	1 medium-size lemon
2 tbsp. lemon juice	1 medium-size lemon
4 tsp. grated orange rind	1 medium-size orange
1 cup orange juice	3 medium-size oranges
4 cups sliced peaches	8 medium-size peaches
2 cups sliced strawberries	1 pint
1 cup soft bread crumbs	2 slices fresh bread
1 cup bread cubes	2 slices fresh bread
2 cups shredded Swiss or cheddar cheese	8 oz. cheese
1 cup egg whites	6 or 7 large eggs
1 egg white	2 tsp. egg white powder + 2 tbsp. water
4 cups chopped walnuts or pecans	1 pound shelled